The
EVERYTHING
Gnostic Gospels
Book

Dear Reader,

I would like to share with you what I have learned about the mystical Gnostics and the roles they played in the birth of Christianity.

After converting to Catholicism in my teens, I devoured books about saints, especially the mystics. I marveled at their reverence for Jesus and a spiritual realm that they could fathom only through their hearts, minds, and imaginations. Though I felt a particular fondness for Mother Mary, I also have been deeply interested in Mary Magdalene as a spiritual role model. Recently, her name has been associated with references to the Gnostics, mystics belonging to diverse sects but sharing some common beliefs. The ancient Gnostic Christians exalted Mary Magdalene and mentioned her with respect and admiration in their sacred manuscripts. I even discovered that a gospel was named after her.

The Gnostic texts had all but disappeared until a peasant at Nag Hammadi, Egypt, in 1945, discovered an earthenware jar buried in the desert. Inside the jar were fifty-two, mostly Gnostic, sacred writings, including some gospels. Scholars have now translated and published these texts. I'll give you Web sites and an extensive bibliography for reading the texts as well as insights into Gnostic contributions to primitive Christianity. I hope you'll find their myths and stories as fascinating as I have.

Meera Lester

The EVERYTHING® Series

Editorial

Publisher	Gary M. Krebs
Director of Product Development	Paula Munier
Managing Editor	Laura M. Daly
Associate Copy Chief	Sheila Zwiebel
Acquisitions Editor	Lisa Laing
Development Editor	Jessica LaPointe
Associate Production Editor	Casey Ebert
Technical Reader	Dan Schowalter

Production

Director of Manufacturing	Susan Beale
Associate Director of Production	Michelle Roy Kelly
Prepress	Erick DaCosta
	Matt LeBlanc
Design and Layout	Heather Barrett
	Brewster Brownville
	Colleen Cunningham
	Jennifer Oliveira
Series Cover Artist	Barry Littmann

Visit the entire Everything® Series at www.everything.com

THE
EVERYTHING®
GNOSTIC GOSPELS BOOK

A complete guide to the secret gospels

Meera Lester

Adams Media
Avon, Massachusetts

Dedicated to the religious mystics of all faiths and all times who tread
the inner path to truth . . . and to my readers.

Author's Note:
Great effort was made to verify the facts in this work; however, scholars sometimes disagree,
and whenever such discrepancies arose in the information for the Gnostic Gospels, the
interpretation of a majority of the sources was the one used in this book.
The quotations in this book were taken from the King James Version of the Bible.

An Everything® Series Book.
Everything® and everything.com® are registered trademarks of F+W Publications, Inc.

Published by Adams Media, an F+W Publications Company
57 Littlefield Street, Avon, MA 02322 U.S.A.
www.adamsmedia.com

ISBN 10: 1-59869-156-2
ISBN 13: 978-1-59869-156-6

Printed in the United States of America.

J I H G F E D C B A

Library of Congress Cataloging-in-Publication Data
available from the publisher

This book is available at quantity discounts for bulk purchases.
For information, please call 1-800-289-0963.

Contents

Top Ten Interesting Facts You'll Learn about the Gnostics / x
Introduction / xi

1 Early Christianity in Conflict / 1
Radical Primitive Christianity **2** • Influences of Other Cultures **7** • Palestinian Jews **9** • A Plethora of Ideas **10** • The Practices of Early Christians **12** • Differing Interpretations of Jesus' Teachings **16**

2 Who Were the Gnostics? / 19
Roots of Gnosticism **20** • Plato's Influence **22** • The Book of Genesis **24** • Sethian Mythology **26** • Tenets of Gnosticism **29** • Five Sacred Rites of Gnosticism **29** • Gnostic Sacramental Rituals **31** • How Gnostic Christians Became Heretics **32**

3 How the Canonical Christian Texts Were Chosen / 35
Gnostic Beliefs in Scripture **36** • Three Views of Salvation: Gnostic, Jewish Christian, Pauline Christian **42** • A Call for Unity **43** • What's in a Gospel? **45** • The Gospels Fight It Out **47** • The Council at Nicaea **48** • Establishment of the Canon **50**

4 Who Were the Authors of the Gnostic Gospels? / 53
Gnostic View of Gender Equality **54** • Who Wrote the Gospels? **55** • Differences Between the Gnostic and the Canonical Gospels **58** • Detractors, Redactors, and Scribes **60** • Textual Inferiority or Just a Different Lens? **62** • Jesus in the Canon and in Gnostic Belief **63**

5   Gnostic Versus Christian Orthodox Views / 65

Diversity and Intolerance **66** • Compilations from Oral Traditions **67** • Defining Heresy Within Christianity **67** • The Canonical Standard **71** • Polemics Against Gnosticism **73** • God's Special Revelation or Man's? **75**

6   The Divine Feminine Ideal / 79

Sophia, the Spirit of Wisdom **80** • Sophia's Fall **81** • Salvation Through Gnosis **82** • Sophia in the Secret Book of John **84** • Sophia as a Message of Hope **85** • The Pistis Sophia **86**

7   The Role of Women in Gnosticism / 91

A Challenge to the Patriarchy **92** • Jesus' Teaching on Gender Equality **94** • Mary Magdalene as Sophia **95** • Mary Magdalene as Female Counterpart to Jesus **98** • Female Officeholders and Bishops **100** • Paul's Revelations about Early Christian Women **101** • Legacy of Mary Magdalene **103**

8   Four Gnostic Schools of Thought / 105

Different Sects Appear **106** • Syrian Discipline **107** • Greek Discipline **110** • The Dualistic Discipline **112** • The Antinomian Discipline **114**

9   Consequences of Heresy / 119

Challenge to Church Doctrine **120** • The Church Deals with Gnostic Heretics **121** • Destruction of Writings by Fire and Water **123** • Excommunication **125** • The Tragic Fate of the Cathars **126** • The Crusades and Inquisition **129**

10   The Nag Hammadi Treasures / 131

Strange Story of Discovery **132** • The Contents of an Ancient Jar **133** • Translation from the Greek into Coptic **134** • Why Bury the Texts in a Jar? **135** • The Obscure Texts Scrutinized **140** • New Source Material for Scholars **142**

11   The Gospel of Mary / 143

No Complete Copy **144** • Mary's Special Revelation **145** • Importance of Mary's Secret Vision **148** • Why Peter Disbelieves **149** • Peter's Bullying **150** • Articulating Jesus' Ideas and Words **151** • Elevated Status of Mary **152**

12   The Gospel of Thomas / 157

Wisdom Interpretation of Jesus' Sayings **158** • Myriad Literary Forms **160** • Who Was the Source for the Gospel of Thomas? **161** • Was Didymos Judas Thomas Jesus' Twin? **161** • The Gospel's Parallels in the New Testament **165** • Jesus Responds to Peter **167** • Making Mary Male **167**

13   The Gospel of Philip / 169

What Is Found in This Gospel? **170** • Who Was Valentinus? **174** • Shades of Valentinian Ideas **175** • Revealing Statements **177** • Much Ado about a Kiss **178** • Was Jesus Married to Mary Magdalene? **179** • Handbook of Gnostic Sacramental Rites? **179**

14   The Gospel of the Egyptians / 181

The Unknowable Divine Being **182** • Divine Characteristics **184** • Five Seals and Gnostic Rituals **188** • Gnosis Through Baptism **189** • Magical Incantations, Gnostic Ritual, and Censure **190**

15   The Gospel of Judas / 193

A Divergent View of Jesus' Betrayer **194** • Jesus Reveals Wisdom, Makes a Request **197** • Sethian Gnostic Teaching **198** • What Jesus Saw in the Stars **199** • Gnosis Is the Point **200** • A Brief History of This Gospel **201** • Radical Departure from Orthodox Christianity's Judas **202**

16 The Gospel of Truth / 207
Could Valentinus Have Written This Text? 208 • Central Ideas and Concepts of the Gospel of Truth 211 • Admonitions to Share Knowledge of Salvation 212 • Ptolemy's Letter to Flora 214

17 A Sampling of Other Gnostic Literature / 217
The Acts of Peter and the Twelve Apostles 218 • The Secret Book of John 220 • The Dialogue of the Savior 224 • Sophia of Jesus Christ 227 • The Apocalypse of Peter 228

18 Gnostic Texts and Early Christianity / 231
A Complex, Vibrant Movement 232 • Conflict, Misunderstanding, and Rising Tensions 233 • Spreading the Good News 234 • The Gnostic Variants 235 • The Gnostics Speak Through Their Writings 237 • The Orthodoxy's Fear of Gnostic Views 238

19 Modern Scholars Examine Ancient Texts / 241
The Original Sacred Documents 242 • Manipulation of the Copies and Translations 243 • Why Mary Magdalene Is Missing 245 • Redaction of the Gospel of John 247 • Forgeries and Falsifications Exposed 250

20 Gnostic Themes and Images in Pop Culture / 255
Gnosticism in Books 256 • Gnostic Elements in Film and Television 259 • Gnostic Influence on Music 262 • Gnostic Imagery in Art 264 • Gnostic Games 264

Appendix A: Glossary / 267
Appendix B: Web Site Resources / 273
Appendix C: Text Resources / 277
Index / 281

Acknowledgments

I wish to express my gratitude to Lisa Laing, my editor, and Paula Munier, director of product development at Adams Media, for having faith in me and bringing me yet another wonderful project. I also wish to thank everyone at Adams Media involved in making this book possible.

I'm deeply grateful to all the scholars of early Christianity and Gnosticism whose work on the Gnostic texts makes it possible for me and all others interested in learning more about them to read translations and commentaries.

Finally, I am appreciative of the support given to me by a group of devoted friends who at various times encouraged, fed, guided, inspired, cajoled, humored, and loved me while I worked on this project: Kathryn Makris, Anita Llewellyn, Jan Stiles, Leeanna Franklin, Becky Cahoon, Sadie Cabrera, Susan Reynolds, and Carlos Carvajal.

Top Ten Interesting Facts
You'll Learn about the Gnostics

1. Gnostic heresies prompted early Christian leaders to refine their beliefs.

2. The Gnostics believed that God the Father of Jesus was not same as the God worshipped by the ancient Hebrews.

3. The earthly realm and physical universe were created in error by a lesser god called the Demiurge, the Gnostics believed.

4. Salvation, the Gnostics believed, did not come from the death and resurrection of Jesus but rather through secret self-knowledge, or *gnosis*.

5. The Gnostics believed that the physical world has entrapped those beings who possess sparks of the divine light (or divine nature) within them.

6. Discovery of the Dead Sea Scrolls and Nag Hammadi library has stimulated worldwide interest in the origins of Christianity and the role played by the Gnostics.

7. Scholarly interpretations and commentary of the recently discovered ancient texts have led to a clearer understanding of the diversity of the early Christian communities, including those of the Gnostic Christians, and the tumultuous period in which they emerged.

8. The Gnostics did not discriminate against women in their worship services or fellowship sessions.

9. Valentinus founded a system of Gnostic belief that flourished and posed a real threat to orthodox Christianity.

10. Gnostic traditions flourished between the second and fourth centuries but the movement all but died out by the middle of the fifth century.

Introduction

▶ A CACHE OF early Christian texts accidentally unearthed in the Egyptian desert over a half century ago put a spotlight on the birth of Christianity, suggesting that it was anything but harmonious and smooth. The death and resurrection of Jesus and tumultuous events that followed triggered a complex, diverse, and contentious process involving groups of early Christians in ideological clashes over interpretations of Jesus' teachings. The earthenware jar discovered by a peasant seeking fertilizer near Nag Hammadi, in Upper Egypt, contained fifty-two mostly Gnostic texts: lost gospels, wisdom literature, poems, hymns, prayers, sayings of the Savior, and apocalyptic material. The writings provided scholars with a lens for viewing primitive Christianity through the beliefs of the Gnostics.

At a time when the proto-orthodox church leaders vigorously defended the church against heresies, punishing and excommunicating their opponents and destroying their religious texts, someone hid the cache of Gnostic Christian books. The ancient monastery of St. Pachomius stood only about fifty miles from the site of the discovery and was known to be a place of significant early Christian activity. Scholars theorize that the Egyptian Christian monks living at St. Pachomius hid the sacred texts, not to destroy them but to preserve them. The documents were put together in ways that suggest the manufacture of them was done with respect and veneration. Many of the texts were written in the Egyptian Coptic script, translated from the original Greek. For these reasons, the monks most likely hid the library for safekeeping.

In this book, you will learn about the Nag Hammadi treasures, the various Gnostic sects and their founders, and their spiritual and ideological differences with orthodox Christianity. You will gain an understanding of the Gnostic view of creation and salvation and why they emphasized an inner, experiential knowledge—gnosis—as a means of salvation. You will also discover their belief in a feminine aspect of God. You may conclude that the threads of their sacred works add to the beauty and vibrancy of the tapestry of early Christianity.

Chapter 1

Early Christianity in Conflict

After Jesus' death, his followers did not immediately establish a new religion. They relied on memory, shared experience, and oral tradition to spread his teachings. The Gospel of Mark was written more than thirty years later. It was the first account of Jesus' life and ministry. Other gospels followed later, but only Matthew, Mark, Luke, and John were selected by church fathers for the canonical New Testament. The Gnostic Gospels, although also written by Christians, were rejected and subsequently lost or destroyed because they presented ideas at odds with orthodox beliefs.

Radical Primitive Christianity

The Gnostics were mystics, deeply interested in spiritual knowledge and wisdom. They sought such information from many sources, including the sacred texts of the Hebrews, the Egyptians, the Greeks and Romans, and others. History reveals they were of Jewish, Zoroastrian, Muslim, and other faiths. In this book, you will read about the Gnostics who were part of the early Christian movements.

The Gnostics believed that God could be known experientially through knowledge of the self. They called this self-knowledge *gnosis* and themselves *gnostikoi*, the Knowing Ones. They felt no need for salvation from one another because they believed salvation came through gnosis when the divine spark within them merged back into the Godhead. The fifty-two mostly Gnostic texts discovered in 1945 cast a new light on the diversity and conflicts of the early Christian communities. The manuscripts dated to the third and fourth centuries and were copied from originals dating to the second century. Early church fathers considered Gnostic writings heretical and banned them, making it dangerous to possess such texts. Because of the inherent danger of protecting such literature, the monks of St. Pachomius, so it is believed, hid the documents in caves near Nag Hammadi in Egypt where the materials were found.

FACT

According to the book of Acts, the word "Christian" was not used until about a decade after Jesus' death. The term first showed up in the language of nonbelievers in Antioch, Syria, a place that later became known as the center of Gentile Christianity. The word "Christian" was used to refer to the followers of Christ. In Greek, the term for "Christian" is *Christianoi*.

To understand these theological conflicts within the earliest communities, it is helpful to place them in the milieu of first-century Palestine. The earliest followers of Jesus were Jews living in Palestine, a land occupied and governed by the Romans. Like their ancestors, these Jews yearned for the

Messiah (literally "anointed one"), who would rescue them from secular rule, restore the kingdom of Israel, and reconcile the Jewish covenant with God. Jesus' supporters became "followers of the Way of the Lord" that Jesus had demonstrated for them. They believed he was the Redeemer whose coming was prophesied in their Hebrew scriptures (the Old Testament). They saw themselves as students of Jesus practicing an alternative form of Judaism.

Jesus' followers lived in a world of rising sectarian tension, religious disputes, increased polarization, and political unrest. While complying with their own Mosaic Law, religious and cultural beliefs, and traditions, Jews were also required to adhere to the laws of the polytheistic Romans who claimed their system originated with Jupiter and functioned with the blessings of their various gods. The Roman governors, as representatives of Rome, wielded enormous economic, political, social, and legal power over their subjects. Roman justice, even far from Rome in Judean territory, was swift and often harsh.

When Jesus began his ministry, his first-century Jewish brethren most likely held widely different views of him. Some perhaps saw him as just another charismatic preacher among the many prophets, exorcists, magicians, healers, and others who traveled through Galilee and Judea. Those who saw him work miracles may have come to believe he was the Messiah, while the more dubious among them may have thought he was simply an accomplished magician. In Jesus' lifetime, many Jews harbored increasing animosity toward others in their communities whom they saw as becoming worldly because of outside influences, primarily from the Greco-Roman culture. The political and religious climate of that time fostered hope among the Jews that the long-hoped-for Messiah was coming to lead the nation of Israel, lifting from it the yoke of Roman rule. It was a time of rising sectarian tensions and apocalyptic expectations.

Modern scholars characterize the Jesus movement as essentially an eschatological movement. "Eschatological" derives from the Greek *eschatos*, meaning "the utmost" or "the end." Many Jews during Jesus' lifetime believed in their ancient prophets' predictions of a coming "day of the Lord" or end-time, and for some, Jesus' words and deeds resonated with those beliefs, heightening expectations of the Apocalypse. It is worth noting that the definition of "Apocalypse" is the disclosure of God in the guise of Messiah, rather than the destruction of the world when the unveiling takes place. Some Jews found elements of Jesus' teachings objectionable, dangerous, and even radical. To them, he must have seemed like a rebel, intentionally shaking up the status quo.

QUESTION?

What is apocalyptic ideology?
Apocalyptic thinking centers around the belief that the end-time is near and that God will judge the righteous and the wicked. Apocalyptic expectation remained high during the time of Jesus and afterward. Many of Jesus' disciples believed that after his death and resurrection, he would return within their lifetimes to establish the kingdom of God on earth.

Jesus' Radical Practices

Jesus' egalitarian view of women, for example, went against the traditional patriarchal idea that women were the property of men. Jewish men could look into their holy scriptures and find male role models. In those texts, they didn't see examples of the great patriarchs treating women as equals. It is likely that the more orthodox Jewish males resisted changing their beliefs about the status of women in Jewish society. Jesus knew that many Jews of his time believed in their Hebrew scripture's admonition "an eye for an eye" (Exodus 21:24), but he taught his followers to "turn the other cheek and do unto others as you would have them do unto you" (Luke 6:28–31).

Jesus ignored purity rules. As he walked to the house of Jairus to raise the man's daughter from the dead, a woman who had had a bleeding condition for twelve years touched the hem of his garment. Jesus healed the woman, but then was considered ritually unclean (according to Jewish purity rules). Even so, he continued on, sought out the dead child of Jairus, and restored her life. Now, because of contact with the dead, he was considered doubly unclean.

Jesus' act of healing on the Sabbath evoked the anger of the Pharisees, a sect of Jews for whom zealous adherence to God's laws and commandments was extremely important. The Pharisees enforced the laws written in the Torah. They felt that all Jews had to obey the purity laws to ensure purity inside and outside of the Temple. Josephus, the Jewish historian writing near the end of the first century, noted that the Pharisees were expert expositors of Jewish law.

Jesus' Radical Followers

After Jesus' death, his followers sometimes acted in opposition to traditional Jewish thinking. The Apostle Paul had a vision to take the gospel to non-Jews (Gentiles). His evangelism converted many Gentiles to Christianity. But dissension arose immediately with the early Christians in Jerusalem (who still saw themselves as a sect of Jews) over whether or not Paul's Gentile converts should be circumcised, obliged to follow Mosaic Law and Jewish dietary laws, and converted to Judaism. The Jews could trace their obligation to be circumcised back to God's commandment to Abraham.

This is my covenant, which ye shall keep, between me and you and thy seed after thee; Every man child among you shall be circumcised. And ye shall circumcise the flesh of your foreskin; and it shall be a token of the covenant betwixt me and you.—Genesis 17:10–11

In the end it was decided that Gentiles could seek the Lord (without all those requirements) if they "abstain from pollutions of idols, and from fornication, and from things strangled, and from blood" (Acts 15:20).

Paul, who became known as the Apostle to the Gentiles, became embroiled in a conflict when he was accused of violating purity laws by bringing Greeks into a Temple area restricted to Jews, thus sparking a riot (Acts 21:16–40). Paul was arrested. Tensions were rising in Jerusalem at the time, perhaps due to widespread apocalyptic sentiment and the political unrest fomented by the Zealot movement, a fringe radical group of militant patriots (some say an offshoot of the Pharisees) who advocated an armed rebellion to overthrow the Romans.

Possibly concerned about Jewish dissension, Paul had his young disciple Timothy circumcised to avoid conflict with the Jews in Lycaonia.

Timothy was the son of a Greek father and a Jewish mother. Paul wanted the young man to accompany him on his missionary travels around the region, but also possibly feared opposition over Timothy's status as an uncircumcised male.

The New Testament letters of Paul reveal schisms, misunderstandings of Jesus' teachings, internecine squabbling, turmoil, and conflict among the fledgling Christian communities and churches that he had established during his missionary travels beyond Palestine in Corinth, Galatia, Ephesus, Philippi, Colossae, and Thessalonia. The New Testament Acts of the Apostles reports that the early followers of Jesus in Jerusalem continued Jewish traditional practices and observances, including attending Temple. But they also followed a routine of attending prayer sessions in homes and participating in dinner fellowship with other believers. By the end of the first century, Christians had established certain rituals and espoused key beliefs. However, they would continue to develop, shape, and clarify their theology over the next few centuries.

QUESTION?

How did early Gnostic beliefs differ from the more literalistic or proto-orthodox beliefs?
The Gnostic groups embraced the idea of gnosis, or self-knowledge, as the path to salvation while the proto-orthodox believed that Jesus died for their sins and his death ensured salvation of those who accepted him as Savior. Some Christians believed that Jesus was a mortal with a divine message, others felt that he was fully human and that Christ dwelled within him. Certain Christians believed that Jesus did not die.

At least one of Jesus' disciples who some might consider a radical follower was Simon the Cananaean (also known as Simon the Zealot). *Cananaean* derives from the Aramaic and means "zealous one." Simon may have been a member of a subsect of Zealots known as the Sicarii, dagger assassins (*sicarii* is a Latin term for a kind of dagger). Like the Pharisees and the Zealots, the Sicarii desired a messiah, descended from King David, who would reclaim the throne of Israel for the Jewish people. The Sicarii were committed to ousting the Romans, using violence if necessary toward achieving that aim.

Although many scholars disagree, some sources suggest that Simon Peter may have also been a Zealot. Most assume that his name, Simeon bar Jona, meant simply Simon, son of Jona. However, Simon Peter's name is spelled in Matthew 16:17 as Barj-jona and the Aramaic word for outlaw, *baryona*, is not a far leap to make. Others believe a more likely candidate than Simon Peter was Judas Iscariot, who betrayed Jesus for thirty pieces of silver. Several sources suggest that Iscariot may have been a corruption of the Latin word *sicarius* (dagger-man), a Roman moniker for Zealot.

When you read the New Testament stories about the followers of Jesus, you begin to see that they were ordinary people living in extraordinary times of social change and religious and political unrest. They saw in Jesus the embodiment of the Redeemer promised by their ancient prophets. They believed his death heralded the coming end-time. They came to believe that his death would bring them salvation. Choosing to follow Jesus meant they now had to live a radical life, one accompanied by great risk, possibly death. The Gnostic scriptures, on the other hand, suggest that the followers of Jesus saw things a little differently than those espousing a literalist view. Their salvation came not from someone else, certainly not from the death of Jesus, but through an inner process of questioning and understanding until enlightenment was achieved. But they did see Jesus as a being of light who came to earth as a revealer to bring gnosis, not from a God who demanded his suffering and death but from the "ageless, unproclaimable Father," as explained in the Gnostic Gospel of the Egyptians.

The divergent ideas of early Christians suggest that birth and evolution of Christianity were fraught with dissension, disagreement, and disharmony as the early church sought consensus on many issues. Common beliefs and unity would help the religion to survive; otherwise a divisive splintering off could only endanger it.

Influences of Other Cultures

Although Roman rulers, oppressors, Gnostic Christians, apologists, and literalistic church fathers each in some way impacted how early Christian theology and practices evolved, equally important were regional cultural and spiritual influences upon the Christian faithful. The lands around the Mediterranean served as fecund ground for incubating and spawning new ideas that influenced earliest Christianity. There were the mystery cults and more gods and goddesses than any one individual could track. Although Christianity clearly had its roots in Judaism, scholars still debate the elements it may have shared with other belief systems such as polytheism, Zoroastrianism, and, later, Mithraism.

- **Polytheism** was widely practiced by the Greeks, Romans, and Egyptians. The death of the king who dies, is buried, and arises on the third day is central to Christian belief but also encapsulates the Egyptian Osiris story.
- **Mithraism** flourished in the areas of Roman rule. Mithras incarnated, according to legend, in 272 B.C. and his coming was prophesied by Zoroaster. Similarities between Mithraism and Christianity can be found in the stories of Jesus and Mithra, who were both born of virgins, share the same birthday, December 25, and have been called "the Light of the world."
- **Zoroastrian** thinking about monotheism and a final judgment with subsequent punishments and rewards in order to gain immortality may have entered Jewish consciousness during Babylonian captivity and thus passed into early Christian thinking.

The spread of religious and cultural ideas became easier and more rapid thanks to Greco-Roman engineering of roads and bridges along with masterful shipbuilding. So influences from those cultures easily spread into Palestine but ideas flowed both ways—that is, also from Palestine into the rest of the world. For example, slaves may have helped the spread of Christianity around the Mediterranean. The Romans and Greeks owned slaves, and the New Testament reports that the Apostle Paul healed a demon-possessed slave girl (Acts 16:16–18). He also sent a letter to Philemon on behalf of Onesimus, a slave who was returning to his owner after becoming a Christian (Philemon 10–16). Further, Paul counseled in his letter to the Ephesians that slaves must be obedient to their masters (Ephesians 6:5–8). It seems likely that Christian slaves, like other converts, contributed to the spread of the new faith.

Palestinian Jews

Although the Romans had political control over the Jewish people, they tolerated the beliefs and practices of their subjects. Palestinian Jews during the first century believed in monotheism, were guided by the Torah, and lived in strict accordance with the Law of Moses. Among the many sects of Jews, several groups were important during Jesus' lifetime: the Pharisees and Sadducees had prominence, but the Essenes and the Zealots were important for their views and contributions (the former were ascetics and the latter were militants).

The Pharisees

The Pharisees believed that God met Moses on Mount Sinai and gave him the Ten Commandments along with numerous laws and knowledge of how to apply them. These laws first passed from one generation to the next through oral tradition and later were written into the Talmud. The Pharisees also believed in a just God who punishes wickedness and rewards goodness in the afterlife. They also believed in a messiah who one day would establish a kingdom of peace on earth.

The Sadducees

The Sadducees, the elitist Jewish group at the time of Jesus, were interested in literal interpretation of the written law found in the Torah and in maintaining the priestly caste and its power to oversee and control temple rituals. Belief in an afterlife was out of the question, since the Torah contained no such idea. Together with the Pharisees, the Sadducees, who descended from the Levi tribe and Zadok family, accounted for the seventy-one Jews making up the Sanhedrin, the highest religious and civil court in Jerusalem.

What is the Apocrypha?
In Judeo-Christian references, the Apocrypha usually refers to a collection of fourteen texts, considered to be outside the canon but included in the Septuagint (the oldest Greek version of the Hebrew scriptures or the Old Testament) and the Vulgate (Latin translation of the Bible from Greek). However, the meaning is broad enough to include religious texts of unknown or dubious authorship.

The Essenes found offensive the beliefs and practices of the Pharisees and the Sadducees and left Jerusalem for the desert. These "Children of Light," as they called themselves, may have been a branch of a sect living in the Qumran settlement near the Dead Sea, now famous as the location where the Dead Sea Scrolls were discovered. The Essenes practiced a rigorous form of asceticism and were vegetarians.

The Zealots

The Zealots were an armed group of revolutionary Jews who advocated the overthrow (violently, if necessary) of the Roman occupiers of Palestine during the first century.

A Plethora of Ideas

In its infancy, Christianity was characterized by disunity, heresies, and schisms because of the varieties of beliefs and practices in its first communities. Different groups of Christians battled for supremacy after Jesus' death. Some of his followers believed that after his mortal body died on the cross, Jesus preached to the dead in the netherworld. Some believed that the price of sin was death and that Jesus' death purchased the salvation of humankind. Others rejected that idea, believing instead that salvation was only possible through self-knowing. Some understood their bodies to be the temple of God and yet others loathed the body as a filthy thing and this world as inhabited by negative spirits. Some Christian communities had women priests, were celibate, and practiced vegetarianism while others believed that male priests could have wives and children.

The developing church of early Christians could not be characterized as one big happy family. Almost immediately after Jesus' death, polarization began around the Apostles. Some of Jesus' followers felt a loyalty toward Peter and became his disciples while others felt a preference for James the Just, the Lord's brother. James remained in Jerusalem after the death of Jesus and, as the first bishop of Jerusalem, oversaw the care of the fledgling Christian community there. Others chose to follow Paul or Mary Magdalene. The point is that the Apostles had their own disciples, whom they must have taught as Jesus taught them through sayings, anecdotes, parables, prayers, and deeds. As you shall see in the discussion of the Gnostic texts, even the Apostles' ideas and understanding of Jesus' teachings sometimes conflicted with one another. In the second and third century, these differences translated into thorny theological issues, causing the literalists among them to accuse the others of introducing and spreading heresies. In turn, such accusations necessarily caused a splintering off of groups of Christians who opposed literalism and desired to vigorously defend and practice their beliefs. What the early Christians did share in common were certain practices that celebrated their faith.

The Dead Sea Scrolls, discovered between 1947 and 1956, consist of over 800 ancient documents, 30 percent of them from the Hebrew Bible. Scholars believe that members of an Essene community hid the texts in caves near Wadi Qumran on the northwestern shore of the Dead Sea. The texts reveal what life was like in the ancient Khirbet Qumran community.

It seems imperative to define how the word "orthodox" will be used throughout this book in reference to the earliest Christian communities. Perhaps the term "literalistic" comes closest to defining the community of Christians who believed in the literal interpretation of Jesus' words. This group included Simon Peter. In the absence of a single authority to determine correctness of belief, this group emerged eventually as the dominant Christian community. Only much later could orthodox and unorthodox practices and beliefs be separated.

The Practices of Early Christians

During Jesus' lifetime, while men studied the scriptures and performed their work, women generally confined themselves to their homes, grinding flour, preparing food, washing clothes, and caring for families. As Jewish women, they were not educated and had no right to engage in discourse about their ancient scriptures the way their men did in the Temple. Still, women would have been expected to kindle the Sabbath candles on Friday night, observe the purity rituals, and train their children to keep God's commandments and to observe Jewish cultural and religious practices.

Jesus brought a shift in thinking about the roles of women. He didn't set out to change their traditional roles, but in many ways women did change. His teachings spoke powerfully to those who had been abused, oppressed, ostracized, and condemned. It is not surprising that these women chose to follow him. After his death, Jesus' followers continued to engage in their Jewish religious and cultural traditions. Simultaneously, they also embraced his more radical and egalitarian ideas. Eventually, Christianity evolved away from its infant identity as a Jewish sect. It remained an illegal religion, however, until A.D. 313 when Roman Emperor Constantine granted religious freedom and Christians could openly celebrate and practice their faith.

Roles of Men and Women

Men and women participated in co-leadership of the house churches (private homes of those loyal to Jesus where the faithful gathered for fellowship, prayer, and a meal). Some scholars and feminist theologians have said that women were especially effective in evangelizing other women and that they served the church well as preachers, teachers, and organizers of fellowship sessions.

Feminist theologian Susan Haskins has observed that by the end of the second century, the early church father Tertullian, amazed that the women of the Gnostic sects were accorded the right to discuss religion, exorcise, heal, and baptize, wrote in opposition to the practices that (in the orthodox Christian churches) women were forbidden to speak in church, baptize, or offer the communion. In other words, women were not to usurp men's tasks. Eventually only Christian men would serve as priests, bishops, and popes, but in Gnostic churches women, even today, serve as hierophants, the equivalent of bishop in the Roman Catholic Church. In ancient Greece, a hierophant was someone who proclaimed and explained ancient sacred rites of worship or who interpreted sacred mysteries. Some modern Gnostics consider that Jesus was a hierophant, inasmuch as he imparted mysteries.

QUESTION?

What are the Synoptic Gospels?

The New Testament Gospels of Matthew, Mark, and Luke collectively are called the synoptic Gospels because each contains the stories of Jesus recounted in essentially the same sequence and often with similar phrasing. The contents of these gospels can be viewed together— hence the term "synoptic," which derives from two Greek words: *syn*, meaning "together," and *opsis*, meaning "seeing."

As the size of Christian congregations began to grow in the first few centuries, larger accommodations had to be found. The patriarchal literalist Christian communities resisted women preaching in public, so when groups of Christian faithfuls moved into larger public places, leadership positions for women declined as men increasingly took over the preaching and the administering of sacraments. Among Jesus' faithful, Mary Magdalene surely emerged as a powerful spiritual role model because of her proximity to Jesus while he was alive and as eyewitness to the Resurrection after his death. As with the male Apostles, she attracted a following and was especially revered by the Gnostic Christians and followers of John the Baptist. Did she and other women conduct baptisms and administer communion? It's a point scholars are still debating, but some feminist theologians believe that women did fully participate in the administering of sacraments.

Many sacramental rites celebrated in the early Christian congregations, including baptism and communion, are still part of church services today.

Baptism

One sacrament central to the new Christian faith was baptism. Just as circumcision was seen as a seal upon God's chosen people in the centuries preceding the birth of Christianity, baptism by water and the Holy Spirit—the latter involving speaking in tongues (Acts 10:44–48)—set apart the followers of Jesus from nonbelievers. However, the rite of purification and sanctification by water was found in many cultures before the first century, and it certainly existed in Judaism long before John the Baptist immersed Jesus in the Jordan River. For example, the Jewish tradition of the mikveh or immersion in a water bath for ritual purification is a very old practice predating Christianity. During the time of Jesus, Christians believed that the baptism by water represented a symbolic washing away of sin but, more importantly, that baptism by the Holy Spirit brought the supplicant into a sacred covenant with Christ, conferring salvation and the promise of eternal life.

The Holy Eucharist

Another Christian sacrament, the Holy Eucharist (communion with bread and wine), had its origins in the Jewish Passover seder (meal or banquet). Some churches call the communion sacrament the Last Supper. Jesus, at his last Passover meal in Jerusalem, asked his disciples to eat bread in remembrance of his body and to drink wine in remembrance of the blood he would shed. Historical scholars debate whether or not Jesus, in linking the redemption symbols of the Jewish Passover meal with the Christian Eucharist, created the new sacred rite where his words were repeated or whether the early Church just attributed those words to him, incorporating them into the liturgy, after the rite was already established.

Catholic doctrine states that Holy Communion is "essential for human salvation." Catholics believe that the communion bread and wine are Jesus Christ, while most non-Catholics believe them to be only a symbol of Christ.

Marriage

Many of the followers of Jesus were married, including some of the Apostles and later bishops and even popes. In Jewish culture at the time of

Jesus, men were expected to take a wife and have children and to not do so was considered unnatural. In taking a wife, men were following the commandment that God gave Adam and Eve.

And God blessed them, and God said unto them, Be fruitful and multiply, and replenish the earth, and subdue it: and have dominion over the fish of the sea, and over the fowl of the air, and over every living thing that moveth upon the earth.—Genesis 1:28

Marriage during the first-century, whether Christian, Jew, or Gentile, was more about family, business, and tribal alliances and ownership of property (wives and children) than it was about love. For followers of Jesus, the emphasis shifted to the taking of one wife and remaining faithful, underscoring a respectful treatment of women that went against patriarchal norms of the day. At a time in history when it was culturally acceptable for husbands to get rid of a wife through divorce or impeachment of her reputation, Jesus showed on numerous occasions his consideration of and concern for the lot of women. We know Jesus must have approved of weddings because he attended one at Cana, which happened to be the location of his first miracle in John's Gospel—turning wine into water.

That miracle was written in the Gospel of John, but not in the synoptic Gospels (Matthew, Mark, and Luke). Today, Holy Matrimony is one of the seven sacraments found in the Roman Catholic Church. Spouses bestow the sacrament upon each other with the priest and family members and friends as witnesses. In Eastern Greek Orthodox tradition, marriage is viewed as one of the Mysteries.

Some of the practices of the early Christians had their origins in Jewish ritual. For example, the antiphonal and responsive singing still practiced in many churches today had its roots in Judaism as an ancient method of performing music. This is also true for prayer and discussion sessions, something that Jesus, as a young Jewish boy, did in the Temple. Some students of biblical history also point out that the pre-Christian Jewish Temple service was made up of four key elements, namely, reading, discussion, singing, and prayer. Early Christians likely adopted the practices, incorporating them into their services.

Differing Interpretations of Jesus' Teachings

Raymond Brown, a respected Biblical scholar, has suggested that early on in the Christian church a schism split the church into two main groups that he designates Apostolic Christians (the orthodox believers) and Secessionists (non-orthodox like the Gnostics). The schism occurred over a disagreement in beliefs held by the orthodox or literalist Christians that Jesus had been sent from God, the Father, as the savior of humankind. The Gnostics refused to change their beliefs to agree with the orthodox Apostolic Christians. The Gnostics held to the dualistic belief in a deity who is the source of light and wisdom and in another entity who created the world full of darkness and suffering. The Gnostics believed that humans must be enlightened to escape their ensnarement in matter. To them, Jesus was a being of Light, the revealer of gnosis, not the Christ to be sacrificed for the sins of humankind.

Others who might not have shared the literalistic or orthodox interpretations of Jesus' teachings were the many Jews who lived outside of Judea and elsewhere within the Roman Empire during the first few centuries after the birth of Christianity. The lingua franca of the Hellenistic world was Greek. The Jewish people of ancient Palestine would have had some contact with the Hellenistic culture of the Greeks and Romans. Scholars note that Greek literary works influenced the writing of Jews in ancient Palestine because texts (and fragments of writing) show Jews adopting some of the literary forms of the Greeks and Romans. So, too, did the writing of certain early church fathers reveal the Hellenistic influence on their contemplation and interpretation about Christian theology. While nearly all the early fathers wrote in Greek, the writing of some (Valentinus, for example) posited theological interpretations at odds with the thinking of the more literalistic or orthodox Christian leaders.

Septuagint was the name of the Greek translation of thirty-nine books of the Hebrew scriptures (or the Old Testament) and certain Apocrypha texts used by early Christians during the first few centuries after the death of Jesus. *Septuagint* is the Latin word for "seventy" and honors the seventy Jewish scholars who supposedly did the translating.

After the last apostle died, the period of their lives in early Christianity became known as the Apostolic Age. With the apostles gone, it fell to early church fathers such as Irenaeus, Hippolytus, Tertullian, Origen, Epiphanius, and other leaders of the Christian faith to protect and preserve the literalistic interpretations of the teachings of Jesus. These particular church leaders opposed the various groups of Gnostics and others with ideas that did not mesh with their understanding of the teachings. Much of the modern scholarship about heretics and heresies that threatened traditional orthodox Christianity in the first few centuries is based on their writings.

Chapter 2

Who Were the Gnostics?

The earliest centuries of Christianity were times of great questioning. Jesus' followers evangelized in lands around the Mediterranean and in Africa and India. Many new converts were culturally, linguistically, and sociopolitically different from the zealous Christians who risked persecution to take the teachings of Jesus throughout the ancient world. As Christianity was translated for people of different cultures, some groups developed beliefs that deviated from the literalist doctrine of the emerging Christian church hierarchy.

Roots of Gnosticism

Aspects of Gnosticism were present from the earliest beginnings of the Christian faith and spread rapidly throughout Palestine, Syria, and elsewhere in the Near East. It developed into a coherent system of thought during the second through the fourth centuries. Gnosticism likely predated Christianity and borrowed ideas and themes from Greek philosophy (especially Plato) and Judaism, syncretizing or merging them with ancient myths and Christian stories. Biblical historians believe that Gnosticism, as a growing movement, originated in the Hebrew-Christian environment because many names, ideas, and idiomatic expressions that occur in Gnostic writings have Semitic origins.

Scholars are quick to point out that within so-called ancient Gnostic materials are religious ideas that are not necessarily the same or in agreement with each other or with tenets of Christianity. There were certainly Gnostic Christians. It would be incorrect to say that the Gnostics were a single group of people in a specific locale, with one religious doctrine, one view of God, one concept of creation and cosmology. Scholar Bart D. Ehrman, who studies the scriptures and faiths of the ancient world and who chairs the department of religious studies at the University of North Carolina at Chapel Hill, asserts that it might make sense to place the origins of Gnostic Christianity inside of Judaism.

For their differences, one thing remained constant about the Gnostics. Regardless of the cultural lenses they peered through, they were spiritual seekers. They sought to acquire knowledge about spiritual beliefs in order to further their understanding of all things divine. They believed that matter was essentially the deterioration of spirit. Through inner intuitive knowledge of the transcendent unknowable God, their souls became liberated. The quest for that special knowledge was the central purpose of life. They sought not the spiritual teachings for the masses (though they were interested in them), but rather secret wisdom from their own inner insights. The Gnostics presented their ideas and beliefs through mythological stories, treatises, gospels, letters, books, acts, sayings, hymns, and other texts much as the Christians did. But unlike the Christian literature, little of the Gnostic tradition survived—that is, until the discovery of a treasure trove of Gnostic writings in a cave near Nag Hammadi, Egypt, in the spring of 1945. The material has since been translated and published, both in book form as *The*

Nag Hammadi Library, edited by James M. Robinson, and on the Internet at *www.gnosis.org/naghamm/nhl.html*. The Gnostics loved myth and storytelling and so it is not surprising that their creation myth puts the forces of light and darkness in perpetual struggle. But their tales use terms that you may not have heard, so before delving too deeply into Gnostic ideas, it may be helpful to know the meaning of words the Gnostics used to tell their stories.

- **Aeons:** God's essence goes through emanations that spontaneously expand into pairs of male and female entities that the Gnostics call Aeons. Gnostics believe that these eternal beings emanating themselves from the Godhead in successive generations result in destabilizing the primordial cosmos.

- **Archon:** The term approximates the meaning of "ruler" in Greek, and the Gnostics believe the archons are rulers that serve the Demiurge. Some call them angels or demons, but they do the work of keeping the divine sparks ensnared in the material world and can create obstacles to prevent the soul from unfettering itself and ascending to the Pleroma.

- **Demiurge:** In Gnostic theology, the Demiurge is the malevolent creator god, craftsman or architect of the physical world that is fundamentally flawed and evil and that imprisons the sparks of the Divine. Other names for the Demiurge are Yaldabaoth (Greek, "Father of Chaos"), Sakla ("Foolish One"), and Samael.

- **Docetism:** Docetism (from the Greek, meaning "to seem") infers that neither Jesus' physical body nor his crucifixion were real (they only seemed real). The Gnostics believed that Jesus, an eternal spiritual being, alternatively known as an Avatar, emanated from the Godhead, and therefore could not come in flesh and could not die.

- **Dualism:** Dualism is the idea that two things that are fundamentally different and often opposing each other—for example, mind/body, heaven/earth, darkness/light, good/evil, and physical/spiritual. Dualistic ideas permeated Gnostic beliefs.

- **Gnosis:** An important term central to Gnostic theology, gnosis means "knowing." In an expansion of the meaning of that term, gnosis has long been understood as an inner experiential knowing of spiritual things, mystical truths. The Gnostics gained the secret knowledge from Jesus that, according to some Gnostic beliefs, he did not reveal to the church.

- **Pleroma:** Pleroma derives from the Greek, meaning "fullness, whole, completion," and refers to the totality of the spiritual universe and all that is Divine. In other words, the Pleroma is the "real" spiritual world where the Godhead and God's powers express through an army of gods (the Aeons) as opposed to the "unreal" or shadow universe that is the physical world.
- **Sophia:** Sophia ("wisdom") represents both the spirit and the feminine side of God. Sophia is a redeemer figure like Jesus, an Aeon who illuminates the way, through the gift of gnosis, for lost souls (divine sparks) to return to the Pleroma.

The Gnostics depict creation as having two main realms. The first is a dark (materialistic) world, full of malevolent forces, including its creator the Demiurge (akin to Satan in Christian theology) and its fellow rulers known as archons. The other is the realm of Light, presided over by the supreme, transcendent God and spiritual emanations of the Divine known as Aeons.

Integral to all Gnostic thinking was the idea that the divine fragment or spark from the realm of Light (a synonym for God) dwells in each human. The spark, in a virginal state of purity, became trapped in the realm of matter or darkness (material world) where it suffered. Only when it returns to the realm of Light through gnosis (inner knowledge) will it be free. There it will dwell while others remain trapped in the dark, evil materialistic world. Aeons like Sophia (the embodiment of wisdom) and Jesus (the embodiment of the Savior) bring secret teachings to help those trapped find their way back to the Light.

Plato's Influence

The Gnostic's conception of a creator god, known as the Demiurge, may have derived from Demiurgos, a figure from Plato's *Timaeus* and *Republic*. Out of chaos, the Gnostic Demiurge created the imperfect copies of the divine model that either purposefully or unconsciously trap divinity in matter. This seems to suggest the pre-existence of particles of matter out of which the universe could be created. Further, they distinguish this evil materialistic world from the Pleroma, the world of wisdom, light, truth, and reality. The human body imprisons the sparks of the Divine, and it is only through the ascent from the physical world back to the Pleroma that the soul finds salvation. A Gnostic savior or revealer is one who comes to awaken those asleep or "slumbering" in darkness.

FACT

Plato, a Greek philosopher, lived from 427 to 347 B.C. He founded the Academy in Athens, emphasizing studies in science, mathematics, and philosophy. He tried unsuccessfully to convert the boy and future king Dionysius II into a philosopher king. Plato's Academy continued for almost 1,000 years but was closed by Emperor Justinian, who saw it as harmful to the Christian faith.

Plato asserted that the cosmos emanated from the transcendent unknowable One and was created by the *Demiurgos* out of passive matter in chaos. The *Demiurgos*, according to Plato (writing in the Socratic dialogue *Timaeus*), is a benevolent entity, a "craftsman," who cobbled together the world out of pre-existing matter that resisted the effort—and thus the world remains imperfect. Plato expressed through his philosophical writing in *Phaedo* the idea that physical bodies are ephemeral and are only imperfect copies of the eternal forms. Also in *Phaedo*, he argued the idea of immortality of the soul. These two concepts resonate in Gnostic thinking.

Gnostic beliefs also reflect Plato's ideas about metaphysics—in particular, his dualistic concept of the world having two aspects, intelligible and perceptual. The intelligible aspect consisted of the world of forms (or "ideas") and the perceptual aspect consisted of the world of replicas of those forms (carbon copies of the original). The true forms/ideas (not copies) can only be comprehended by the intellect, and such comprehension of reality is the goal of all knowledge.

Plato espoused that the essence of something (for example, a Judean date palm) was its form. The plant could grow through all the stages from a seed to a young palm and then a frond-covered mature tree laden with succulent dates, but through each stage or change in substance, the tree's essence (its form) is always present and is only being embodied by substance. This resonates with the Gnostic idea of the divine spark, unchanging, though embodied in matter. The object of knowledge is to break through to the underlying reality behind false forms of this world, and to understand that reality—that world of being that always is and never changes—is comprehended by the mind, not the senses or the imagination.

Plato's dualism expresses the idea that the human body is different than the soul. The body is simply a container or temporary housing for the soul. Plato suggested that the soul came from the world of ideas, a spiritual realm, before it entered the body. Once in the body, it became the overseer of the human. A saying of Plato reflects this idea of dualism perfectly: "Man is the soul which utilizes the body." In *Timaeus*, Plato offers further clarification.

Now God did not make the soul after the body . . . for having brought them together he would never have allowed that the elder should be ruled by the younger. . . . Whereas he made the soul in origin and excellence prior to and older than the body, to be the ruler and mistress, of whom the body was to be the subject.—Timaeus, 34

Christian theology was anchored in monotheism, or the belief in one god, a concept that early Christians shared with Judaism. Monotheism was also the basis of Islam. In opposition to the concept of the Demiurge, most early Christian fathers rejected the idea that any being other than God created the cosmos. They believed that a benevolent God created the world out of nothingness, unlike Plato's Demiurgos who created the world out of matter that already existed in the chaos.

The Book of Genesis

The Gnostics were fascinated by creation myths. The book of Genesis, the first book of the Hebrew scriptures, which represents a monotheistic God but immediately presents ideas of dualistic creation, may have particularly appealed to them. The eternal God alone in existence created heaven and earth. Earth was dark and formless. After establishing light and separating it from darkness, God established a firmament called heaven. God continued the process of creating, often observing that "it was good" until finally creating human beings out of "his own image, male and female," the first pair.

And the Lord God formed man of the dust of the ground, and breathed into his nostrils the breath of life; and man became a living soul.... And the Lord God caused a deep sleep to fall upon Adam and he slept: and he took one of his ribs, and ... made he a woman, and brought her unto the man.—Genesis 2:7–22

Not surprisingly, the Gnostics interpreted the story of Genesis differently than did ancient Jews and Christians. For the Gnostics, Adam and Eve were not historical people, the predecessors of humankind, or the original couple who brought sin upon humanity, but rather the personification of two principles indwelling in humans. While Adam personified the soul, Eve represented the spirit. Adam represented the "lower self" and Eve the "higher self." Right away, you can see the problem that orthodox Christianity might have with this idea because it places Eve in a superior position to Adam.

The Gnostics viewed Eve as Adam's numinous "awakener." The second century Gnostic text titled Apocryphon of John reveals that Adam was covered in the "drunkenness of darkness" and he awakened when Luminous Epinoia (or Eve) appeared and "lifted the veil which lay over his mind." Ancient Hebrews called the first woman by the name of Eve (in Hebrew, the name means "life"), but the Gnostics knew her as the "mother of all living."

Before orthodox Christianity established the belief in the Trinity—that is, belief in the Father, the Son, and the Holy Spirit—and the belief subsequently became part of the orthodox Apostles' Creed and the Nicene Creed (the first written sometime around A.D. 215 and the second in A.D. 325), some early Christian communities venerated a deity named Luminous Epinoia as the Divine Eve. The word "luminous" suggests light, so Gnostics undoubtedly saw her as a "light bearer," empowered to illuminate the sacred in their lives. The Apocryphon of John states that she is humanity's capacity to know God. The narrator of the Apocryphon of John asked Jesus if every human receives her, to which Jesus replied, "Yes."

This Gnostic Eve stands in dramatic contrast to the Orthodox Christian view of Eve as a weak, impressionable woman, powerless to resist the Serpent's temptation to eat from the tree in the center of the Garden of Eden. Eve "saw that the tree was good for food . . . pleasant to the eyes, and a tree to be desired to make one wise" (Genesis 3:6). She wanted those things. Consider this in the cultural context of the times of Jesus, when women were considered the property of men. Because of the times in which they lived, women were not educated and likely not well versed in the ancient scriptures, although they would have had some knowledge in order to train their children and practice the faith themselves. Until Jesus came along with his egalitarian beliefs and practices, women were not thought capable of understanding the deep wisdom of the scriptures. Many Jews and Christians saw Eve's act of defiance at disobeying God, of eating the apple, and of involving Adam by offering him a taste as a sin against the Father God. The second chapter of 1 Timothy describes the blame assigned to Eve for desiring knowledge and partaking of the forbidden fruit.

Sethian Mythology

There were many groups of Christians in the first few centuries. One important group—the Sethian Gnostics—aspired to mystical knowledge that they interpreted through wisdom, stories, themes (in particular, Genesis), and myths of various religious and philosophical traditions in order to find their way back to the Godhead. The fifth chapter of Genesis details the genealogy of the Hebrew patriarchs, among them a son of Adam. When Adam was 130 years old, he bore a son "in his own likeness, and after his image; and called his name Seth" (Genesis 5:3). The Sethians saw Seth as a savior figure much as Christians viewed Christ. The Sethians began as a Messianic religion (with the expectation of the coming of a savior/messiah) much as the Jewish Christian movement did. Contact with the earliest forms of Christianity brought Christian elements into the Gnostic Sethians' belief and practices.

Gnostic Sethian mythology features a number of characters who play out roles in an epic story that serves as a "pre-story" to Genesis. Gnostics did not believe that human sin brought humanity into enslavement in the material world, but rather that this enslavement was the fault of the creator. The Sethian myth attempts to offer a Gnostic explanation of the downward shift from God to human, from Spirit to matter.

FACT

Sethian Gnosticism is so-called because of references to Seth, the child of Adam and Eve, one who provided special knowledge. Sethian Gnostic writings include Zostrianos, The Three Steles of Seth, Apocalypse of Adam, Allogenes, The Reality of the Rulers, The Gospel of the Egyptians, The Apocryphon of John, The Threefold First Thought, and The Thunder, Perfect Mind.

Several Gnostic texts share a cluster of common beliefs that relate to Sethian mythology:

- The Holy Trinity is made up of the Invisible Spirit (Father), Barbelo (Mother), and Son (the Demiurge).
- Gnostics have gnosis that they are collectively the spiritual kernels or seeds of Seth.
- Seth is the Savior of his seed.
- The Demiurge Yaldabaoth attempts to destroy the seed of Seth.
- There are three Ages, and the Savior comes in each Age.

One version of the Sethian myth opened with an Aeon named Barbelo. This Aeon was perhaps the original emanation of God and possessed both a masculine and feminine side. Barbelo was a kind of master parent of all the other emanations or Aeons, and they, too had masculine and feminine aspects. And so, each emanation split off into more emanations that continued the process. All of these emanations, dividing and multiplying like a cell undergoing mitosis, fragmented God until the primordial universe became unstable. That's when the Aeon Sophia appeared in the story.

Sophia means "wisdom" in Greek; as her name implied, she wisely considered her position so far removed from the Godhead and pondered on how to get back to the center of divine nature closest to God. She decided to imitate God's original action of emanating. She did not seek permission. Her act of creating a copy of herself caused something of a crisis to occur within the Pleroma and as a result, the Demiurge known as Yaldabaoth (sometimes pictured as a serpent with a lion's head) was born of Sophia. She created a throne for him and wrapped him in a resplendent cloud, where the monstrous being lived, isolated and without knowledge of the higher realms—of the Pleroma Reality.

QUESTION?

How was Yaldabaoth similar to Yahweh, God of the Hebrews?
Yaldabaoth, ignorant of any other god, declares some variation of: "I am a jealous God; there is no God but me." The Hebrew's Yahweh makes a similar statement in Exodus 20:4–5. The Gnostics accorded Yaldabaoth and Yahweh the status of inferior gods.

Yaldabaoth stole some power from his mother to create the material universe. Unknowingly, he created a carbon copy of the Pleroma, but his world simply reflected reality. It wasn't the real deal. He, as inferior creator, created the imperfect physical world and the beings in it mirrored those above. In that way, his mother's power became encapsulated into human forms and humans became ensnared in the material universe. This sets the stage for Yaldabaoth to create man in the image of God.

One version of the Gnostic myth is that God tricks Yaldabaoth to transfer some of his mother Sophia's power into the inanimate Adam, who at that point had no spirit. This breathing of life into Adam was the initial step in making all humans animate and more powerful than Yaldabaoth's beings or cosmic forces. Those beings then banished Adam into the lowest realms of matter. But all is not lost, because God takes pity on Adam and inspires him with a divine thought on how to extricate himself from matter and ascend to his true home.

Tenets of Gnosticism

For the Gnostics, the primary purpose of life was the search for enlightenment. In this regard, Gnostics were not very different from other religious mystics. In their search for enlightenment, they established certain principles. Because of the diversity of early Christian communities espousing Gnostic ideas, it is difficult to present a specific list of beliefs that could be called the tenets of Gnosticism. Still, some diverse early communities of Gnostics, including the Naassenes, Ophites, Simonians, Cerinthians, Docetists, Arianists, Manichaeans, and others shared some ideas in common. Certainly Gnostic groups in the first few centuries of early Christianity did share some basic ideas, including beliefs in:

- A doctrine of immanence
- A doctrine of reincarnation
- A group of powers called archons
- A concept of resurrection
- The process of salvation
- A doctrine of "emanations"
- The nature of humanity
- The idea of a revealer

Scholars agree that immediately following the death of Jesus there was no single version of Christianity with an established creed and set of orthodox dogmas. There was no New Testament to consult. There had not yet been a battle of theological ideas that would eventually include in the tenets of Christianity original sin, the divinity of Jesus, and the virgin birth, but exclude Gnostic ideas of immanence (God in each human as opposed to only being transcendent), a revealer who brings secret knowledge, and reincarnation.

Five Sacred Rites of Gnosticism

The following list includes the Gnostic religious rites mentioned in the Gospel of Philip. Some of the Gnostic religious rites may have been drawn from other spiritual traditions around the Greco-Roman world. These Gnostic rites (some would call them sacraments) ideally liberated the person's indwelling divine spark, putting him on the right path to enlightenment and his "real" home in the Pleroma. The Gnostics could not embrace the Christian belief that they could get to heaven simply by having enough faith and behaving well on earth. Gnostic sacraments listed in the Gospel of Philip included:

- Baptism (ritual immersion in water)
- Chrism (holy rite of anointing with olive oil)
- Bridal Chamber
- Holy Eucharist
- Redemption
- Extreme Unction or Anointing at Death
- Holy Orders

Many Gnostics saw themselves as the Christian faithful. They did not view their religious practices or sacramental rites as acts of heretical defiance against the beliefs and practices of other Christian communities. Indeed, there was not yet a body of the Christian church to formally challenge the Gnostics. However, beginning in the second century, certain Christian church fathers wrote polemics against the Gnostics.

It might seem that there were many similarities between the baptism and Holy Eucharist rites of the Christians (Gnostic and other communities), and pagan Mystery rituals. At least one source of material on ancient Christianity noted bluntly that the early fathers for many centuries after the death of Jesus—from the Apostle Paul through Saint Augustine—would have to explain the close resemblances.

Persecution of the Gnostics and purges against Gnostic communities for heresies drove the Gnostics underground to practice in secret. Gnosticism resurfaced through the ages in various countries and in the lives of various groups of people to the present day. Modern Gnostics not only have these ancient sacraments to link them with the past; they also have, thanks to the work of scholars, translations of their spiritual ancestral writings collected in *The Gnostic Bible* by Willis Barnstone and Marvin Meyer. On the Internet, you can find Gnostic versions of a creed, mass, and rosary as well as prayers.

Gnostic Sacramental Rituals

As the first step on the initiate's spiritual journey, baptism was likely the most important of the Gnostic rituals. With its origins in Jewish purification rites, baptism symbolized a spiritual "washing" with the purpose of weakening the control of the archons' powers over the initiate's mental life (emotional, psychic, and intellectual). According to the Valentinian Gnostic belief, loosening the grip of this false world's ideas freed the initiate of entrapment in matter and the prison of darkness.

FACT

The Apostles' Creed evolved as a profession of faith by baptismal candidates. Early church father Irenaeus's "Rule of Faith" and the later baptismal service of Hippolytus are strikingly similar to the Creed. In the Christian churches of the first few centuries, candidates would be dunked three times and expected to answer affirmatively each question asked of them about faith.

The Gnostic rite of baptism welcomed the individual into the church, just as it does today in most Christian places of worship. But the symbolic immersion in water did not mean the Gnostic initiate would experience immediate enlightenment. The religious candidate thereafter would undertake a regular practice of meditation, contemplation, spiritual study, and other activities in pursuit of that goal.

The ritual least understood by historical and biblical scholars is mentioned in the Gospel of Philip as the "Bridal Chamber." Gnostic texts note that a couple once joined in the bridal chamber is to never again separate. Scholars suggest it may be a sacred ritual between a woman and man, or an allegory for some type of a mystical union of the individual Divine spark (bride) and its Source (bridegroom).

How Gnostic Christians Became Heretics

The more literalistic of the Christian communities, in an effort to preserve the "integrity" of stories about Jesus and his teachings—or at least their interpretations of those teachings—differentiated themselves from other Christians who espoused Gnostic ideas. Their term for the latter was "heretic" and their ideas came to be called heresies. Some early Christian fathers sought out heresies to vigorously oppose them. Lacking ancient sources of original Gnostic documents, prior to Nag Hammadi modern scholars have had to rely on the writings of those early Christian heresiologists (individuals who study and write about heresy) to provide information about Gnosticism in their writings.

The most notable among the heresiologists was a church father named Irenaeus, bishop of Lyons, who sometime around A.D. 180 wrote a treatise in five volumes titled *On the Detection and Overthrow of the So-Called Gnosis*. The work is commonly referred to as simply *Against Heresies*. Other church fathers, such as the Tertullian (bishop of Carthage) and Hippolytus of Rome, also made contributions to what is known about Gnosticism by writing against it. You will read more about these individuals and the heresies they particularly found offensive in other chapters. For now, suffice it to say that the majority of Gnostic texts were destroyed in order to suppress the movement. Little survives to modern times, though copies of Gnostic texts discovered within the last half-century have shed more light on what is known about Gnosticism.

Gnostic Syncretism

Syncretism means the merging together of distinctly different (often opposing) ideas and fusing them into one concept. The Gnostics used syncretism from the already existing traditions of the ancient world to develop their ideas about cosmology (origin and structure of the universe) and theology. From roughly the second to the fourth centuries A.D., their sects flourished. It is believed that in some cases entire congregations may have shared

Gnostic ideas but in other cases only an individual or a few people within a congregation might embrace Gnostic beliefs, since there was no Gnostic collection of teachings gathered in one book like the Bible.

Gnostic Religious Writings

The Gnostics wrote diverse works, including many gospels about Jesus, his life and his teachings, and his companions (Mary Magdalene, Thomas, Philip, Judas Iscariot, et al.). Banned for centuries, copies of Gnostic texts resurfaced in 1945 at Nag Hammadi. A peasant stumbled upon a clay jar containing fifty-two ancient papyri texts. These ancient texts discovered only a half century ago offer a snapshot of earliest evolving Christianity in Palestine in the first few centuries. Among the codices (leather-bound papyrus manuscripts) found were The Gospel of the Egyptians, Pistis Sophia, The Dialogue of the Savior, The Book of Thomas the Contender, The Apocryphon of John, The Gospel of Philip, The Gospel of Thomas, and The Thunder, Perfect Mind. Taken together they show the extreme diversity and divisions in early Christian thinking and writing. Find these Gnostic texts at *www.gnosis.org* or in the book, edited by James M. Robinson, titled *The Nag Hammadi Library: The Definitive Translation of the Gnostic Scriptures Complete in One Volume.*

Gnostic Equality Between the Sexes

Did the Gnostics believe that men and women were equal? Most likely, since it is known that the Gnostics especially revered Mary Magdalene and held her in the highest esteem. They featured her prominently in their writings. She even has a Gnostic gospel named after her. The Gnostics depicted the Supreme God in male and female imagery and therefore saw the Divine in women as well as men. In the Gnostic scriptures, it is often Sophia, goddess of wisdom, who calls out in a Gnostic myth or proverb or shines behind the "lens" that Mary Magdalene holds in her discussions with Jesus.

Chapter 3

How the Canonical Christian Texts Were Chosen

Early groups of Christians possessed many sacred texts. Their religious material included letters, gospels, acts, manuals, epistles, hymns, apocalyptic literature, and treatises and were as diverse as the people who possessed them and the times and cultures in which they lived. Some of these writings made it into the New Testament canon; others were rejected, suppressed, and destroyed. Through the process of selection over many years, the documents collected into the canon offered a particular view of Christianity, but there were other documents and other views as well.

Gnostic Beliefs in Scripture

Even before the end of the Apostles' lifetimes, problems arose within the fledgling Christian communities. The New Testament letters of Paul and the Acts of the Apostles reveal many of these early problems. From reading them, you can see that the first Christians had to grapple with a host of issues: what they believed about Jesus, sin, Gentiles and Jews, the roles of women, and behavior and cultural practices that were not acceptable in or compatible with Christian ethical and moral ways. Nothing inflamed the early orthodox Christians more than heresy.

FACT

Heresy (from the Greek *hairein*) means "the act of choosing." It has been used throughout history to highlight a point of doctrine or opinion that is at variance with the more generally accepted doctrine or teaching. Most often, the word is used within the context of religious ideas, beliefs, or systems.

Scriptural Letters Written to Oppose Gnosticism

Prior to his martyrdom around A.D. 107, a Syrian living in Antioch named Ignatius wrote a number of letters to the Christian communities of Ephesus, Magnesia, Tralles, Rome, Philadelphia, and Smyrna. Ignatius exhorted these Christians to be ever vigilant against the spreading heresies of Gnosticism and Docetism (believers in those systems thought that Jesus the Christ was only a spirit with a phantom body). Such heresies threatened Christian unity, and the letters of Ignatius show that he was trying to create Christian unity. The letters suggest that he was sold on hierarchy and doctrine, but that the churches he visited were not. Ignatius asked Christians to obey their bishops. This was very early in the history of the church, but it is clear that a three-tiered hierarchy of leadership (bishops, priests, and deacons) was already established and that an orthodox viewpoint was in place. Those vested in unity based on apostolic succession and orthodox ideas used the power of the pen on papyrus to oppose Gnosticism and other ideas at variance with their beliefs.

Irenaeus, a presbyter in the southern Gallic city of Lyons, lived during a time of protracted persecutions of Christians between A.D. 120 and A.D. 203. It also happened to be a time when Gnosticism in general and Valentinism specifically, with its doctrine of dualism, were fashionable and flourishing. Irenaeus opposed the Gnostic idea of a lesser God doing the work of creation. He believed that the creation God of the Hebrew scriptures and the redemption God of the New Testament were the same God embodied in Christ. He particularly hated the hypocrisies of Marcion and Valentinus and forcefully argued against the Gnostic heresies in a five-volume work titled *On the Detection and Overthrow of the So-Called Gnosis*, also known by the shorter title, *Adversus Haereses* (or *Against Heresies*). This book contains precise and abundant quotes from a majority of the texts that made it into the New Testament. Irenaeus also wrote *The Demonstration of the Apostolic Teaching* (a text thought to serve as an instruction guide for baptism candidates into the early orthodox Christian religion). But mostly, Irenaeus's writings were against Gnosticism.

The Basilidians and Valentinians claimed that Jesus was a spirit, not a man. Other groups included Marcionists, Montanists, Ebionites (Jewish Christians opposed to abandoning Judaic customs and rituals), Arianists, Sethians, Thomasines, Mandaeans (followers of John the Baptist), Manichaeans, Ophites, Cainites, Carpocratians, Borborites, and Naassenes (mystics who claimed their teachings came from James, Jesus' brother).

Writings Favoring Gnosticism

Marcion was one of the most famous Gnostics. Much of what is known about Marcion has come down through the writings of those who opposed his teachings. He traveled from Asia Minor to Rome in A.D. 139. He was a Christian who adopted Gnostic beliefs and within five years was excommunicated. Marcion saw the God of Hebrew scriptures (the Old Testament) as weak and cruel whereas the God that Christ revealed was merciful and good. Marcion believed that of all the Apostles, only Paul truly understood the gospel teachings. The others were too steeped in Judaism. He practiced a severe ascetic life—the Gnostics thought that the body was polluted, loathsome, and evil and that asceticism countered such evil. Marcion established a sect of followers who believed in his particular view of Gnosticism. They shunned marriage, flesh, and wine (even from the Holy Eucharist). He developed his own canon, throwing out the Hebrew scriptures altogether. In Marcion's canon were ten letters of the Apostle Paul (minus the letters to Timothy and Titus known as the three pastoral Epistles), the Gospel of Luke (but he edited out all the references to the God of the Hebrew scriptures as the Father of Christ), and some of his own writings. Marcion and his followers could not accept the idea that Christ could have appeared in the flesh. Flesh was evil, but Christ was good and, therefore, how could he have come in the flesh? Marcion decided to accept the doctrine of Docetism. He may have been raised in a community of Jesus' followers who for generations had accepted such ideas.

QUESTION?

What are polemics and apologetics?
Polemics, in reference to religion, is the art of waging controversial arguments against a particular ecclesiastical doctrine or opinion. Apologetics are explanations and defenses of Christianity. Several early Christians—Justin Martyr, Origen, and Augustine—are recognized as Apologists. Even the Apostle Paul made two apologies, one before Festus and the other before Agrippa (Acts 24:10; 25:8, and 26:2).

Tertullian converted to Christianity roughly between A.D. 197 to 198. His writings—there are about thirty-one—illustrate a brilliant mind that could seize upon new ideas. Initially, he was a faithful follower of the orthodox Christian way, a great Christian writer in Latin (which earned him the moniker of the Father of the Latin Church), and formulator of the term "Trinity," a term that endures to today. Tertullian's writings include polemics against heresies and apologetics against Judaism and paganism. In particular,

Tertullian zealously wrote five books against Marcionite heresies. Modern scholars consider them an invaluable source for information about Gnosticism of his time. Later in life, Tertullian broke with the orthodox Christian Church to become a Montanist. Members of that sect, after falling into ecstatic states to directly experience the presence of the Holy Spirit, would proclaim inspired messages.

Arius was a gifted theologian and writer from North Africa (A.D. 256 to A.D. 336). He sought to resolve a problem with the Christian doctrine. Both the Jews and the Christians had one God, but in Christianity, the Father God and his Son are both worshipped as God. Arius's attempt at resolving the doctrinal problem (so that Christianity would not be a bitheism, i.e., a religion with two gods) focused on the nature of God and the relationship between the Father and his Son. The orthodox Christians took the position that both were distinct Persons, but were one God. Arius reasoned that the Son was not eternal and, further, that he was subordinate to the Father (see 1 Corinthians 15:24–28.) His philosophy attracted a lot of support. However, the Council of Nicaea (the first ecumenical conference of bishops that was convened in A.D. 325 by Emperor Constantine I) established the canon. After significant debate, showing the strength of Arius's position, the Council voted his view into heresy. It bore the name of Arius and gave rise to polemics against it by the orthodoxy.

Other Significant Scriptural Writings

The earliest writings contained in the New Testament belong to the Apostle Paul, a Pharisaic Jew and Roman citizen, according to Acts. He never met Jesus, but experienced a powerful conversion and became an ardent believer. In his letter to the Galatians, he opposed those who argued in favor of making Christianity a synthesis between keeping faith in Christ and keeping the (Mosaic) law of the Jews. Paul called the proponents of such ideas "the Judaizers." Paul's thoughts in Romans are later developed into the doctrine of "original sin" by Augustine and others. About the death and resurrection of Jesus, he wrote that Jesus "was delivered for our offenses, and was raised again for our justification" (Romans 4:25). He also explained how salvation comes through one's faith in Jesus (as opposed to adherence to Mosaic Law). Paul's belief in the divine nature of the Christ marks him as one of the first to offer this idea. Another Pauline offering was the concept of the Holy Spirit. But was Paul's thinking aligned more with the orthodox or Gnostic beliefs?

Paul reveals in 2 Corinthians 12:2–5 that he was "caught up to the third heaven . . . caught up into paradise, and heard unspeakable words, which it is not lawful for a man to utter." The Gnostics relied on dreams and visions for inner insights, and when they spoke of their theology, it was often in terms of inspired revelation from an inward-oriented spiritual experience.

That his letters would be included in the New Testament suggested the importance and acceptance of his views by the orthodox church fathers, but modern religious scholar Elaine Pagels, writing in *The Gnostic Paul*, posits an interesting theory for Paul being a Gnostic. Unquestionably, his influence on the early church was so powerful that someone wrote forged letters from Paul (the pastoral Epistles to Timothy and Titus) to make it appear that Paul held beliefs in compliance with the orthodox interpretation rather than the Gnostic view. A passage in a letter that Paul supposedly wrote to Timothy makes a point about the expected behavior of women in church and reads as though Paul preached ideas consistent with literalist Christianity in the first century.

Let the woman learn in silence with all subjection. But I suffer not a woman to teach, nor to usurp authority over the man, but to be in silence. For Adam was first formed, then Eve. And Adam was not deceived, but the woman being deceived was in the transgression.—1 Timothy 2:11–14

Clement of Alexandria was an orthodox early church father claiming to have more than one version of the Gospel of Mark. One of them contained a secret teaching imparted to the Apostles by Jesus. The teaching passed down from the Apostles through secret transmission to a few spiritually advanced individuals who were ready to receive and be changed by gnosis. A letter attributed to Clement to someone named Theodore apparently to refute "unspeakable teachings of the Carpocratians" contained manuscript pages with unknown passages of Mark's Gospel. In the letter, Clement claimed that the secret, more spiritual gospel was for the use of believers being perfected in Egypt. So valuable was this gospel that Clement noted the church in Alexandria had to keep careful guard of it and to allow only those spiritually advanced individuals who had undergone initiation into the great mysteries to read it.

The only reference scholars had to this secret teaching of Jesus was the one mention of it in the letter attributed to Clement. Authorship of the letter has been the focus of a heated scholarly debate in recent times. Some Christians find the letter to be theologically offensive because of its homoerotic overtones and the reference to a great sound inside the tomb of Lazarus *before* Jesus removed the stone and raised him from the dead. Could Lazarus have called out or signaled Jesus in that great noise if he were already dead? Although some Clementine scholars believe the letter to be written by Clement, other biblical scholars say the letter is a forgery.

QUESTION?

Which version of the Gospel of Mark known to Clement is the one in the New Testament?

Of the three versions—the longer "secret" version aimed at those spiritually advanced, the shorter version for new Christians, or the suspected forgery—it is generally accepted that the shorter version is the one included in the canonical New Testament.

As the spread of Gnosticism in the second and third centuries gathered steam, the orthodox element of the literalist Christian church worked to define and maintain its identity as distinct and apart from that of the Gnostics. Helping in that effort was a young presbyter from Caesarea by the name of Eusebius, a scholar with an interest in antiquities, who in the fourth century wrote a ten-volume history of Christianity that proved invaluable to the orthodox church through the ages and greatly aided the work of modern biblical scholars.

Three Views of Salvation: Gnostic, Jewish Christian, Pauline Christian

The Gnostics believed that salvation came through the grace of God and the secret spiritual knowledge that Jesus the Christ (redeemer figure) imparted to humankind. The Gnostics also believed that humans were imperfect and therefore could not secure salvation by themselves through good deeds. They believed that through self-discovery and inner knowledge that came from direct contact with the Divine, their sacred spark could awaken from beneath the dark spell of the Demiurge to return to the realm of Light. The inner spiritual resurrection, not the physical, gave each seeker access to God without the intercession of priests or the death of Jesus.

The Jewish Christians, those closest to Jesus, who saw themselves as a sect within Judaism, believed that salvation came from following Mosaic laws and abiding by the rules governing purity, diet, behavior, and sacrifice in the Temple as well as honoring the Jewish holy days and the Sabbath.

An early Christian view of salvation can be found in the Gospels of Matthew, Mark, and Luke (collectively known as the synoptic Gospels because of their similarities in content, language, and style). These gospels reveal part of the message that salvation comes through individual good deeds and kindly treatment of others, especially the poor (Matthew 25:31–46 and Luke 10:25–27). The Gospel of John emphasizes salvation through faith in Jesus as the Son of God: "Behold the Lamb of God, which taketh away the sin of the world" (John 1:29). The early Christians did not elaborate on exactly what one needed in order to be "saved," but Paul believed that salvation came from belief in the Son of God (see 2 Corinthians 5:10–21) and faith in Jesus. He wrote to the Corinthians about the certainty of the resurrection of the dead: "For since by man came death, by man came also the resurrection of the dead. For as in Adam all die, even so in Christ shall all be made alive" (1 Corinthians 15:21–22).

The Pauline Christian view of salvation stresses belief in Jesus, son of God, who died for the sins of humankind, and was resurrected. Pauline Christianity describes the beliefs, theology, moral behavior, and acts of faith necessary for salvation as espoused by the Apostle Paul in his letters and supported also by the writer of the book of Acts of the Apostles. Pauline

Christianity today is expressed through Roman Catholicism but also Protestant denominations as well.

FACT

Soteriology is the study of the biblical doctrine of salvation through Jesus Christ. The term "salvation" derives from the Greek word *sōtēria*, which can also mean redemption. When humans satisfy the condition of faith in Christ, they receive salvation (see Paul's letter to the Romans 1:16–17).

A Call for Unity

Early Christian communities, while endeavoring to stay close to Jesus' teachings and words of wisdom, began to diverge as they developed their own ideas and traditions. Both the canonical and the Gnostic Gospels reveal instances when Jesus, within his own inner circle, had to clarify particulars of his teachings, patiently explain a point, or redirect a disciple whose frustration and anger required a rebuke. There were twelve disciples in Jesus' inner circle—twelve witnesses to informal conversations, private teachings, and talks before multitudes. Yet these twelve often disagreed and at times were contentious with each other.

The disciples all had been raised in the patriarchal society of first-century Palestine. In that milieu, women were not usually educated nor considered equal to men, yet the Gnostic texts portray Mary Magdalene as having a special relationship with Jesus, and spiritual insights and understanding better than all her co-disciples. Her spiritual comprehension shines in *the Pistis Sophia*. The Gospel of Philip stresses her personal relationship with Jesus. In the Gospel of Mary (Magdalene), while Peter and the others are mourning Jesus, he tells Mary that he (Peter) and the others know that Jesus loved her more than them and urges her to share any words the Savior might have told her. She offers a secret teaching that Jesus gave her, and afterwards Andrew disbelieves her and Peter is incredulous, asking those gathered if Jesus would speak secretly with a woman. It is Levi who calms everyone and reminds Peter that the Savior made her worthy and it was not Peter's place to reject her.

The canonical texts reveal that there were disagreements among members of Jesus' core group while he dwelt among them and that dissension continued after his death. Each Apostle had his own group of followers. After Jesus' death, the Apostles separated. Those adhering to their Jewish traditions remained in their sect of Judaism, which they now considered "reformed." Pauline Christians evangelized to non-Jews. Paul found himself at odds with Peter and James, head of the community in Jerusalem. Community leaders had to deal with rising tensions over what was expected in Christian belief and practice. In an effort to counsel, instruct, and unite the Christians of Ephesus, Paul sent a letter telling them that the death of Jesus united Jew and Gentile. In this letter, he also laid out clear guidelines for all to follow.

I, therefore, the prisoner of the Lord, beseech you that ye walk worthy . . . forbearing one another in love; endeavoring to keep the unity of the Spirit in the bond of peace. There is one body, and one Spirit . . . One Lord, one faith, one baptism, one God and Father of all, who is above all, and through all, and in you all.—Ephesians 4:1–6

Many Christian leaders, including Gnostic, Jewish Christian, and literalist Christians, understood that the unity of the faithful depended on agreeing upon key elements of doctrine. There was a growing consensus among many Christians by the late second century that the Gospels of Matthew, Mark, Luke, and John represented inspired narrative and the best authoritative accounts of Jesus' life and teachings as well as his divinity. These four gospels, although they portrayed differing understandings of Jesus, served as a means of unifying different communities of Christians in the absence of a canon.

The literalist Christians focused on the group and growing its "family," while the Gnostics continued to emphasize the individual and the process of inner spiritual discovery. This may partially account for the decline of Gnosticism after several centuries, while Christianity continued to grow even in spite of persecution, but there was another reason as well. Through a process of selection over several centuries Christian leaders chose some texts over others for the emerging church. Those that they considered tainted by heresies were destroyed prior to the reign of Constantine. The fifty-two once-suppressed Gnostic texts found at Nag Hammadi indicate that some Gnostics must have defied the order to destroy those sacred writings and instead hid them in a jar in the desert cave to be discovered at some future time. The writings of Nag Hammadi were collected by Christians. The texts took many forms, including among them hymns, acts, myths, prayers, and gospels.

What's in a Gospel?

Jesus charged the Apostles with a commission to go into the world and share the gospel. Gospel was initially oral teaching—an imparting of "good news." The word "gospel" is usually thought of as a written account of Jesus' life and teachings. More generally, a gospel may simply be a teaching or doctrine of a religious teacher. The New Testament contains only four (Matthew, Mark, Luke, and John) out of the many circulating in the first few centuries. In the Gnostic Bible, there are six: the Gospels of Thomas, Philip, John, Truth, Mary (Magdalene), and the Secret Supper. In the collection of Gnostic texts found in the clay jar at Nag Hammadi, there were five: the Gospels of Truth, Thomas, Philip, the Egyptians, and Mary. These gospels, along with other texts in the jar, offer glimpses into ancient Judaism and early Christianity as well as into the life of Jesus. Of course these gospels, like the canonical texts, can only reveal how Jesus' life was described by later followers. There is no way to know about the actual details of the life of Jesus and his followers, whether they were Jews, Egyptians, or Gentiles, or Gnostics from around the Greco-Roman empire.

The Canonical Gospels and the Synoptic Problem

The synoptic Gospels (Matthew, Mark, and Luke) possess similar stories about Jesus' life and sayings attributed to him told in similar phrases and, in some cases, identical wording (the Gospel of John is quite different in literary style and content). So, were the three similar gospels separate accounts by three different writers or was one account written and the others generated from it? An eighteenth-century German scholar named J. J. Griesbach positioned the three gospels in a three-column table (a "synopsis") to study their relationship. It became apparent that not only were many of the same stories occurring in the same sequences but being told in the same or similar ways.

FACT

While the canonical and the Gnostic Gospels had differences, they also had some areas of agreement. One of those was the practice of asceticism. It was a moral and religious behavior that both groups respected and practiced, although some biblical scholars say the point was played down or sidestepped in polemics against Gnostic heresies.

Scholars have debated many different reasons for the similarities. It is plausible that the gospels are written versions of popular stories about Jesus that were told and repeated innumerable times. However, they would have been told in Aramaic, Jesus' language, and the New Testament was written in Greek. The synoptic Gospels share many of the same Greek words, suggesting that perhaps one gospel was written, and the other two either were written independently, borrowing from a third source or simply from the original gospel. Modern scholarship indicates that Mark was likely the first gospel written, and that Matthew and Luke depended on it as a source.

The "Q" Source

A collection of the sayings of Jesus' deemed "Q" by some scholars and called the "Sayings Gospel Q" by others, provides sayings contained in Matthew and Luke that are not found in Mark. The Sayings Gospel Q is part of the "Two Source theory" solution to the synoptic problem surrounding the three synoptic Gospels. Most scholars agree that the Gospel of Mark was written in the late 60s A.D. , and that Matthew and Luke both borrow from Mark. In addition, both Matthew and Luke use the hypothetical Q source to attribute sayings to Jesus. Finally, both Matthew and Luke use their own original oral source material not contained in Mark. The Gospel of Matthew may have been written around A.D. 70 to A.D. 100 and the Gospel of Luke may have been written around A.D. 80 to 100 (many scholars believe it was circa A.D. 85).

The Gospels Fight It Out

Imagine churches spread out in lands all around the Mediterranean and into Africa. Perhaps many of these churches had sacred texts that had been translated or copied by scribes from original source material. Or perhaps itinerant preachers making their pilgrimages around the region brought new ideas, pieces of texts, a different version of a particular gospel account, etc. into these fledgling Christian communities and churches. The gospels in these churches may not have been exactly the same as their earliest versions. Errors may have been introduced, scribes might have edited out or redacted material to shorten passages, translations might not have been exact, and new material could have been inserted.

The Gnostics were influenced by and perhaps borrowed ideas from a variety of other belief systems available to them during the first and second centuries, including the cults of Isis and Osiris, Attis and Cybele, Mithraism (based on Mithras, ancient god of light), and Zoroastrianism.

Certainly, there were lots of gospels circulating in the early centuries of the church. If a gospel bore the name of an Apostle, it would have more of an impact on the early Christians than one that didn't. The authorship and authority of many of the gospels were questioned. Had they been altered to reflect a particular viewpoint? Had material been added or deleted? Even in the early centuries of the church, everyone knew that if someone wanted others to notice his ideas, he could put an Apostle's name on his gospel. As you already know, many of the Gnostic Gospels do bear the name of someone close to Jesus.

The process of selecting the gospels that would be included in the New Testament took centuries to complete. It required collecting, scrutinizing, accepting, and rejecting. The gospels had to fight it out. In many ways, the battle against heresies helped the leaders of the fledgling early church refine exactly what they did believe and enabled them to determine which texts best represented their understanding of the truth about Jesus, his life, times, words, and ministry.

In the second century and much later, a group of gospels known as the Infancy Gospels began to circulate. They focused on the life of young Jesus. None of those gospels made it into the canon, and so are designated as apocryphal texts. They include the Gospel of Pseudo-Matthew, Gospel of James, Infancy Gospel of Thomas, and the Life of John the Baptist, History of Joseph the Carpenter, and the Arabic Infancy Gospel. Sometimes a gospel deviated too much from the literalist positions of what was then an acceptable doctrine to some Christian leaders and faithful followers. If it were deemed at variance with acceptable ideas of the emerging core community of Christians, it would remain outside the canon. Many such gospels were excluded for this reason. Other reasons that a gospel would not be considered useful is if its authorship was dubious or thought to be an outright forgery. Marcion (who died in circa A.D. 160) was said to have edited his version of the Gospel of Luke, and he, in turn, thought that Matthew, Mark, and John were forgeries. Early church father and historian Irenaeus of Lyons (about A.D. 130 to about 200) did not hesitate to call Marcion a heretic.

The Council at Nicaea

Did the Christian leaders during the three hundred years after Jesus' death decide one day that things were getting a little out of control and they needed to call a meeting during which they would establish for all time what Jesus had said and meant? Was their intent to iterate a canon, excommunicate those who disagreed with it, and thereby establish what all Christians of future generations would believe? Biblical scholars say it was more complicated than that, but basically that is what happened.

A pivotal moment in church history took place in A.D. 325 when a dispute that had long been brewing over the Christology of Jesus erupted between two branches of the early church, prompting Emperor Constantine to convene a council of Christian leaders. The Father, Son, and Holy Spirit represented then, as it does now, the Trinity of the Godhead. Bishop Alexander of the church of Alexandria, Egypt, and his followers believed in the divinity of Jesus. For Alexander, the Son existed co-eternally with the Father and was of the same substance as the Father. Arius, a well-respected presbyter of the time, opposed the idea of a divine Jesus. Arius and his followers believed that the Son, though a most spectacular and perfect creation, was still a creation. The Son, the Arians reasoned, was created after the Father and therefore could not be eternal.

FACT

Some Gnostics believed that the Redeemer/Savior dwelled within Jesus from his birth, while others thought the Savior descended upon him at his baptism and departed before the moment of death. Still others taught that the wrathful Demiurge caused Jesus' death. Finally, some Gnostics believed that Simon of Cyrene died in place of Jesus.

Alexander believed that the words "born," "begotten," and "created" all meant the same thing. Arius disagreed. Alexander and his followers argued that Arius was defying the unity of the Godhead as expressed in the Gospel of John, chapter 10, verse 30, in which Jesus says, "I and my Father are One." The divinity of Jesus became the critical boiling-point issue around which the leaders of the church would come together to resolve for all future time this theological problem and others.

Who Attended?

Roman Emperor Constantine convened the meeting, which was modeled upon Roman senate sessions, and empowered the Council with the power of the state to enforce its resolutions. This was a critical turning point in the development of Christianity. Prior to the convening of the council, church leaders and authors could argue strongly for a doctrine, but had no way to enforce it. Of the 1,800 Christian bishops invited, only 250 to 300 from both the eastern and western provinces attended. This was the first large gathering of Christians following the Edict of Milan in A.D. 313, when Emperors Constantine and Licinius decreed an end to Christian persecution. Some of the bishops at the Council of Nicaea still bore marks of persecution. Many priests and acolytes accompanied their bishops for the session, which lasted more than a month. Emperor Constantine attended as an observer but did not vote.

What Was Decided?

During the month-long convocation, a host of issues were decided and conflicts resolved. The council overwhelmingly agreed with Bishop of Alexandria and against Arius (only two voted for the Arian position). Arius was excommunicated, declared a heretic, and exiled. The council also reached an agreement on the Christian Passover. Henceforth they called it Easter and would celebrate on the first Sunday following the first full moon after the vernal equinox. The council voted to prohibit young women in the homes of clerics, self-castration, usury among clerics, kneeling during the liturgy on Sundays and during the fifty days of Pentecost, and the removal of priests. Among other actions, it voted to establish a minimum term for catechumens (those who studied the faith in preparation for being initiated in the sacred mysteries), recognize the Holy See of Jerusalem as having honorary rights, establish the highest authority for the bishops of Alexandra and Rome and their regions, allow two annual synods to be held, ensure that bishops and presbyters receive the Holy Eucharist before deacons, and declare the invalidity of baptism by Pauline heretics.

Establishment of the Canon

For the first time, the assembled bishops sought to unify all Christian factions and formulate one creed that articulated Christian beliefs. They sought a statement using scriptural language that precisely represented the church's orthodox doctrine and excluded any heresies (particularly the Arian heresies). Subsequent councils would deal with other heresies. They began with the baptismal creed used by Bishop Eusebius of Caesarea, adding clarifications as they worked through it. This newly formulated creed became known as the Nicene Creed.

New language in the creed included phrases such as "God from God, Light from Light, true God from true God; begotten, not made; from the substance of the Father." Arius and his followers could recite other creeds but could not truthfully recite these precise words. Emperor Constantine followed through with a statement that anyone refusing to sign the creed would be exiled. Arius, Theonas of Marmarica in Libya, and Secundus of Ptolemais refused and were excommunicated and exiled. Arius's works were ordered to be destroyed.

Out of a response to heresies, the young Christian church had together established rules for itself and a creed. Their next challenge was to establish the New Testament canon.

Chapter 4

Who Were the Authors of the Gnostic Gospels?

The New Testament offers one version of Jesus' life and times. It is a view that has been supported by the church for over 2,000 years. Modern feminist scholars say the church and its patriarchal traditions have all but erased the contributions of women who also followed Jesus. Gnostic-influenced communities in the earliest centuries of the church had a more egalitarian social structure than the more patriarchal Christian communities. The Gnostic Gospels offer another approach to Jesus, his women followers, and the early groups that believed in him.

Gnostic View of Gender Equality

The Gnostic writings celebrate women as bearers of truth, wisdom, and light. The Gnostic God is often regarded in the context of a dyad possessing both masculine and feminine attributes. The orthodox Christians speak of God the Father and his Son. For the Trinity, the Holy Spirit is added. Mary, the holy mother of Jesus, is not accorded the same stature as God the Father, though she may be reverently referred to as "Mary, Mother of God," according to religious scholar Elaine Pagels, an expert on the Gnostics. But Mary is not considered the same as God the Father in feminine form. Yet the Jewish wisdom literature in the Hebrew scriptures (Ecclesiastes, Proverbs, Sirach, the Wisdom of Solomon, etc.), in which Christianity has roots, personifies Wisdom as a female.

FACT

Of the fifty-two Gnostic texts found at Nag Hammadi, four feature the feminine spiritual aspect of God. They are The Sophia of Jesus Christ, The Thought of Norea, The Exegesis on the Soul, and The Thunder, Perfect Mind. The texts survive in Egyptian Coptic but were originally written in Greek.

The Gnostic Gospel of Truth addresses both the masculine and feminine forms of God as Father and Mother. In the Dialogue of the Savior, God appears in the text as "Mother of All." The Divine Mother in Gnostic tradition was called by many names. She was Helena to Simon Magus (a magician and sorcerer mentioned in the book of Acts); Barbelo (Mother) in the Gnostic Holy Trinity and also in the Secret Book of John; Sophia to Valentinus; and Thunder in The Thunder, Perfect Mind.

In the Gnostic Gospels, it is clear that women are as capable as men of receiving and understanding spiritual teachings. In The Dialogue of the Savior, Jesus gives a special teaching to some of the disciples. Mary Magdalene asks him why she has come into the world of matter, to which he replies that she "makes clear the abundance of the revealer." How might she make abundance clear unless she was conveying or transmitting a teaching that the

Savior has revealed to her? The Gospel of Mary, of which there are three copies in existence but no complete version, shows that female followers of Jesus served as teachers. That gospel with others—Gospel of Philip, Dialogue of the Savior, and Gospel of Thomas—show Peter, Jesus' chief male disciple, as a man somewhat intolerant of women, especially Mary Magdalene. When, during a session with Jesus and the other disciples, he complains of Mary Magdalene talking too much (presumably usurping the time available for men to ask questions), Jesus rebukes not Mary Magdalene but Peter.

Who Wrote the Gospels?

The authorship of the gospels (both the New Testament and the Gnostic) is generally attributed to the Apostles, but most scholars agree that the authorship of the ancient sacred texts is not known. Scholars have been able to piece together information about the gospels that suggest possible authorship for some. Early church fathers writing polemics against certain Gnostic texts, among them gospels that some Christians claimed to possess, have made modern scholars aware that such texts existed, but only recently with the Nag Hammadi find have many of these texts become available to scholars to translate and study. Sometime in the second century, the gospels were given their names. Generally, the names given were associated with the Apostles or others important to the early church. Many New Testament scholars agree that the Apostles did not write the gospels that bear their names.

Authorship of the New Testament Gospels

John Mark, the attendant of Peter, is widely considered the best candidate for the authorship of the New Testament Gospel of Mark because he was familiar with Palestine, the language of Aramaic, and Jewish customs, culture, and institutions. Matthew, originally written in Greek, probably was written for Jews rather than Gentiles. Some sources consider it the "most Jewish" of the four New Testament gospels. Its author is unknown, but he obviously relied heavily upon the Gospel of Mark (thought to be the first of the New Testament gospels written) as well as a large body of material not found in Mark but closely corresponding to the Sayings Gospel Q.

The earliest known version of Luke dates from the second century, since it is clear that Marcion used it. Early church fathers believed that Luke, a physician and companion of the Apostle Paul, wrote the Gospel of Luke and also the Acts of the Apostles. Clement, the early church father, called the Gospel of John the "spiritual gospel." Tradition assigns the authorship of that gospel to John, son of Zebedee. Some scholars, however, challenge that attribution, citing the sophistication of theology in that gospel. The Gospel of John varies greatly from the synoptic Gospels in the stories that are told and their sequence. It is written in a highly symbolic and literary style and features a splendid prologue. No baptism of Jesus takes place in that gospel, and the gospel is full of signs. Some biblical scholars assert that if not written by John, son of Zebedee, then possibly it was written by a Greek convert to Christianity.

Paraenesis is a term often used by scholars to describe the advice or exhortation of a moral nature found within a sacred text. It also can mean an urgent warning of impending evil. Several of the ancient Christian scriptures contain such a warning, especially for new initiates and converts to Christianity.

Authorship of the Gnostic Gospels

The Gospel of Thomas features 114 sayings of Jesus in the form of wisdom sayings, prophecies, parables, and rules. The Gospel of Thomas is attributed to Didymos Judas Thomas the twin, because the gospel itself states as much. Didymos (in Greek) and Thomas (in Aramaic) both mean "twin." Scholars say that in the Syrian church this Thomas was known as Jesus' brother. Gnostic scholar Marvin Meyer writes in the introduction to *The Gospel of Thomas: The Hidden Sayings of Jesus* that there is some speculation that this gospel was used (perhaps even written by) the Manichaeans, followers of Mani who were Gnostic mystics.

The Gospel of Mary (Magdalene) is the only Christian gospel bearing the name of a woman. The work reflects tensions in early Christianity.

The Gospel of Mary was written in Greek and dates to the second century. Significantly, it was in the latter part of that century that the orthodox communities of Christians established the apostolic hierarchy of leadership within their churches and left Mary out of it. The Gospel of Mary affirms the death and resurrection of Jesus but interprets his teachings in ways that depart radically from orthodox interpretations.

The Gospel of Truth most likely dates to the middle of the second century. Although the authorship is unknown, Valentinus, a Gnostic teacher who lived in the early part of the second century, has been suggested. The teachings of Valentinus seem to correspond to the Gospel of Truth. That gospel is not precisely a gospel in the sense that it tells the "good news," because it moves between narrative and warnings of imminent evil. The early church father Irenaeus may have been referring to this gospel, among others, when he accused the Gnostics of possessing more gospels "than there really are."

QUESTION?

How many gospels are there?
Scholars are aware of more than fifty complete gospels, including the four canonical gospels, but have fragmentary information on only sixteen others, including Peter, Philip, Matthias, Hebrews, Egyptians, Thomas, Nicodemus, the Twelve Apostles, Basilides, Valentinus, Marcion, Eve, Judas, Teleiosis, The Writing of Genna Marias, and the Proto-Evangelium of James.

Egyptian churches during the second and third centuries may have used the Gospel of the Egyptians as a sacred text. The gospel advocates a return to a primordial and androgynous state through celibacy. The authorship of this divinely inspired gospel is listed as Seth, an interesting attribution considering that the heavenly, mythological Seth has been referred to as Father of the Gnostic race.

The Secret Gospel of John (also known as the Apocryphon of John) is a secret teaching of the Savior given to John, who declares himself brother of James, one of the sons of Zebedee. The tractate offers a narrative mythological revelation of creation, the fall, and salvation of humanity. It focuses on the origin of evil and how to escape it in order to return to heaven. It has been described as offering the most insightful detailing of dualistic Gnostic mythology so far found, and, as such, is notable among the tractates found in Nag Hammadi discovery.

The Gospel of Philip appears to be a collection of excerpts from a Christian Gnostic book of sacramental catechisms. The text is not organized in any helpful or obvious way. It contains a few stories about Jesus and offers meanings of sacred names, discusses the significance of sacramental rites, reveals meaning in Biblical passages, and provides a few of Jesus' sayings that fit into a Gnostic context and warnings of evil (paraenesis). Authorship is unknown.

Differences Between the Gnostic and the Canonical Gospels

Orthodox Christians labored in the first few centuries to root out the Gnostics and the taint of Gnosticism as well as other heresies in their sacred scriptures. It was work that did not cease for over 2,000 years as new heresies and challenges arose. The Gnostics now again have a voice through the discovery of their hidden sacred texts found at Nag Hammadi. Interestingly, some of their texts, such as the Second Treatise of the Great Seth, Testimony of Truth, and Apocalypse of Peter, decry orthodox Christians as ones who don't know who Christ is, are unknowing and empty, and lead astray those who seek the freedom of gnosis. Both the Gnostics and the orthodox Christians recognized the authority of Jesus and share some common linkage. However, the differences between them and their interpretations of Scripture were often great.

For example, the Gnostic Valentinus separated Jesus (the man) from Christ (the Savior figure). He believed that Christ descended upon Jesus when he was baptized but left before Jesus expired on the cross. Of course, early church father Irenaeus argued against the idea that Jesus and the Christ were separate and of two substances. He did not believe that there was a divine spark in humans to rekindle. There was no self-knowledge that equated with God-knowledge. Valentinus and the conservative leaders in the early Christian church believed in Jesus and his words, but they just interpreted him and his teachings differently.

There is no canonical equivalent to the Gospel of Thomas. The sayings of Jesus in the Gospel of Thomas are similar to those found in the New Testament Gospels, although some do conflict. The Gospel of Thomas declares that the sayings offer salvation if you correctly understand them. Further, those who do understand them will not "taste death." This salvation is available through individual effort. Jesus, in the Gospel of Thomas, suggests that you need to know yourself at the deepest level, for it is there you get to know God. Early church father Irenaeus stated that in order to approach God, you must come through the church, or there is no salvation. The Gospel of Thomas did not make it into the canon for at least a couple of possible reasons. The canonizers may have thought its content was heretical and possibly believed that the gospel was not authentic.

Early church father Irenaeus provides the first mention of Cerinthus in Against Heresies. Cerinthus was a Gnostic, belonging to the Ebionites. He may have been Egyptian. Although none of his writings survive to today, his doctrines have been described by hostile sources as mixing Judaism, Gnosticism, Ebionitism, and Chiliasm.

The canonical Gospel of John has been the subject of vigorous scholarly debate. Was the author a Gnostic, like Cerinthus, even though the canonical Gospel of John presents anti-Gnostic theology? The Gospel of John is written in a literary style similar to Gnostic writing in its use of opposites (light/dark, death/life, flesh/spirit, etc.). Could orthodox Christian scribes have edited it? Was it based on an earlier Gnostic text that did not survive? Scholars debate these and many other questions about this gospel.

The canonical Gospel of John provides some mystery. The prologue is a beautiful hymn that was undoubtedly adapted and added to open the gospel. More than one author might have worked on this gospel, with one of them writing in a different style of Greek than found in the rest of the text. Scholars noticed the discrepancy in chapter twenty-one. Also, there are two endings to the time Jesus spent discoursing in the Upper Room with his disciples. Chapter 14:31 reads, "But that the world may know that I love the Father; and as the Father gave me commandment, even so I do. Arise, let us go hence." Chapter 18:1 states, "When Jesus had spoken these words, he went forth with his disciples over the brook Cedron, where was a garden, into the which he entered, and his disciples."

Detractors, Redactors, and Scribes

Ancient writers were known as scribes. From the earliest centuries, they copied from the Greek or translated the written material of the sacred texts. Scribes sometimes shortened works while aiming for clarity and attempting to remain close to the original in meaning and message. Scholars have a job deciphering some of those texts because of a lacuna or hole in the papyrus where a word should be found. Scholars must then guess the meaning to supply the right word. In these ways, sacred works are sometimes changed.

Both the Gnostic and the canonical scriptures began as oral traditions and early writings that were handed down through the ages. Sometimes a text was written and in some cases (at least in the canonical gospels) a little was added or a small amount removed as the text was used. Some Biblical scholars suggest that the author of the Secret Gospel of John (who wrote about John's vision of the Holy Spirit in female terms) may have been a Gnostic, and that Gnostics in the second century may have used that gospel as one of their sacred texts. They argue that the author's writings shared similarities with two other Gnostic Gospels, Thomas and Philip. Some experts suggest that the Apostle John may have written the original Gospel of John only to have it vigorously edited by others with a more orthodox Christian view. The editing may have even been done at Ephesus, where John wrote Revelation. However, some people feel that there is little support for the idea that John wrote both the Gospel bearing his name and also Revelation.

The Secret Gospel of John reveals a vision that the grieving disciple has after the death of Jesus in which he sees a dazzling light and hears the

Savior's voice speaking to him, asking whether or not John recognizes him. Then the voice declares itself as the Father, Mother, and Son. John is first shocked, then realizes that the Divine Mother is the Holy Spirit in the feminine aspect. Of course, the canonical gospels did not espouse the Divine Mother as the third person of the Trinity but rather the Holy Spirit.

In the beginning was the Word, and the Word was with God, and the Word was God . . . All things were made by him; and without him was not any thing made that was made. In him was life; and the life was the light of men. And the light shineth in darkness; and the darkness comprehended it not.—John 1:1–5

Some modern readers of the Bible have said that John, son of Zebedee, was not educated enough to write the Fourth Gospel. John was one of three in the core group of Jesus' disciples. Passages in the New Testament suggest that some thought John, a former fisherman, to be ignorant and without the benefit of a higher education. Acts 4:13 makes a point of Peter and John's ignorance: "Now when they saw the boldness of Peter and John, and perceived that they were unlearned and ignorant men, they marveled; and they took knowledge of them, that they had been with Jesus." Yet John is widely credited with the authorship of the Gospel of John, the most spiritual and sophisticated (from a theological and literary standpoint) gospel of the New Testament. Scholar Ramon Jusino has an interesting theory that Mary Magdalene may have been the author or served as the eyewitness source for the Fourth Gospel. See *http://ramon_k_justino.tripod.com/magdalene.html.*

Some of the early literalist Christians would not have been comfortable with portrayals of powerful women in their sacred texts. Particularly offensive would be the portrayal of a woman with status and authority or as an expression of the Divine. Such mention of a woman, outside of a traditional subordinate role, might have warranted an orthodox redaction or some editing that would bring the offending passage back in alignment with the Christian literalist viewpoint. But the Gnostics' dualistic concepts embraced the feminine as the necessary complement to the masculine, whether as expressed through the Divine or through humans.

The Gospel of John and the book of Revelation are similar in both language and theology. However, one theory suggests that a disciple of John, rather than the Apostle himself, wrote the book of Revelation.

Textual Inferiority or Just a Different Lens?

The patristic early fathers called the Gnostic writings textually inferior because they contained blasphemies and heresies. But perhaps the very texts against which they felt they must vigorously defend the faith were simply providing another lens for viewing fledgling Christianity. For the young Christian church with its patristic views and an emerging male hierarchy, Mary Magdalene presented something of a conundrum. Her central role as eyewitness to the resurrected form of Jesus would have been well known in oral tradition and also in the later gospel accounts. But some feminist theologians have stated that her story may have been edited to marginalize her presence and minimize her power and leadership. In the Gnostic texts, however, Mary Magdalene is honored and venerated. What were the early orthodox fathers to do with Gnostic texts like the Gospel of Mary, the Dialogue of the Savior, and the Gospel of Philip, among the early Christian writings that presented Mary Magdalene as Jesus' pre-eminent disciple with a thorough grasp of gnosis?

Mary Magdalene saw a vision of Jesus and asked him how it was that she could see him, whether it was through the spirit or soul. He answered, "Through the mind." The Gnostics learned to interpret their visions as spiritual insights into the "real" world, the inner realms of truth, rather than the apparition of the material universe.

The orthodox Christian church emerged as the dominant religion and its canon, creed, and sacred texts are those that endure. The powerful and dominant record history as they want it remembered, excluding historical accounts that do not support their view. After Constantine, orthodox leaders ordered sacred texts known to contain blasphemies and heresies to be burned or otherwise destroyed.

Jesus in the Canon and in Gnostic Belief

Jesus is the most important figure in Christianity. Variously called Master, Lord, Messiah, Son of God, and Savior, everything the church teaches revolves in some way around Jesus. In the canon, he is the Bridegroom and his bride is the church. The church teaches that sinners authored and administered the sufferings that Jesus had to endure during his crucifixion. The cruel and violent death did not come about as the juncture of certain circumstances coming together, but rather as a part of the mystery of God's plan. Jesus' death enables sinners to reconcile with God. The Gospel of Matthew says that John the Baptist baptized Jesus in the River Jordan and the Spirit of God descended upon Jesus like a dove (Matthew 3:15–16). John in the Gospel of John sees Jesus approaching and calls him the Lamb of God (John 1:29). The "Lamb of God" phrase alluded to the redemption of Israel at the first Passover and also to the prophecy Jesus was fulfilling as the Son of God, permitting himself to be led to slaughter for the sins of the multitudes. Jesus transformed the Passover meal into the Last Supper with a new blood covenant. That Eucharist would forever after symbolize his sacrifice. The mission of Jesus the Christ and the Holy Spirit arrive at completion in the church. In Roman Catholicism today, the church is called the Temple of the Holy Spirit. Christ is the light of the church, and he endows it with holiness.

The term *ecclesia* is a Greek word meaning "an assembly," but when used in a Christian context, it is almost always translated as "church." In contrast, the word "church" derives from the Greek word *kyriake* and also the German word *kirche*, meaning "what belongs to the Lord."

Salvation flows to those who accept him as their Lord and Savior. He is head of the church and the church is his body. Converts are welcomed in the family that is the church. No salvation is possible outside of the church. This has been the position of the church for centuries. It is no accident that the gospels and the other sacred texts selected for inclusion in the New Testament support this position.

The Gnostic Gospels offer a different view of Jesus. He comes to humanity as a Savior bringing gnosis to those who seek knowledge and desire enlightenment. In this way, Jesus is the Redeemer who helps humans save themselves from the pull of the material world. He gives knowledge (secret to those spiritually adept), inspiring souls to turn inward and seek the Light. He is the divine Light Bearer who illuminates the way from darkness, inspiring the soul to rise to enlightenment. Gnostics saw the cosmos as the very embodiment of God. The path to finding God was to them an inward path. They may have pointed to the Gospel of Luke for verification from Jesus' own words.

And when he was demanded of the Pharisees, when the kingdom of God should come, he answered them and said, The kingdom of God cometh not with observation: Neither shall they say, Lo here! or, lo there! for, behold, the kingdom of God is within you.—Luke 17:20–21

The Gnostics distinguish between rational and experiential knowledge, or, in other words, that which must be directly, intuitively experienced in order to be known. Jesus is a vessel carrying the secret knowledge (gnosis) to enable and empower them on the soul's inward and upward journey. Jesus is the inward guide, and when they reach the stage of enlightenment where the darkness has fallen away and their divine spark has merged into the ocean of Light, they, too, will have become Christ, no longer different or separate from him.

Chapter 5

Gnostic Versus Christian Orthodox Views

In the Second Treatise of the Great Seth (a text discovered at Nag Hammadi), the narrator explains how he (presumably Jesus Christ speaking as Seth) came to earth, endured the crucifixion, and returned to the Pleroma. Scholars say that the narrative is both a Christian work and a Gnostic polemic. It agrees with parts of the New Testament, but states that the way to salvation is through gnosis. It refutes the claim by orthodox believers that their church is the "true church."

Diversity and Intolerance

The orthodox Christians believed that Jesus died so that his death and resurrection could bring salvation to humanity. The Second Treatise of the Great Seth (along with many of the Gnostic Gospels and other writings) maintains that salvation was possible not through Jesus' death but through the secret knowledge that he brought. The narrator of the Second Treatise of the Great Seth spoke of the orthodox Christians as those who hated the "perfect and incorruptible ones" (the Gnostic believers), while they were themselves empty, ignorant, incapable of understanding (the Gnostic way) and thought they were "advancing the name of Christ."

The minority viewpoints in early Christianity did not receive much coverage in the narrative of the church. Biblical scholars and theologians have known about the diversity of the early Christian groups from the writings of orthodox leaders who penned polemics against them, but they haven't had much of an in-depth view from the other side. The Nag Hammadi discovery has helped rectify that imbalance. Scholar Elaine Pagels has pointed out in her writings that while the orthodox scriptures speak of sin and redemption, the Gnostic texts address illusion and enlightenment, and also that Jesus came not to die for humanity's sins but to bring knowledge and access to spiritual enlightenment.

Within the diversity of the early Christian communities, those leaning toward more literalistic (what some might call orthodox) views gained dominance through intolerance to Sethian Gnosticism and other points of view—not just pagan and the mystery traditions, but also other Christian sects whom the orthodox hated for their heresies. They branded as heresy any works divergent from their views and destroyed the offending material. After the Council of Nicaea in A.D. 325, the orthodox leaders had the power of Emperor Constantine and the state behind them. As history has shown, orthodox Christianity prevailed while other Christian sects declined or died out due to persecution.

Compilations from Oral Traditions

Before sects had texts, they had stories. The stories from the Hebrew scriptures and the New Testament derive from stories about Jesus' life and times that were handed down orally from one generation to the next. Later stories recounted the acts of the Apostles and their martyrdoms. Itinerant preachers, teachers, and others carried the stories to distant lands. The stories may have changed (it is unlikely that they would have been memorized verbatim), but they still maintained the central idea.

FACT

Knowledge of self was central to Gnostic thinking about God and cosmology. The Gnostic stories were filled with revealers, saviors, and personifications of the Divine as mythical religious archetypes dished up in wisdom tales, proclamations, poems, sayings, and sacred hymns.

Because the stories in the New Testament came first out of oral tradition and later from the written gospels, their historical accuracy is questionable. Oral storytellers could have added elements that reflected their own interpretation of the story or changed the meaning when they changed any of the words. Translation of the stories from one language to another necessarily meant meaning could have been lost. The gospels, which came after the earliest Christian writings and after the life and death of Jesus, disagree on many points.

Defining Heresy Within Christianity

The squabbling that went on between sects of Christians with the orthodox early fathers foreshadowed internecine troubles that would plague the church for centuries. The orthodox fathers formulated the Nicene Creed to clarify for all time their articles of faith, or at least they hoped for such an outcome. In fact, a long string of disagreements and councils followed. The creed became a safeguard against sects, such as the Arians, spouting beliefs opposed by the orthodox Christians. The creed described Jesus Christ as

"God from God, Light from Light, true God from true God." This essentially stated his divinity. In order to assert his divine eternalness and that a lesser God did not make him nor was he a lesser God, the following words were chosen: "begotten, not made."

Two terms: *homoousios* and *homoiousios*, from the Greek root *ousia* (substance or essence), were at the heart of the pre-Nicene controversy. Bishop Alexander and his followers espoused homoousios (Son and the Father were the of the same substance and co-eternal). The Arians and others claimed Father and Son were not identical. The Homoiousians compromised, saying that the essence of Father and Son were similar.

In the final blow directly aimed at countering what the orthodox fathers saw as Arian heresy, they added: "one substance of the Father." Thus, the majority of the church leadership in attendance defined the divinity of Jesus and formulated a profession of faith that specifically expressed the beliefs that the bishops held in common. The church, which had been diverse and pretty much inclusive, eventually excluded those (the Gnostics and other groups) who could not profess the faith as laid out in the Nicene Creed. The dominant orthodox faction of the church had the power of the state to aid in enforcement. But the Nicene Creed did not stop the infighting, nor did it put an end to heresy as the orthodoxy desired.

Theodosius Tries to Eradicate Heresy

Emperor Theodosius in A.D. 381 convened a second council at Constantinople. He wanted to unite the eastern bishops and desired to condemn all versions of pagan and Gnostic belief, in particular those sects that were resistant and rapidly spreading, including Arianism (especially the extreme form known as Eunomianism), Apollinarianism, and Macedonianism. Theodosius sought to establish the pre-eminence of the Constantinople bishop behind the bishop of Rome, and Constantinople as the New Rome. The Emperor, before closing the council, issued an order that those errant bishops who would sincerely confess their belief in the equal divinity of the Father, Son, and Holy Spirit could return to their churches. Still, the factions could not agree.

Theodosius convened another council in A.D. 382 and again in A.D. 383. He particularly sought to unite all the various groups of Christians through the teachings of the orthodox early church fathers whose leadership produced the Nicene Creed. But, from among the eastern churches, a group of Arians resisted all efforts toward reconciliation with the orthodoxy. Their extreme brand of Arianism became known as Eunomianism, after their leader Eunomius. He served as Bishop of the Orthodox See of Cyzicus in Mysia for a time before being deposed and exiled. His sect was subjected to persecution after being excluded from the edict of religious tolerance.

FACT

Athanasius, who opposed Arianism, became known as the Father of Orthodoxy. He was the first individual to establish the twenty-seven books of the New Testament that became the canon. His was the first surviving list identical to that used today. He set forth the list in his Easter letter of A.D. 367.

Emperor Theodosius eventually turned to brutality and extreme measures to eradicate the heresies of paganism, Arianism, Gnosticism, and other spiritual beliefs and practices he thought undermined orthodox Christian beliefs. His representative traveled through Asia Minor, Egypt, and Syria to destroy temples and disband unorthodox religious groups. The persecution drove some unorthodox groups underground and obliterated others, but accusations of heresy among groups of Christians persisted.

Further Persecutions

The orthodoxy, having gained the dominant position in Christianity and with the power of the political authority behind it, hurled accusations of heresy against other Christians who remained outside of the now well-established church. Such sects included:

- **Apollinarianism:** This fourth-century sect was founded by Apollinarius the Younger, who served as bishop of Laodicea in Syria. Apollinarius asserted that the divine and human could not coexist in one being; that, in turn, jeopardized the doctrine of incarnation, death, and atonement, bringing upon the sect formal condemnation in A.D. 381.

- **Neoplatonism:** Plotinus was the founder of this third-century Roman sect that believed that Jesus was born human but ascended through mystical levels of being until he reached deification. That type of thinking evolved into a Christian mystic spiritualism in the fifth century under Dionysius the Pseudo-Aeropagitem, against whom some levied charges of Pantheism.

- **Nestorianism:** The Patriarch of Alexandria Nestorius espoused the belief that Jesus was two persons, one human and the other divine. The sect was condemned in A.D. 432 at the Council of Ephesus. Nestorianism was branded heretical and was anathematized.

- **Monophysitism:** This fifth-century sect believed that Jesus possessed only one nature and it was divine. Leo the Great at the Council of Chalcedon in A.D. 451 condemned the sect and its founder Eutyches.

The Spanish Have Their Say

Spanish Christians in A.D. 447 inserted a three-word phrase known as the "*filioque* clause" into the Nicene Creed. The phrase, consisting of the words "and the Son," entered the creed as a way to counter the Arian Christian heresies. The use of the clause spread to France, where the Arians flourished. The manner in which the *filioque* clause was inserted (against the rules of the canon of the Third Ecumenical Council in A.D. 432) brought charges of heresy in the tenth century from the Patriarch of Constantinople against the Pope in Rome. Despite a concerted effort by the Christian orthodoxy to stamp out Arianism, it continued through the Middle Ages and into the Reformation.

The Canonical Standard

At some time in the Christian historical narrative, twenty-seven books of the New Testament became the chosen texts to convey the accepted teachings of Jesus and the Apostles. The literature about early Christianity suggests that many of these texts were already in use by the early orthodox fathers. They gave weight to both oral and written revelation and proclamation. The Gnostics used many of the same texts; however, they interpreted the scriptures in different ways, according to their "fuller" understanding of Jesus' teachings within the Gnostic tradition. It seems that Jesus, in his references in the Old Testament to the many Hebrew scriptures, signaled his acceptance of the texts and their usage. But he had already died before the writings of the New Testament took place. So when and how was the canon established and by whose authority? Can it ever be changed? These are questions that some theologians and biblical historians still consider worth discussing.

After the Apostolic Age, no decisive list of sacred texts that constituted a canon for the orthodoxy existed—or if it did, it did not survive. As mentioned in a previous chapter, the Gnostic Marcion in the second century gathered together sacred texts into his version of a canon that included the Gospel of Luke, which he edited, and ten of Paul's letters (excluding the first and second pastoral Epistles of Timothy and Titus, plus the letter to the Hebrews). Marcion excluded any texts with which he disagreed. In their rejection of Marcion and his Gnostic theology, the early church fathers were forced to think about their own beliefs and to clarify them for their Christian churches and communities. Paramount among their concerns were the sacred texts that were circulating (which ones were acceptable and which ones weren't), the relationship between the Jewish Christians and the Gentile Christians, and heretics and their heresies, as well as reliability of sources (texts versus inspired dialogues, visions, etc.) for information about Jesus.

The Muratorian Canon was a list of sacred texts compiled, possibly in Rome, by an unknown individual just before the end of the second century, although some argue that the Muratorian Canon is actually a fourth-century list. The canon bears the name of L. A. Muratori, the Italian scholar who discovered the canon. Found in the eighteenth century in a library in Milan, the document includes all of the books of the New Testament as being canonical with the exception of Hebrews, James, and the second book of Peter. The Apocalypse of Peter, a Gnostic text, was included but later was rejected.

Not until the fourth century did the term "canon" come into usage as a religious term to refer to the sacred texts of both the Hebrew scriptures (Old Testament) and the New Testament. By then, the early church fathers perceived a need for an authoritative corpus of writings to support the church's religious rules on issues relating to faith and practice.

FACT

The word "canon" derives from the Greek *kanon*, meaning "rule" or "standard." This word appears in Paul's writings in the New Testament but he does not use the word in reference to the scriptures. The Apostles expected the end-time within their lifetimes. They probably never considered the need for a canon.

By the latter half of the century, after John, the last Apostle, had died, the Christian fathers recognized the importance of two groups of documents: Paul's letters and the Gospels of Matthew, Mark, Luke, and John. These items must have carried great significance as authoritative texts. But the four gospels could be said to be for a Jewish audience (especially Matthew) while the Pauline letters targeted the Gentile communities of Christians. It was the Acts of the Apostles, the second of Luke's two-volume work, that bridged these the four gospel accounts with Paul's letters. Luke stressed in Acts that Christianity, like Judaism, deserved Rome's fair treatment and tolerance. The following is a timeline for the New Testament.

CHAPTER 5: GNOSTIC VERSUS CHRISTIAN ORTHODOX VIEWS

Approximate Composition Dates of New Testament Texts

Date	Book of the New Testament
Circa A.D. 49	Paul's first letter to the Thessalonians
Circa A.D. 51	Paul's letter to the Galatians
Circa A.D. 52	Paul's second letter to the Thessalonians
Circa A.D. 55–56	Paul's first and second letters to the Corinthians
Circa A.D. 59–63	Paul's letter to the Philippians
Circa A.D. 59–63	Paul's letters to the Colossians and Ephesians
Circa A.D. 60–63	Paul's letters to the Romans and Philemon
Circa A.D. 63–67	Pastoral Epistles (attributed falsely to Paul): books 1 and 2 of Timothy, Titus, book 1 of Peter, and Hebrews
Circa A.D. 65	Q, or the Sayings Gospel Q, source for Matthew and Luke
Circa A.D. 70	Gospel of Mark
Circa A.D. 80–100	Gospel of Matthew
Circa A.D. 85–95	Gospel of Luke and Acts of the Apostles
Circa A.D. 95	Revelation
Circa A.D. 100–125	Gospel of John
Circa A.D. 150	The four Gospels gathered together as an embryonic canon
Circa A.D. 367	Thirty-ninth Festal Letter of Athanasius offers a list of texts for the New Testament canon

Polemics Against Gnosticism

The orthodox polemics against the Gnostics had a threefold effect: it pushed the Gnostics away from the Christian congregations, destroyed their writings and sacred texts, and effectively dispersed and disbanded their sects. The orthodox Christians excluded and reviled their Gnostic brethren. The patristic fathers used the power of their oratory and their writings to destroy any interpretation of the sacred texts and the Christology of Jesus that the Gnostics espoused when it went against the orthodox position.

The heresiologist Origen launched point-by-point, page-by-page refutation of Gnostic heresy that seems excessive to modern readers, but he wasn't alone. The orthodox father Hippolytus of Rome wrote the ten-volume *Refutation of All Heresies* to expose the heresies of his day that he perceived as coming out of Greek philosophy (philosophers are known as "lovers of wisdom"). Irenaeus of Lyons wrote five volumes titled *Against Heresies*. Tertullian wrote five volumes titled *Against Marcion* (a well-known Gnostic), and a single volume against each of the other heretics that he despised. The dogmatic and practical Origen needed eight volumes to dispute the assertions of Celsus, a second-century author of *The True Word* and an opponent of Christianity.

Celsus accuses Jesus of having "invented his birth from a virgin," and upbraids Him with being "born in a certain Jewish village, of a poor woman of the country, who gained her subsistence by spinning, and who was turned out of doors by her husband . . . she disgracefully gave birth to Jesus, an illegitimate child . . ."—*Contra Celsus* 1:28

Celsus had knowledge of Gnosticism and the Gnostic sects. He was also aware of Marcion and his writings as well as the Christians and their differences, and used his knowledge in his own polemic against Christianity. What scholars today know of Celsus, they have learned by reading Origen's polemic *Contra Celsus* (Against Celsus) in defense of Christianity. Origen provides Celsus's words almost verbatim.

From their writings it is clear that the orthodoxy must have genuinely feared their Gnostic opponents. Whether the heresiologists were tearing apart a Gnostic myth for its literalism (even though the Gnostics did not treat their myths and legends as literal) or attacking the concept that the God of the New Testament was superior to the God of the Old Testament (such as Marcion believed), they used every weapon available to them, including logic, sarcasm, ridicule, outrageous accusations, and suggestions that Gnostic ideas contaminated the true Christian message.

God's Special Revelation or Man's?

The ancient Christian legacy is a set of common beliefs: one God who created heaven and earth, whose Son Jesus was both human and divine and whose death and resurrection (as foretold by Old Testament prophecies) brought salvation. It is a belief held by many modern Christians as well as those of ancient times that the one God of all inspired the sacred writings of the Hebrew scriptures and the New Testament. These beliefs belong to the orthodoxy (which means "right belief"), and the holy books they use and revere are those that survived the conflicts among the many early versions of Christianity. The sacred texts of other unorthodox Christian sects, such as the Gnostics, did not make it into the canon.

Some modern Christians swear that every word in the Bible is the true word of God and that it contains no errors. Yet Biblical scholars note that no original manuscripts of any of the gospels exist. There is no proof that the Apostles wrote them. The gospels that exist today are several generations of texts removed from the authors whose names they bear.

Even fewer fragments and pages of Gnostic texts survived. The Gnostic Gospel of Peter, Secret Gospel of Mark, Dialogue of the Savior, and Egerton Gospel each exist in only a single manuscript, although fragments of the Gospel of Mary survive in both the Coptic and Greek versions (no complete version of that gospel exists). While the entire Gnostic Gospel of Thomas is preserved, it exists only in the Coptic, although three Greek fragments make it likely that it was originally a Greek composition.

FACT

The earliest fragment of the New Testament that survives today is the Rylands Library Papyrus P52, also known as Saint John's fragment. It contains lines from the Gospel of John, 18:31–33, written in Greek, and it dates between A.D. 125 and A.D. 160. Another fragment from the Gospel of Mark (7Q5, found at Qumran) may date to no later than A.D. 68, although this dating is debated.

Jesus and his Apostles spoke Aramaic, although some scholars say they most likely spoke Hebrew in the synagogue. The first oral stories of Jesus' life and ministry were almost certainly in Aramaic. Paul, a Hellenistic Jew, spoke and wrote Greek, and his letters, the earliest writings of the New Testament, were written in Greek. So what theologians, biblical scholars, and historians have to work from are mostly translated copies or fragments. Some are in Greek, but many are in the Egyptian Coptic language that has been described by some ancient language experts as a kind of shorthand for translating Greek into an Egyptian language with Greek characters. Christian missionaries used the Egyptian Coptic to evangelize Egyptian peasants, so many of the sacred texts they used were translated into that language.

Scholars say there is no evidence that Jesus ever wrote anything for his disciples or for posterity. Some who believe that the New Testament literally contains the word of God sometimes refer to 2 Peter 1:21: "For the prophecy came not in old time by the will of man: but holy men of God spake as they were moved by the Holy Ghost," and also 2 Timothy 3:16: "All scripture is given by inspiration of God, and is profitable for doctrine, for reproof, for correction, for instruction in righteousness." While some Christians believe that every word contained in the New Testament is the infallible word of God, others point out that the process of choosing those New Testament texts took centuries. They were chosen amid an ongoing conflict between those who believed the orthodox texts represented Jesus' words and deeds, while others, the Gnostic Christians, were just as certain that orthodox writings had an inferior understanding of the true knowledge Jesus brought. Most modern scholars hold the opinion that Jesus' words and teachings were disseminated orally for decades before others began writing them onto papyrus or in codices (leather-bound books).

QUESTION?

Why did the Gospel of Peter not make it into the canon?
There are several possible reasons why this popular gospel, mentioned by the orthodox second-century fathers, was rejected by Seraphim of Antioch and others: it contained anti-Jewish accusations, included Docetic inferences (which cast doubt on Jesus' suffering on the cross), and glossed over Pilate's role in the crucifixion.

As the conflict raged on, the scriptures were translated, copied, recopied, widely circulated, and passed down through generations. Human error accounted for mistranslations, misspellings, and omissions. When mistakes were caught and corrections made, the attempt (for example, words out of sequence) sometimes changed the meaning of the entire sentence.

Scholars say there are even forgeries called pseudepigrapha ("false writings") that circulated in the ancient world and later appear in the apocrypha and even in the canonical New Testament. The latter has two—the first and second letters of Timothy and Titus (known as the pastoral Epistles). Paul supposedly wrote the letters; however, historians and Biblical scholars say that they were most certainly penned after his death.

Chapter 6

The Divine Feminine Ideal

The divine feminine occupied an important place in Gnostic theology. Certain sects of Gnostics eschewed eros (sexual longing to be united with another) in favor of agape (unconditional, self-sacrificing love). They practiced celibacy and aceticism. Those who engaged in lovemaking viewed their female partner as the embodiment of the divine feminine. The Gnostics' God was both masculine and feminine, and created humans in that divine image. Eventually, the concept of the divine feminine all but disappeared, while "the bride of Christ" came to mean the collective soul of the church.

Sophia, the Spirit of Wisdom

The Gnostics, like the Hebrew mystics, believed that wisdom also was a feminine attribute of God. The Gnostics saw wisdom as an Aeon who dwelled in the Pleroma, and they called wisdom by the name of Sophia, the "Mother of All Creation." In Hebrew, her name was Hohkma; in Latin, it became Sapienta; and in Greek, she was Sophia. Some spiritual seekers called her God's female soul, his creative power or energy, and wisdom. Others claimed that the dove that descended upon Jesus after his baptism symbolized baptism by the Holy Spirit, not male, but female. In the ancient Near East, the dove has traditionally served as a symbol of the feminine and as a sign of baptism in which the soul becomes purified.

Mary Magdalene for many modern women symbolizes the Gnostic idealized divine feminine. She was the first eyewitness to Jesus' resurrected form. She has an important yet brief role in the canonical Gospels, but in the Gnostic texts she is revered. She is called Mariham, Mariam, Mariamne, Miryam, and Mary. Jesus called her "the Woman Who Knows the All."

In many ancient sacred texts, the personification of wisdom was nearly always female. For example, The Book of Wisdom (a deuterocanonical— or Apochryphal—book, also known as the Wisdom of Solomon), found in the Hebrew scriptures refers to wisdom (the noun is female) throughout as female. She is "resplendent and unfading . . . and . . . readily perceived by those who love her" (Wisdom 6:12). In the Secret Book of James (also known as the Apocryphon of James), Jesus refers to himself as the son of the Holy Spirit and says to "become better than I; make yourselves like the son of the Holy Spirit." The Hebrew word for spirit is *ruach*, a feminine-gender word; however, in the Greek-language New Testament it becomes *pneuma*, a neuter noun. The notion that Jesus had one male parent goes against the symbolism of God as "mother" and "father" that existed in certain traditions at the time that the new Christian religion emerged. The Gospel of Philip asserts that whoever becomes Christian gains both "mother" and "father" because Spirit (ruach) is the mother of many. "Wisdom ["mother"] is known by her children" (Matthew 11:19).

Sophia's Fall

The story of Sophia's fall begins with the idea of an original and unknowable First Parent (also known as Godhead, Forefather, Unknowable One, Monad, Root, Logos, All Begotten, First Mystery, and Aeon). The Godhead emanated pairs of "lesser" beings, quasi gods, of which Sophia and Christ were the youngest/lowest pair. These lesser gods with the Godhead made up the fullness of Pleroma (heaven). Following her emanation from the Godhead, Sophia feared losing knowledge and the light of the One. She longed to return to it. In her passion and longing, without either the help of her male counterpart or permission from the Godhead, she undertook the action of "emanating" a being—the Demiurge, a formless entity outside of the Pleroma.

This is the crisis in the story of Sophia. It came about not because of a sexual creational act but because of a masculine/feminine imbalance. Sophia's action disturbed the harmony of the Pleroma. The early Gnostics, as already noted, considered Christ the masculine counterpart of Sophia. The masculine name for Sophia is Lucifer (hēlēl in Hebrew, which means "shining one"). Some have equated the Demiurge, her offspring, as Satan.

FACT

Three types of humans exist in this material world, according to Valentianian Gnosticism. They include the hylics, in which humans are bound to matter (evil), psychics, in which humans are bound to the soul (and only partially evil), and pneumatics, special people capable of attaining enlightenment through gnosis.

Sophia imparted in the Demiurge a divine spark, or *pneuma* (Greek, meaning "wind," "air," or "spirit"). She hid the Demiurge away in a cloud, beyond the awareness of other immortals. Ignorant of Sophia, his "Mother

God," and using the power of Spirit, the Demiurge created the physical world. This caused the divine sparks (or spiritual longing) to become trapped in matter. Sophia's counterpart, Jesus, helps her to again see the light of the Godhead and helps her in understanding spirit.

The Greco-Roman philosophers believed that they could claim wisdom through reasoning alone, but the Gnostics believed that wisdom could only be achieved through inner, intuitive experiential knowing. The Gnostics told their stories in creation myths and in other literary forms. The fall of Sophia and her subsequent restoration to the Pleroma resonates in several well-known fairy tales and myths, both ancient and modern, including Persephone, Orpheus, Cinderella, and Sleeping Beauty.

Salvation Through Gnosis

In Gnostic traditon, Christ helped Sophia to see the light of the Godhead. Christ then left the Pleroma and descended into the world of matter in the form of Jesus. There he imparted his secret knowledge—gnosis—so that humans could turn away from the material world and find their way back to the Pleroma or the Fullness of God. In his letter to the Ephesians, the Apostle Paul pointed out that Christ's love bestows knowledge that gives the fullness of God. Could the "knowledge" that comes from loving Christ of which Paul wrote be gnosis? Paul addressed the need for unity of the church in Christ. In his letter, he wrote of seven unifying factors: spirit, hope, faith, church, baptism, one Lord, and the one God. Further, he expounded upon the idea that Christ's gifts are meant to lead to growth and renewal and that the light of Christ illuminates various aspects of human life. Although that particular Pauline letter seemed to be a straightforward plea to members of the young Christian church at Ephesus, the Gnostic symbolism is unmistakable. The orthodox early church fathers claimed Paul as one of their own, but modern Gnostic scholar Elaine Pagels suggests that Paul may have, in fact, been a Gnostic whose gnostic views were later covered up by the church.

According to the Gnostics, Jesus also taught them secret teachings that he did not give to the church. The church believed he was born of the Virgin Mary and God, with Joseph serving as his stepfather. But the Gnostics believed that Jesus was actually the offspring of God and Spirit/Sophia and with them made up the Trinity. He entered Mary's body through Mary and

Joseph's lovemaking. That Gnostic belief and others caused animosity with the orthodox church that was further exacerbated by the Gnostics' rejection of the need for bishops, priests, and deacons, although they did allow women to serve in church leadership positions. Some scholars have noted that the Gnostics would draw straws to see who would officiate in their church/fellowship/prayer sessions. There was no established hierarchy of leadership. Many refused to make the sign of the cross. They did not believe that Jesus had suffered and died for their sins. They thought that there could be no separation of spirit from matter and, furthermore, that matter was evil. Jesus' suffering was simply a symbolism for the dark condition of humanity.

That Christ may dwell in your hearts by faith; that ye, being rooted and grounded in love, may be able to comprehend with all saints what is the breadth, and length, and depth, and height; and to know the love of Christ, which passeth knowledge, that ye might be filled with all the fullness of God.—Ephesians 3:17–19

In Judaism, Christianity, and many ancient pagan belief systems, salvation was through faith and good works and through obedience to the will of God. The Gnostics set themselves apart from those other groups. If the Jews were God's chosen people, the Gnostics held a special place as well, as "the people who know" or the *gnostikos.* Their work on earth was to free themselves from the physical realm of matter. Their salvation came through secret, inner knowledge.

One of the tractates found at Nag Hammadi is titled A Valentinian Exposition (Codex XI, 2), On the Anointing, On Baptism A and B, and On the Eucharist A and B. Religious scholars believe the text to be a secret catechism used as an initiation into gnosis. The early Gnostic Christians viewed transcendence as a central tenet of their faith. They believed that the resurrection of the spirit had already taken place in this evil and alien world. Freedom and salvation came through the secret wisdom of gnosis. Several of their texts held that view of spiritual reality, including the Treatise on the Resurrection, the Exegesis on the Soul, and the Gospel of Philip.

The Hagia Sophia (or Church of Divine Wisdom), built in A.D. 360, celebrated Sophia's attributes of wisdom and light. For over a thousand years, it served as the Cathedral of the Ecumenical Patriarchate of Constantinople. Forty windows around the dome's base allow light to reflect into the nave's interior. The quality of light has been described by pilgrims as soft and mystical, like a divine presence.

Sophia in the Secret Book of John

In the Apocryphon of John, a text of mythological Gnosticism discovered at Nag Hammadi, Sophia's desire to know the One leads her to emanate the Demiurge (God of imperfect creation) and subsequently causes the disturbance of the Pleroma. After the crisis, the Father of Everything emanates a new Aeon pair, Christos (masculine) and Holy Spirit (feminine), who stabilize the Pleroma and emanate a new Aeon, Jesus. Also, the Aeon Achamoth (lower Sophia) comes into being. So the new Aeon pair is Jesus/Sophia or Savior/Wisdom. Sophia then brings forth the god Psyche. This is a very simplistic way of explaining the complex cosmology of the Gnostics, which includes increasing stratification of heavens and planes of existence, complete with gods.

QUESTION?

How does the Apocryphon of John describe the Unknowable God?
The purported author, John the son of Zebedee, offers a metaphysical exposition on the Gnostic creation myth in the Apocryphon of John, describing the Unknowable God as the Monad with "nothing above" who is the father of everything as well as the incorruptible and pure light, into which "no eye can look."

Using Genesis and Revelation as a basic framework, the Apocryphon of John details humanity's creation, fall, and subsequent salvation. Scholars say that although the early church historian Irenaeus wrote about the teachings found in the Apocryphon of John, he did not know of that particular tractate. However, Irenaeus wrote Against Heresies about A.D. 185, so those particular Gnostic teachings must have already been circulating, and biblical scholars suggest that the Apocryphon of John can be dated prior to A.D. 180.

Sophia as a Message of Hope

Sophia's fall and redemption is also the story of the soul's bondage in matter and subsequent liberation through gnosis. Sophia's story features a message of hope that all of humankind can escape its entrapment in darkness and negativity once an awakening (an inner longing for the return to light and the Godhead) occurs. For a while, Sophia suffers in the bondage of ignorance. Her own light (the divine spark within her) calls her back to the Pleroma. This suggests that each individual soul can also awaken and be liberated. Sophia in The Thunder, Perfect Mind reveals that she is the one called "truth."

Her essence of oneness underlies all things, even those with the appearance of duality. Although appearing as both light and dark, good and evil, strength and fear, male and female, knowledge and ignorance, and foolish and wise, Sophia remains unchanged. She epitomizes the mysterious and enigmatic embodiment of Divine Wisdom.

During her fall, Sophia wandered around bondage and ignorance. Her search for the Godhead symbolically represented each soul. The Gnostics saw Sophia's fall as the soul's fall from God. The distance between the soul and God brought suffering upon the soul, but suffering produced strength of will in the face of adversity, and that refined character. Ultimately, a strong character and the desire to move toward God inspired hope.

The Thunder, Perfect Mind has been called a "female revelation" that made it unique among all the texts found at Nag Hammadi. It has closest resonance to the Valentinian version of Gnosticism and also the Bible's wisdom hymns. It puts forth paradoxical proclamations, each beginning with the words, "I am." For example, "I am the whore and the holy one." Some scholars have defined the female narrative voice in The Thunder, Perfect Mind as the higher and lower Sophia figures or the Eve found in other Gnostic writings.

And not only so, but we glory in tribulations also: knowing that tribulation worketh patience; and patience, experience; and experience, hope: and hope maketh not ashamed; because the love of God is shed abroad in our hearts by the Holy Ghost which is given unto us.—Romans 5:3–5

In their book *Jesus and the Lost Goddess: The Secret Teaching of the Original Christians*, authors Timothy Freke and Peter Gandy assert that the main women in the New Testament Gospel accounts, namely Virgin Mary and Mary Magdalene, symbolize respectively the higher Sophia and the lower Sophia, two aspects of the single character in the Sophia myth. Some Gnostics believed that Mary Magdalene embodied Sophia or Holy Wisdom. She showed an insightful inquisitiveness and understanding of Jesus' wisdom teachings. In one, Jesus explained the origin of the the name Pistis. Jesus noted that in their descent from the immortal world to the corruptible one, Christ and Sophia revealed a brilliant light—the divine soul. Jesus called the light by its male name, Begetter of All Things and by its female name, Begettress Sophia, or Pistis.

Gnostics understood Sophia as the longing for return to the Godhead. The awakening and the thirst for knowledge and its acquisition, according to Gnostic belief, resulted in the realization that a savior was needed. That savior was Jesus. The sacred journey of returning to the Godhead was not made in one leap but in steady increments. The return, however, is the goal of life.

The Pistis Sophia

The Pistis Sophia (Faith Wisdom or sometimes translated as Faith of Sophia) dates to A.D. 250–300 and is one of those Gnostic scriptures that was once thought to have been destroyed by the orthodox early church but has survived. The text suggests that Jesus did not ascend to the Pleroma but stayed on earth for eleven years, teaching his disciples until he had brought their knowledge up to the first level of the mystery. The text explains the falling and rising of the soul, Gnostic cosmology, and desires that must be overcome for one to achieve salvation. Sophia's descent symbolizes the descent of the power of redemption in the divine feminine. Three Biblical female images express this power. They are Eve, the Virgin Mary, and Mary Magdalene.

FACT

Patristic Christian leaders in the fourth century banned the Pistis Sophia. The British Museum acquired a copy from a doctor in 1795 who got it from an unknown source. Written in Upper Egyptian Sahidic dialect translated from Greek, the text shows Jesus instructing his disciples in esoteric mysteries, in particular, Sophia's fall and repentance, symbolic of the predicament of individuals.

In the Gospel of Philip, a text that covers the topic of marriage as a sacred mystery, Mary Magadalene is called the "companion" of Jesus. It states that there were three Marys who always walked with him: his mother Mary, her sister (presumably the Virgin Mary's sister or sister-in-law), and Mary Magdalene, "the one who was called his companion."

Peter Challenges Mary Magdalene

In the Pistis Sophia, Jesus' last teaching takes place on the Mount of Olives twelve years after his death and resurrection. Here, he teaches his disciples (Martha, Matthew, Philip, Peter, Mother Mary, Mary Magdalene, and Salome, among them) about many realms of the invisible world. He instructs them in esoteric mysteries. At one point during the discourse, Peter, Jesus' hot-tempered, impulsive disciple (whom some have labeled a mysogynist and others have called tender-hearted), complained to Jesus that he and the other disciples cannot endure Mary Magdalene because she talks too much, depriving them of the opportunity to speak.

Two things are notable about this passage. The first is that Jesus treated his female disciples as equal participants with the men in his discourse sessions. The second reveals Peter's intolerance of Mary Magdalene. Her questioning of the Savior and her ongoing discourse is not to Peter's liking, nor would it have been tolerated by the orthodox Christian fathers who followed Peter after Jesus' death.

Mary Magdalene tells Jesus that she is afraid of Peter, because he threatened her and because he hates her sex. The Pistis Sophia, along with the Gospel of Thomas, the Gospel of the Egyptians, and the Gospel of Mary, illustrate tensions between these two important disciples of Jesus. The tensions between these two echo outward into the earliest groups of Christians, before the orthodoxy had established itself and ordered the destruction of any texts offering competing viewpoints.

References in Sophian teachings of the holy bride usually mean the presence and power of the Divine (Sophia) as embodied in each human, with Christ as the masculine counterpart. Mary Magdalene has been called the Sophia or "Divine Wisdom" of Jesus Christ.

The conflict between Mary Magdalene and Peter indicates differences in viewpoints and interpretations of Jesus' esoteric teachings by two of his closest disciples. Both of them possessed an understanding of what the Lord had taught them. But Mary Magdalene was a mystic and visionary and Jesus empowered, emboldened, and magnified her while he often rebuked Peter for his brashness and cowardess. Nevertheless, in Peter, he saw a tender-hearted man, someone who was solid and courageous (especially after the Pentecost).

Mary Magdalene spoke boldly and in openess about her fear of Peter. But Jesus made the ultimate promise to Mary when he told her that because her heart was pure and strained toward heaven more than her brother and sister disciples, he would complete her, bestowing upon her all the divine mysteries.

Mary Magdalene as Jesus' Elect

In the Pistis Sophia, Jesus calls Mary Magdalene "blessed." He praises her spiritual understanding, saying that she is more spiritual than the others. Jesus tells Mary Magdalene that she will inherit the whole Kingdom of the Light. Some feminist theologians believe that Jesus, in his enthusiastic support of Mary Magdalene, intended for her to be his spiritual heir over his ministry. They say that Mary Magdalene occupied a special place in his heart, and that he told her she was blessed beyond all the women upon the earth and would be the "perfection of all perfections." Some translations say she would be the "completeness of all completions." Mary Magdalene asked him if she could speak directly and he told her to speak in openess and not be afraid. He told her to ask him any question and he would reveal the answer to her.

According to the Gospel of Mary, after Jesus had been put to death Peter asked Mary Magdalene to share some words or teachings that Jesus had given her but not the others. This indicates that Peter knew that Jesus and Mary Magdalene shared a close, intimate friendship.

Mary Magdalene may have served in many roles in the life and ministry of Jesus, but only her role as the victim of demon possession that Jesus healed and her role as the eyewitness to the Resurrection are recorded in the New Testament Gospels. However, mention is made that she was among a group of women followers who supported Jesus' mission out of their means (finances).

QUESTION?

Was Mary Magdalene the leader of a sect of early Christianity?
Some feminist theologians and religious scholars say that she stood out as a likely candidate. In widely circulated early Christian writings, Mary Magdalene was depicted as a mystic, someone close (perhaps closest) to Jesus, who grasped his most esoteric lessons, had visions, and articulated his teachings to others.

According to John's Gospel, after death Jesus chose to appear to a certain woman, his pre-eminent female follower. Her testimony that he had risen inspired hope in the Christians. Her words of comfort turned their minds toward God and away from grief. It would have been difficult to downplay or erase Mary Magdalene's central role in the Resurrection, and, indeed, there are fourteen references to her in the canonical Gospels. But there is no mention of other roles that she may have had, such as leader of one important branch of Christianity, or of her teaching and preaching.

Chapter 7

The Role of Women in Gnosticism

During the earliest era of Christianity, Jewish and Roman women alike lived under the subjugation of men. Some sources say that during Jesus' lifetime, women ranked lower than beasts of burden in importance in that society. Christianity had its roots in Judaism, and most Jewish women of those times were neither educated nor allowed to have discourse with men in the Temple. The Torah and strict purity laws dictated how women and men were to conduct themselves.

A Challenge to the Patriarchy

Many women undoubtedly accepted their fate without much resistance because they lived in a society with rules enforced by men and passed through a lineage of Jewish patriarchs. Their lives mirrored the lives of their mothers and grandmothers. Yet the less fortunate women who had no men to define them and their place in society, such as widows, and those who were lame, chronically ill, slaves, or prostitutes became disenfranchised. They had no safety net and no easy way out of their miserable existence. In Jesus, they saw a new kind of man, one who accorded them respect, empathy, and the means of health and empowerment.

Jesus challenged the patriarchy in its treatment of women. He witnessed every day how women were treated in his world. A woman was not allowed to let a man other than her husband see her with her hair unbound, eat with a strange man, or talk with a man in public. Yet Jesus explained the Scriptures to women, offered them hope (as the woman at the well in John 4:4–42), protected them from being stoned to death, and healed them.

And a woman having an issue of blood twelve years, which had spent all her living upon physicians, neither could be healed of any, came behind him, and touched the border of his garment: and immediately her issue of blood stanched.—Luke 8:43–44

Until Jesus came along, they were cast off, ostracized, and disenfranchised. He showed a remarkable, radical egalitarian treatment of women. He treated them with respect. He accepted them even when they were considered ritually unclean or filled with sin. Jesus did not abuse them or treat them as servants or as sex objects. He never dehumanized or depersonalized them. He spoke to them in public, and also in private, and they taught him things. Women around him were grateful. They anointed him with perfumed oil and provided for him out of their means. They became his disciples. One woman—Mary of Magdala—became his closest friend and confidante (as the Gnostic Gospels argue), was eyewitness to his resurrection, and served as his designated messenger to the male apostles who, according to popular belief, may have fled into hiding after Jesus' death in fear of their own lives. Jesus may not have intended to emerge as a social reformer and he did not change Jewish law, but he showed through example a more equitable way to treat women.

Orthodox Christian women conform to roles of women reflected in the Bible. They see themselves as followers of Christ, wives and mothers, spiritual educators of their children, and workers and missionaries in the world. They see in the mother of Jesus a spiritual exemplar of piety and virtue.

As the first Christian communities grew, the Gentile communities expanded faster than those of the Jewish Christians. However, when the faithful gathered, they most likely did so in small groups so as not to alert the authorities. They met in house churches at table fellowships modeled upon the Jewish table tradition. Men and women worshipped with prayer and prophecy, healed, and did whatever they had known Jesus to do. They likely shared food and drink after their worship session in a communal fellowship. Because there were Jewish Christian groups that ate kosher foods and Gentile groups that consumed a more open diet, the evolution of the church away from its Jewish roots into the Gentile realm likely found the food choices becoming less restrictive. The New Testament Gospels depict Jesus at table fellowship with people who were disenfranchised or marginalized in the Palestinian society of the first century. His social interaction with such individuals, disregard for washing purification before eating, and lack of regard for tithed bread rankled Jewish leaders, who labeled Jesus a glutton. The fourteenth chapter of the canonical Gospel of Luke shows how Jesus felt about the restrictions put upon him and others in Jewish society. In one instance he challenges the status quo by naming those who should be invited to a feast.

But when thou makest a feast, call the poor, the maimed, the lame, the blind: and thou shalt be blessed; for they cannot recompense thee: for thou shalt be recompensed at the resurrection of the just.—Luke 14:13–14

Three women traveled with Jesus. Luke 8:2–3 mentions Mary Magdalene, Joanna (wife of Chuza, Herod's steward), and Susanna. In the Gospel of Philip 59:6–11, there were three who always walked with Jesus, and they were all Marys. Presumably many other women also followed him. He brought them words of wisdom in the parables, sayings, and prayers that he taught them. In the Lost Gospel of Q, also known as the Sayings Gospel Q, Jesus speaks the true sayings that are attributed to Wisdom. That Gospel shows how closely Jesus is associated with Wisdom, a feminine attribute of God. In the Dialogue of the Savior, he reveals that whatever comes from truth does not perish.

Jesus' Teaching on Gender Equality

While the Hebrew scriptures or Old Testament and New Testament both assert that God and humans are separate, some of the Gnostic scriptures proclaimed that the Self and the Divine are the same, a truth that can be discovered through gnosis. In Gnostic Christian circles, such as one that Mary Magdalene may have led, women were prophets and leaders. The Apostle Paul in his New Testament letters greeted women and referred to them as co-workers. He even called one a deacon, although the feminine form would be deaconess, and praised another—Junia and her husband Andronicus, who were "my kinsmen, and my fellow-prisoners, who are of note among the apostles, who also were in Christ before me" (Romans 16:7). According to the Acts of the Apostles, in some cases women owned the houses where early Christians met. So among the many sects of Christians that emerged following Jesus' death, women were full participants in religious activities.

By the early second century, the patriarchal leaders had pushed women from their roles as prophets and priests and bishops and forced them back into patriarchal subjugation, as can be seen from reading 1 Timothy, chapter 2. The patristic leaders established rules and a hierarchy that limited women's roles or excluded them completely (such as serving as bishops and priests). They enforced their rules through their teachings, sermons, and writings, and, later, councils. Some scholars have noted that the contributions of women were eliminated from the official texts of the church. Not until the fourth century would women again be able to become deaconesses (just below the level of a priest), though they were still barred from entering the priesthood.

FACT

Leaders in the early Christian churches were called *episkopos* (bishop, overseer), *presbyteros* (elder), and *diakonos* (deacon). Qualifications for bishops are listed in the New Testament (1 Timothy 3:1–7): a man must be blameless, be husband of one wife, have good moral values, rule well over his house, be in control of his family, be spiritually mature, and be held in high esteem by nonbelievers.

It's difficult to imagine how the Christian church might have evolved if women's roles had not diminished, if the divine feminine aspect of God had not been eliminated, and if women's contributions had not been devalued or discarded. Gnostics believed in enlightenment but also ignorance. While the orthodox Christians labeled the Gnostics *heretics*, the Gnostics claimed that the orthodox were ignorant. Valentinus, in particular, believed that ignorance was the root of the material world and without it the world would cease to be. For Valentinus and his followers, the physical or material world was what kept the soul trapped from returning to the realm of Light.

Mary Magdalene as Sophia

The Gnostics had an image of divine feminine that was purged from the Christian texts of the early church fathers. However, she did appear often in the Gnostic writings as Mary Magdalene allegorized as Sophia/Wisdom/Goddess. She was portrayed as Jesus' most trusted apostle and companion

(Gospel of Philip), as a visionary and prophet who possessed a secret teaching that Jesus gave her but not the other disciples (in the Gospel of Mary), as the "woman who knew the All" (in the Dialogue of the Savior) and as the Sophia, the brilliant questioner of Jesus (in the Pistis Sophia). Two Gnostic texts—On the Origin of the World and The Hypostasis of the Archons—proclaim that Sophia alone produced the Judeo-Christian God. A God who would send his only Son to be crucified was unthinkable to some Gnostics, who preferred to contemplate a transcendent God as Goodness and Light.

Followers of Valentinus and his disciple, Marcus the magician, believed that God is indescribable but could be imagined as having two aspects: the masculine (variously called the Primal Father, the Ineffable, and the Depth), and the feminine, seen as the Mystical Eternal Silence, Incorruptible Wisdom, and Mother of All. Marcus claimed his visions of the divine being were female.

The wisdom texts of the Hebrew scriptures often personify wisdom as Sophia or *Hokhmah*. She articulates knowledge through the proverbs, riddles, and sayings found in those texts. The Apocryphal book of Sirach, for example, states that the Lord "poured her [Wisdom] upon his works" and every living thing and also on his friends (Sirach 1:8).

Mary Magdalene's Divine Wisdom

Mary Magdalene, the disciple of Jesus, sought wisdom; as Sophia, she expressed the divine attribute of Wisdom (as in the Pistis Sophia). Yet in the Gnostic Gospel of Thomas (verse 114), Peter tells Jesus that Mary Magdalene was not worthy of being an Apostle because she was a woman. Peter was married, yet in the Gnostic literature he is the one most often at odds with Mary Magdalene. But to the Gnostics, Mary Magdalene was filled with wisdom that the Lord poured upon her. For Gnostic women, she must have stood as a powerful spiritual example. The Naassenes, one of the early Gnostic sects, possessed a lesson containing initiatory teachings of Jesus from the Last Supper, which mentions Mariamne [Mary Magdalene].

To understand how the Gnostics might have seen Mary Magdalene as the personification of Sophia, an understanding of a few (of the great number) of the roles Sophia played in ancient times might be in order. In the Ptolemaic tradition, Sophia, the Aeon known as Wisdom, was called Achamoth, or Mother of the Seven Heavens. To the followers of Valentinus, Sophia was represented as higher aspect—Lightsome Mother—and a lower one—Achamoth. In the Gnostic Acts of Thomas, she is the focus of the Eucharistic Prayer. As such, she becomes the ancient goddess known as Astarte or Isis (both were called goddesses of wisdom). The symbol for Astarte was the dove, which is also the symbol of the Holy Spirit.

Gnostic Women and Sophia

It is difficult to say with certainty what theological views about Sophia, the Divine Mother, and other feminine references to God meant to Gnostic women going about their daily activities within their communities. It seems clear that, in the spiritual realms, they did officiate at church fellowship gatherings, prophesied, and performed functions that their conservative counterparts reserved for priests. They likely prepared foods for a simple or celebratory meal for Christian fellowship. But the Gnostic texts for the most part bear the names of men.

QUESTION?

Who conducted baptisms in the house churches of different congregations in different urban areas of the Diaspora?
The Apostle Paul with co-workers evangelized communities and established individual homes as "house churches" where he baptized the house-church owners or residents and, they, in turn, baptized the others. Women not only baptized but also may have presided over the Eucharist.

Scholars still seek answers about how Gnostic women lived their lives on a daily basis and how much equality with men they really had. Patriarchy had not disappeared. Slavery still existed. Roman domination and persecution continued at least until the reign of Emperor Constantine in the fourth century. While much of what survives in ancient literature offers conflicting images, it is likely that the zeitgeist did not change much while they went about their lives while inwardly searching for the special spiritual knowledge that would set them free.

Mary Magdalene as Female Counterpart to Jesus

Timothy Freke and Peter Gandy, authors of *Jesus and the Lost Goddess*, suggest that the "All," as Mary Magdalene is called in the Dialogue of the Savior, represents the Goddess, who was prominent in the ancient world from the pagan mysteries. Goddess worship had its roots in the Egyptian cult of Isis, the Sister-Bride of Osiris. Their child, known as the God of Light, was named Horus. The Gnostics' assigning of Goddess status to Mary Magdalene may be a reflection of their tendency to borrowing themes, ideas, myths, and practices from other traditions and syncretizing them into their own belief system. In the Egyptian legend, Isis discovers that her husband has been murdered and mutilated. Osiris descended into the underworld, struggled with evil powers, and on the third day rose again. He became equal to Râ, the Sun God. The similarities with Jesus' suffering, death, and resurrection cannot be missed. Scholar Margaret Starbird maintains that in the anointing, death, and resurrection of Jesus is the reworking of an old partnership paradigm found in the ancient myths of the Sacred Bride and Bridegroom. She asserts that the Isis and Osiris myth serves as one example.

Mary Magdalene's anointing of Jesus with special oil places her in the Egyptian shamanic tradition as a great priestess. Authors Freke and Gandy suggest that the Gnostic beliefs about Mary Magdalene as the Goddess-consort to Jesus' God-man so threatened the early orthodox church's vision that the church sought to "brutally suppress" such ideas. The church, however, does call Mary Magdalene "Apostle to the Apostles."

For the orthodox Christians (Catholics and Greek Orthodox), the feminine archetype is embodied in the Blessed Virgin Mary. However, in Gnostic Christianity, Mary Magdalene personified the archetype feminine counterpart to Jesus. The Gnostic texts place Mary Magdalene in a position that the orthodox texts reserve for Peter—that is, as Jesus' closest, pre-eminent, and most trusted disciple. The Gnostic Gospel of Thomas mentions six disciples: Thomas, Matthew, Peter, James, Salome, and Mary Magdalene.

Irenaeus of Lyons, Tertullian of Carthage, Hippolytus of Rome, and others labeled Gnostic beliefs (for example, God as the Sacred Feminine) absurd, their myths ridiculous, their corruption of orthodox scripture dangerous, and their women officiating over the Eucharist deviant. Women were to remain silent and Gnostic texts were to be destroyed.

The Gnostic Gospel of Mary reveals that Jesus' inner circle knew of her elevated standing with Jesus. In a scene from that Gospel, Peter disbelieves Mary Magdalene after he has asked her to share words or a teaching that Jesus may have given her and not him. When she does, he disbelieves and asks whether or not the others think that Jesus would tell her, a woman, something that he would not tell the male disciples. Levi defends Mary Magdalene and asks Peter who he was to reject her if the Savior made her worthy. Levi reminds Peter that the Savior "knows her very well." Levi suggests that instead of being contentious with Mary, they should "put on the perfect man" and do as Jesus had commanded them (Gospel of Mary 18:10–20).

Some Internet Gnostic sites proclaim an understanding of Mary Magdalene as Jesus' wife and co-Redeemer. They point out that in the canonical gospels, Mary Magdalene's name appears first in lists of women (but behind the Virgin Mary), indicating her important stature. They make note of the Gnostic Gospels' elevation of her over other disciples and point to the Gospel of Philip's statement that Jesus kissed her often on the . . . , inserting the word "mouth" where the lacuna appears. For others to see Mary Magdalene as a consort or counterpart to Jesus would have dismayed and worried the Christian orthodox fathers because she stood for freedom of the individual over the need of clergy to secure salvation. She represented dangerous ideas that were reprehensible to the church, including sacred marriage and sexuality rather than virginity and abstinence.

Female Officeholders and Bishops

Jesus helped women. He restored them to wholeness. He gave them hope and treated them fairly. Jesus welcomed them into his small but growing movement. According to some Biblical scholars, many of the first Christian sects treated women as Jesus had shown through example. They allowed women to serve in Christian house-church worship sessions as presbyters, deaconesses, and bishops. But at the close of the first century of Jesus' ministry, with the dominant branch of Christianity emerging as orthodox, women's roles began eroding. The Gnostic sects, by allowing women to officiate in churches, stood in direct opposition to the ban against women speaking in church enforced by the orthodox Christian groups. Paul, in his first letter to the Christians in Corinth (a community he established in circa A.D. 51), spells out clearly the behavior expected of women. In his letter, he writes forcefully with all his apostolic authority about how to deal with community issues, such as women who wished to speak to those assembled.

Let your women keep silence in the churches: for it is not permitted unto them to speak; but they are commanded to be under obedience, as also saith the law. And if they will learn any thing, let them ask their husbands at home: for it is a shame for women to speak in the church.—1 Corinthians 14:34–35

Yet, in seeming contradiction, women in the orthodox version of the faith must have served in some leadership roles according to various references in the texts of the New Testament, especially Acts and the letters of Paul. Those texts reveal that women were helpers, workers in the faith, and prominent leaders. Some scholars believe that an unknown individual at a later, unknown date inserted the quote above into the text of the letter to the Christians at Corinth to enforce (by Paul's authority) the suppression of women as full participants in church. If this proves true, then the quote cannot be construed as authoritative.

Paul's Revelations about Early Christian Women

In the years following Jesus' death, the Apostle Paul recognized the contributions of women working with him as ministers and apostles. Paul made a profound and vigorous assertion of equality between men and women as God's children in Christ in his letter to the Galatians. The letter suggested that gender was dissolved through baptism in Christ. The words he uses in the letter are from a baptismal formula belonging to the Jewish Christian "church" that he had joined.

For as many of you as have been baptized into Christ have put on Christ. There is neither Jew nor Greek, there is neither bond nor free, there is neither male nor female: for ye are all one in Christ Jesus. And if ye be Christ's, then are ye Abraham's seed, and heirs according to the promise.—Galatians 3:27–29

Paul participated in the Christian fellowship meetings that took place in private homes. In his letters in the New Testament, Paul often began his letters with a greeting to his hosts. It was not unusual for him to recognize the contributions of women, and it seems, since women ruled over the domain of the home, that women provide the food and drink for these religious/social gatherings. All who had an interest or desire to participate could join in sessions of fellowship and prayer.

In the Gnostic Christian fellowship gatherings, all were encouraged to participate. Women and men drew lots to choose who would serve as prophet, priest, or bishop. But by the second century in the literalist Christian churches, Jesus' pattern of gender equality changed. Women, after Jesus' death, had claimed spiritual power and served as spiritual leaders. They had baptized, healed, shared discourse, and performed exorcisms, according to a polemic against them by second-century church father Tertullian, who called them "audacious," "without modesty," and "bold." With the apostolic hierarchical structure firmly in place and vigorous verbal and written attacks mounted against the Gnostics by the orthodox dominant group of Christians, the religious roles for women receded.

In Paul's letters to the churches that he had established in various communities, he singled out women for greetings and praise. Christian women leaders in his epistles include:

- **Apphia:** a leader in a house church along with Archippus and Philemon.
- **Chloe:** a wealthy woman with some stature in her Christian community, where she was possibly a leader of a Corinthian church.
- **Euodia and Syntyche:** missionaries who were equal with Paul in the work they did.
- **Mary:** one of Paul's workers.
- **Persis:** a woman who worked hard for the faith and for whom Paul felt an especially deep fondness. He commended her for her efforts.
- **Junia:** wife of Andronicus; they were a missionary couple. Paul called her "outstanding among the apostles," which clearly shows that the early Christian church had female apostles. He said she was imprisoned.
- **Phoebe:** a high-class woman, likely a patron of Paul's that he singled out as a helper. She may have provided financial assistance to him in his missionary work as well as done some preaching and teaching as the diakonos, or leader, of one of his churches.
- **Prisca:** wife of Aquila, who served as leader with her husband of house churches in Corinth, Ephesus, and Rome. They were a missionary couple that risked their lives for Paul. He accorded her a superior position to her husband by regularly mentioning her name before his.
- **Typhaena and Tryphosa:** possibly sisters and workers in the faith.
- **Nympha:** a hostess and leader of a house church, possibly a widow.

Like Paul, the Gnostics argued for gender equality and supported the right of women to lead services, prophesy, and preach.

Legacy of Mary Magdalene

Some Gnostic sects saw Mary Magdalene as a lover, and perhaps even a wife, to Jesus. For them, she was the Illuminatrix or Light Bearer. Jesus' pure light and hers would pour into each other in the rite of sacred marriage known as hieros gamos. Hers was the presence her followers invoked in silence to guide them on their inward journey out of darkness toward the light of the Pleroma. She was the wisdom chalice that contained all of Jesus' teachings. Though the Gnostics did not have a hierarchy like the more dominant orthodox group of Christians, Mary Magdalene for them would have been the Apostle from whom all future generations of her followers could trace their ancient spiritual lineage. Even the orthodox Christians called her the "Apostle to the Apostles." Later, the Greek Orthodox Church bestowed upon her the title of "Holy Myrrh-Bearer" and "Equal-Unto-the-Apostles." Like the Roman Catholic Church, the Greek Orthodox Church celebrates her feast day on July 22.

In the Dialogue of the Savior, when Mary Magdalene asks why she has come to "this place," Jesus tells her she "makes clear the abundance of the Revealer." Some modern Gnostics take that to mean that she brings forth into consciousness what is already there. There is no practice beyond turning inward in silence to experience the mystery.

Modern advocates of women in the priesthood say that Jesus called women to both discipleship and leadership. By revealing his risen transcendent form to Mary Magdalene and entrusting her to carry his resurrection message to the other disciples (some say, the first command to preach), he upheld the place of women in his ministry after his death. The texts that esteem Mary Magdalene and reflect her as the guarantor of the tradition of women leaders in the faith, exhort them to share with others their sacred visions and significant words. Modern Catholic women who love their faith but seek change within the church call out her name. Mary Magdalene would have known the power of the numinous Presence. As one modern

Gnostic explained, Gnosis is as close as the heartbeat and in silence the spirit recognizes and experiences that Holy Presence.

Future Church, an organization seeking reform with the Catholic church to raise awareness of Mary Magdalene's central role in the early church and to allow women who are called to serve into the priesthood, maintains a Web site at *www.futurechurch.org*. The organization cites evidence from fourth-to sixth-century churches that women served as priests.

Chapter 8

Four Gnostic Schools of Thought

The Gnostics taught a basic doctrine that included belief in a transcendent deity, the duality of matter and spirit realms with linkage between them, a Pleroma where the Fullness of God existed, the Demiurge as the creator of the world of matter, a divine spark within each human upon birth, and an awakening through inner self-knowledge that leads to the merging of consciousness back into the Divine. However, certain sects formulated variations in these basic core beliefs.

Different Sects Appear

Gnosticism emerged and took root in a Judeo-Christian milieu. It synthe-sized ideas from other sources, including Syrian, Greco-Roman, and Egyp-tian. As a religious movement, it most likely started in the first century and flourished from the second to the fourth centuries. Contrasted with the early orthodox Christian organization, Gnosticism stressed individual effort toward understanding truth (enabled by the assistance of a savior figure who brought secret knowledge) that helped the individual to obtain libera-tion or enlightenment. They refused to align themselves or their beliefs with the God of the Hebrew Scriptures, Yahweh or Jehovah. They interpreted Jesus' teachings in ways that were radically different from orthodox Chris-tianity. They believed that Christ was a divine spirit descended to earth to inhabit Jesus' body. As such, Christ did not die when Jesus was crucified but departed Jesus' body to return to the divine world. Because of this belief, the Gnostics eschewed the idea of salvation through the death of Christ and literalistic interpretations of the Gospels.

The Gnostic Gospel of the Hebrews and the Gospel of Thomas each reveal a thread connecting the Holy Spirit with the Divine Mother. Epiph-anius, a fourth-century writer, preserved a few quotations of Hebrews in his text Panarion. Earlier, in the second century, Irenaeus referred to a version of Matthew's gospel (Gospel of the Hebrews in Aramaic) that the Gnostic Ebionites used.

The orthodox Christians stressed the importance of their own interpreta-tions of Jesus' teachings. They imposed upon their followers the obligation to follow orthodox doctrine, creed, and hierarchy of clergy as the church's authority. Both the Gnostic and orthodox groups saw Jesus as a Savior/Redeemer figure. They both shared some of the same sacred New Testament texts. But there were many differences between them in belief and practice. The orthodox Christians established unity through the structure of a hierarchy of priests, deacons, and bishops by the second century while the Gnostics, for the most part, had no organizational structure and appeared to be more of a conglomeration of many different sects. The one Gnostic group that rose in popularity was Marcionism. Marcion developed his own version of the New Testament, but without a core of missionaries to spread the faith, Marcionism ultimately failed to thrive like many of the Gnostic sects. Differences in Gnostic interpretation of whichever scriptures they possessed and used broadly separated the many different sects into four main groups.

Syrian Discipline

Some historians place this school at the beginning of Gnosticism, making it the oldest. This group of Gnostic sects opposed the Jewish God, espousing a belief that the God of Good (of the New Testament) must take the place of the rigidly righteous, harsh God of the Jewish people (of the Hebrew scriptures). They rejected the latter, believing that the God of Good called upon believers to serve Him through his Son Jesus Christ. The Syrian Gnostics borrowed from Platonist sources, viewing the material or physical world as inherently evil and markedly inferior to the good world of the Pleroma. This group of Gnostics shunned meat and often chose asceticism and celibacy over marriage and children. They included the Naassenes, Ophites, Sethians, Peratai, Saturnilians, and the Cainites.

Naassenes

The Naassenes saw themselves as disciples of Jesus and claimed that their mystical spiritual teachings came from James the Just, Jesus' brother. Their sect became one of the first accused of heresy by the orthodox Christians. Heresiologist and church father Hippolytus branded their doctrine as the root of all heresies and wrote a refutation against what he believed to be their delusional ideas.

Book five of Hippolytus's aggressive refutation of the Naassenes contains the secret sermon presented to them by Jesus at the Last Supper. Mark H. Gaffney, in his book *The Gnostic Secrets of the Naassenes, the Initiatory Teachings of the Last Supper*, offers a look at the sermon that Hippolytus claimed to record word for word. Gaffney, in his book, masterfully decodes and deciphers the spiritual meaning from the message that Jesus supposedly imparted to his inner circle of disciples during their last meal together. Hippolytus noted that James handed down many discourses to Mariamne, and he (Hippolytus) desired to silence the ideas that the Naassenes were spreading.

FACT

The word "Naassene" derives from the Hebrew word for serpent, nahas or nahash. In the ancient world, the serpent universally symbolized wisdom, redeeming power, and knowledge. The serpent (of wisdom) tempted Eve to taste the Tree of the Knowledge (of good and evil) in the Garden of Eden. Orthodox Christianity branded her act the Original Sin.

In some ways, the Naassene symbolism of water as the spirit world and the upward flowing of the river that can make humans like gods resonated with ideas found in the practice of Kundalini yoga in the Hindu tradition. The concept of reversing the flow of energy (along the spine) upward—toward enlightenment—instead of downward into the material world is found in both Buddhism and Hinduism (and may also have some resonance in the Gospel of Mary in the secret teaching that Mary reveals to Peter). The latter two systems promote a belief in a dormant, divine energy, coiled three and one-half times at the base of the spine. There the divine energy remains asleep. Once awakened, it moves upward like a snake to the top of the head and bestows cosmic consciousness, or a merging of the individual consciousness into the Divine. To the Naassenes, individual effort was vital to reversing the downward pull of the material universe so that the spirit could ascend into the realms of gods. The Gnostic rite of the Bridal Chamber might have facilitated this ascent.

Ophites

The Ophites revered the serpent (in the tale of Adam and Eve) as the giver of knowledge and Divine Wisdom and as Achamoth. The Ophites lived in Egypt and Syria circa A.D. 100. Like the Naassenes, the Ophites rejected the God of the Hebrew scriptures because he forbade the first couple to eat from the tree of knowledge in the Garden of Eden. At least four early church heresiologists polemicized against the Ophites—Hippolytus, Irenaeus, Origen, and Epiphanius. Ophite sects included the Sethians, Peratai, Borborites, Naassenes, and Mandaeans, a religious sect active in modern Iran and Iraq.

Sethians

The Sethians worshipped the serpent as the redeemer of Eve from the power of gross matter. Followers saw Seth, the third son of Adam, as the father of all spiritual seekers, or *pneumatikoi*, rather than men attached to the material world and carnality. They viewed the world as having three divisions: darkness, light, and the spirit realm between the two. Many of the Gnostic texts discovered at Nag Hammadi are considered to be Sethian writings.

Peratai

The Peratai was a Gnostic group founded by Euphrates, Celbes, and Ademes. Like the Sethians and Naassenes, the group revered the serpent, and its symbol figured prominently in their rituals and practices. Modern scholars refer to them as one of the "Serpent Gnostic" sects. They saw themselves as pilgrims passing through the material world as visitors from their true home in the spirit realm. They believed in the power of the number three. For example, their Trinity was the Father, the Son (the Cosmic Serpent), and the world of Hyle or matter. Their beliefs are symbolized by the triangle within the circle. Heresiologist Hippolytus denounced the Peratai school of Gnosticism and its astrology and mathematical elements. He blamed the serpent as the root of all Gnostic thinking.

Euphrates knew a great deal about astrology, and thus his sect believed that individual karma is linked to a person's horoscope and the position of the sun, planets, and moon at birth. The Peratai wore talismans adorned with serpents to ward off evil.

Saturnilians

Saturninus founded a Syrian Gnostic sect that believed in the duality of the universe with the unknowable God as one pole and Satan, ruler of created matter, as the opposite. Saturninus came from Antioch and practiced a severe version of asceticism, encratism, which he may have introduced to early Christians. His followers abstained from marriage and meat-eating. He taught a creation myth that revealed angels or divine architects made the human bodies. A savior (in male form) rescued those with divine sparks and destroyed the archons or those of evil powers. Justin Martyr, one of the patristic fathers writing in A.D. 150 to 160, mentioned Saturninus along with other well-known Gnostic leaders, including Basilides, Marcion, and Valentinus.

FACT

The Mandaeans were a Gnostic Christian sect that vigorously empha-sized baptism and fertility. Although the sect likely had its roots in Juda-ism and Christianity, and is later influenced by Islam, it eschewed all three. The sect continues today in areas of Iran and along the Tigris and Euphrates rivers.

Cainites

The Cainites, a second-century Gnostic sect that venerated Cain, believed that it was good to resist God, the evil power. Followers saw Cain as a being whose existence derived from superior power unlike Abel, Cain's brother, and that Cain was the victim of the Demiurge (Jehovah of the Hebrew scrip-tures), whom many Gnostics saw as evil. Several patristic early Christian fathers—Irenaeus, Epiphanius, Hippolytus, and Tertullian—mentioned the Cainites in their writings about heretics.

Greek Discipline

The Greek or Hellenistic school of Gnostic belief tended to be more con-ceptual and philosophical and less rigidly ascetic than the Syrian. Two indi-vidual leaders gained power and notoriety within the Hellenistic Gnostic sects: Basilides and Valentinus. Some scholars say Basilides was born in Antioch but went to Alexandria where he founded his sect in circa A.D. 130.

Others report that he was an Alexandrian native. His son Isidore continued and built upon his father's work. Valentinus spent some time preaching in Alexandria, but in circa A.D. 160 he traveled to Rome, where he developed an intricate Gnostic cosmology based in part on sexual dualism during the process of emanation. Sophia and Christ figured prominently in Valentinian doctrine.

Basilidians

The main source for what is known about the Gnostic patriarch Basilides, his teaching, and his followers are the polemics of the orthodox early church fathers, since only fragments of his own work have survived. The Basilidians thrived in Egypt. Some members of the cult lived along the Nile delta, according to writings of Epiphanius. Basilidians observed Jesus' feast day, celebrating it annually on the day of his baptism. They observed a five-year silence, did not partake of food offered to false gods and idols, and wore amulets featuring the word "Abrasax" or the number "365."

Basilidians inscribed the word "Abrasax" on their talismans, amulets, and gems. Hebrew meanings for the first three letters in the acronym—Ab (Father), Ben (Son) and Ruah (Spirit, in the Hebrew feminine gender)—spell out the Trinity. Another source notes that the Basilidians believed in 365 heavens. The sum of the numeric value of "Abrasax" is 365.

The Valentinians

Valentinus, the founder of the most popular of the Gnostic groups, had many followers in his lifetime. He borrowed many of his ideas from the Apostle Paul, Plato, and Greek scientific thought. Initially, he subscribed to the orthodox Christian doctrine, but later veered from it and incorporated his own views, for which he was later excommunicated. Valentinians believed in the one unknowable God who, through the process of emanation, created pairs of gender-opposite beings known as Aeons. Sophia was one. Valentinians espoused the idea that humans live under subjugation of the material, or *hylic*, world and must free themselves from the pull of nature so that the inner, divine self can ascend to the spiritual world. Christ and the Holy Spirit came to earth with the mission of human redemption. However, Christ did not have a body, and therefore did not suffer or die on the cross, according to Valentinus. The mysterious "Bridal Chamber" was a rite belonging to the Valentinians.

QUESTION?

What did Heracleon see in the Gospel of John that resonated with his Valentinian ideas?
Heracleon read his own meanings into the Fourth Gospel, subtracting from it any actual historical events. In that gospel, he saw much Valentinian symbolism in references to spiritual light, darkness, and mysteries, particularly of numbers.

Branches of Valentinianism spread throughout Egypt, Syria, Italy, and southern Gaul (today's France). Two followers of Valentinus became the focus of polemical writings against Gnosticism by the patristic fathers: Ptolemy (who wrote the Gnostic text known as Letter to Flora) and Heracleon, a powerful Gnostic thinker and writer. Historians and Biblical scholars note that Heracleon's ideas aligned more closely with orthodox thinking than did Ptolemy's. The African patristic father Tertullian wrote against Ptolemy, and the orthodox leader Origen bridled against Heracleon. Both Origen and Heracleon wrote commentaries on the Gospel of John. Another prominent follower of Valentinus was Marcos, an Egyptian patriarch, though little is known about him.

The Dualistic Discipline

Marcion, son of a Christian bishop in Asia, was one of the early architects of the belief in Gnosticism that there were two gods. He was born in about A.D. 85, which means that not all of Jesus' apostles had yet died. Because of his merchant activities, Marcion amassed a fortune. Unfortunately, either due to misunderstanding or youthful indiscretion, he was accused of defiling a virgin. He left his home in Sinope, Asia Minor, in shame, excommunicated from that church. Marcion went to Rome and offered the conservative Roman church a gift of 200,000 sesterces. Perhaps it helped smooth his initial acceptance into that church, but once the patristic fathers understood how divergent Marcion's views were to their orthodox Christian beliefs, they gave back the money, branded him a heretic, and expelled him from the mother church in Rome in A.D. 144. Marcion then embarked upon a mission to establish his own churches in Rome, Carthage, Syria, Nicomedia, Smyrna, Phrygia, Antioch, and elsewhere.

Marcionites embraced the idea of an eternal struggle between good and evil. They rejected the God of the Hebrew scriptures as being the Father of Jesus. One of Marcion's followers named Apelles called the god of the Hebrew scriptures an angel of evil (arch enemy of Good) while another of his students asserted instead that "eternal matter" was the root of evil. Of major importance, however, is the Marcionite belief that Jesus brought secret knowledge that he did not share with the masses but rather taught to a select group of chosen ones. Marcion, in compiling his own canon of acceptable sacred texts, completely eliminated the old Hebrew scriptures from his canon. This set him apart from the orthodox Christians who relied on the Hebrew scriptures and regarded Old Testament prophecy as fulfilled in the life and ministry of Jesus.

Marcionites wanted nothing to do with Jewish practice, belief, or influence. Toward that aim, Marcion excised all positive references to the Jews in the letters of Paul and the Gospel of Luke, retaining and using his heavily redacted version in his teachings. Marcionites believed that the Demiurge was an inferior god, the cruel God of the Jews and the Hebrew scriptures who made women suffer in childbirth. The Father God who created Jesus, however, was a god of grace, love, goodness, and forgiveness.

Another important Marcionian idea refuted by the orthodoxy was that Christ appeared to be human but, in reality, was not. Thus, no Resurrection of the Flesh, Second Coming, or Judgment Day could be considered plausible. Finally, Marcionites shunned marriage, engaged in fasting, and observed strict asceticism.

The Antinomian Discipline

Antinomian (which derives from anti, meaning against, and nomos, meaning law) groups embraced a doctrine of unlimited licentiousness in opposition to the rigid ascetic practices of some of the other Gnostic sects. Their doctrine refuted and rejected the ancient Hebrew Mosaic Law that governed the ethical and moral actions of Jews. Basically, antinomians took the idea that just as good works do not bring salvation, neither do evil works prevent it. Once people become Christians, they are sanctified and cannot lose that sanctification.

Carpocratians

The Gnostic Carpocratians are one group of antinomians mentioned by several of the heresiologists for their disregard of human laws and lack of respect for good works. They were thought to be libertine in the extreme and believed that the God of Good secretly was to be found within the human spirit. They believed that humans, in order to free themselves from the trap of material existence, had to go through every possible human experience. They practiced magic and manipulation of the demigods, and had sex with whomever they wanted. Patristic father Tertullian called them fornicators. The Carpocratians believed that if they went through the entire gamut of all of human experience in one lifetime, they would never again have to reincarnate. Action was of little significance, they believed, if individual intent was right. Reincarnation was the Devil's work and his way of keeping humans in bondage. Human fate dictated the imprisoning of the immortal spirit and it was only through the teachings of beings like Jesus and Carpocrates that humans could find their way to their divine home again.

Carpocrates did not give much credence to the idea that God would impregnate the Virgin Mary or that Jesus would enter the world through virgin birth. He declared what he believed was obvious, that Jesus was Joseph's son. Carpocrates saw God manifested in the Greek philosophers such as Plato, Aristotle, and Pythagoras. He held Jesus in high esteem and saw him as a man of purity and godliness, qualities Carpocrates attributed to the divine wisdom Jesus possessed. Carpocratians believed that Jesus remembered his bodiless soul in the divine realm of the Unbegotten from which he came. Salvation for Carpocratians was not *through* Jesus but by *becoming* a Jesus themselves, remembering their true home as Jesus did.

FACT

Carpocrates, philosopher and founder of the movement that carries his name, lived and preached in the first half of the second century. His son Epiphanes expressed their sect's belief in communal sharing of property and women in *On Justice*. Epiphanes died in Kefalonia, Greece at age seventeen.

Much of what is known about the Carpocratians today comes from those who opposed the sect's beliefs, including Clement of Alexandria and Irenaeus of Lyons, the latter writing in *Against Heresies*. Both polemicized against them. Allegedly, the Carpocratians possessed two items of interest to the church and also to modern scholars: a painting supposedly of Jesus by Pilate and a copy of the Secret Gospel of Mark. Patristic father Clement accused Carpocrates of stealing the Gospel from the library in the Alexandrian church and then manipulating its text to suit his own "carnal" teachings. As noted in a previous chapter, the Secret Gospel of Mark has only been known about since 1958 through a mention in a letter by early church father Clement that was discovered by scholar Morton Smith.

Simonians

Simon Magus, a magician, was the founder of the Gnostic sect known as the Simonians. Early Christians took note of his ideas at variance with orthodox beliefs. Several patristic fathers, including Irenaeus, Justin Martyr, Hippolytus, and Clement, excoriated him as being a heretic, and, in fact, called him the patriarch of the heretics. However, Simon's followers believed he was God incarnate, perhaps because he portrayed himself as a kind of divine emanation. He had a reputation as a great sorcerer. He once offered money to purchase the Holy Spirit from the Apostles. (This is the origin of the term "simony," which is the buying or selling of sacred objects.)

Then Simon himself believed also: and when he was baptized, he continued with Philip, and wondered, beholding the miracles and signs . . . . . And when Simon saw that through laying on of the apostles' hands the Holy Ghost was given, he offered them money, saying, Give me also this power, that on whomsoever I lay hands, he may receive the Holy Ghost.—Acts 8:13–19

Simonism blended paganism with Greek and Babylonian religious elements and practices and syncretized them into Christianity. Simon was a contemporary of Peter and Paul and was baptized by Philip, so had intimate contact with the earliest versions of Christianity. He attempted to set up a universal religion, calling it Christianity because he was a Christian. Simon and his cult represented a major challenge for the Apostles and early church orthodox fathers because his brand of Christianity was greatly at odds with the teachings of the Apostles. They and generations of patristic fathers after them would work to discredit Simon and eliminate his cult as a wild offshoot.

Simonians' theological view of good versus evil asserted that nothing in and of itself was necessarily good or bad. Simonians believed that to be blessed in the world after death was to have the grace of Simon (as the god Zeus) and his female counterpart Helena (Athene) imparted to them. The Simonians as a sect thrived in Syria, and also in parts of Asia Minor and Rome. At least two strong groups grew out of Simonism—Dositheans and Menandrians. Dositheans followed Dositheus, the Samaritan teacher of Simon Magus. He did not believe in Simon's doctrine of rejecting the Hebrew scriptures. Dositheus claimed to be sent by God and was considered by his followers to be a great prophet. Menander asserted that the architects or angels sent by Ennoia (the Divine Mind) created the material world. Salvation of Menandrians came through baptism (by Menander) and the perfection of the art of magic.

According to one story, Simon supposedly could levitate and fly at will. Flying, inevitably became the means for meeting his death. He soared in the air while performing in a stunt to prove to the Emperor Claudius that he was a god. While he was still airborne, the Apostles Peter and Paul prayed for his flying to stop. Simon fell to his death. The event became immortalized in the painting of an altarpiece for the Compagnia di San Marco in the mid-fifteenth century.

Chapter 9

Consequences of Heresy

After the Crucifixion, the Jewish follow-ers of Jesus continued to see the move-ment as Jewish, albeit a reformed version of Judaism. The Apostle Paul saw it as a movement that welcomed all Jews and Gentiles, and he proselytized mainly to the Gentiles. The Apostles had disagree-ments among themselves that required resolution. But that was just the begin-ning of the trials and tribulations that the Jesus movement evolving into the infant Christian church would have faced.

Challenge to Church Doctrine

Perhaps the reason that so many gospels and other texts were written over the fifty years or so after Jesus' death was due to squabbling among the disciples. Each would have wanted to set into record his time with Jesus and interpretations of his teachings. Without Jesus to lead them, the group of Apostles struggled to stay together in spite of their differences. Peter and Andrew considered going back to their fishing enterprise. Mary Magdalene, according to the Gnostic gospel bearing her name, had sought them in their hiding places, consoled them in their grief, and admonished them to turn their minds back upon the teachings of Jesus. But who would be the new leader? To whom were they to turn now that Jesus was gone?

FACT

The modern Catholic Church teaches that only a Christian who rejects the church's teachings can commit heresy. A schismatic is someone who turns away from the authority of the church but still believes its teachings, and an apostate is one who completely rejects Christianity. Members of other faiths cannot be Christian heretics.

The Jesus followers did what Jesus had commissioned them to do. In their work of sharing Jesus' teachings with others, they established new communities of Christians. Initially, those communities may have stayed close to the teaching they had been given, but what happened as those communities evolved and new ideas or questions emerged? It seems logical that if they had a copy of a gospel account or some other sacred writing about Jesus' teachings or sayings, they would use it to inspire each other and try to grapple through any issues that troubled them. Who was to say if they were following the faith correctly or not?

Undoubtedly, differences of opinion would have become more problematic when interpretations by new cults of believers calling themselves Christians and living around Palestine, the Mediterranean, Egypt, and Syria threatened the emerging orthodox Christian church. The earliest writings of the New Testament, Paul's letters, clearly show the struggles faced by the new converts when cultural or other religious influences clashed with Paul's understanding of "Christian" belief. Paul, of course, never uses the word Christian. Not only Paul during his lifetime, but later the orthodox early fathers had to clarify and redefine who they were and what they believed in order to defend their doctrine when new ideas threatened to change it.

For there is no difference between the Jew and the Greek: for the same Lord over all is rich unto all that call upon him. For whosoever shall call upon the name of the Lord shall be saved. How then shall they call on him in whom they have not believed? And how shall they believe in him of whom they have not heard? And how shall they hear without a preacher?—Romans 10:12–14

Early church father Irenaeus used the term "haereses" in his *Against Heresies*, in which he describes his opponents and their beliefs as opposed to his own orthodox ideology (which became the position of the church). "Orthodox" comes from the Latin words *ortho*, meaning "straight," and *doxa*, which means "thinking."

The Church Deals with Gnostic Heretics

Some of the earliest ideas that orthodox Christians found heretical dealt with the Trinity and the nature of Jesus and the Father. The Trinity basically is a belief that God is three beings having one essence: the Father, Son, and Holy Spirit, with Jesus being both human and divine. The Trinity is a Christian mystery—a matter of belief and faith rather than a rational conclusion. The orthodox early church believed that Christ died and that his death was a Paschal sacrifice that redeemed humanity by taking away the sins of the world. The church considered Christ's sacrifice as a gift from God, the Father, and at the same time a gift that the Son of God offered humanity by giving life to the Father through the Holy Spirit.

As Christianity spread and flourished, the orthodox fathers had to vigorously defend assaults of heresy, particularly against the Gnostics. Among the various communities of Gnostics could be found a variety of under-standings and portrayals of Jesus. The Valentinians, for example, saw him as a savior figure while Gnostic believers in Seth viewed Jesus as the incarna-tion of Seth. The diversity of beliefs among Christians extended into other areas of belief as well.

As already mentioned, the role of women as church leaders, according to some modern scholars, was seen as a threat to the version of Christianity that was growing ever more powerful in the early second century. Women themselves were not mounting any kind of threat, but whatever gains they may have made began to erode. Still, some Gnostic sects allowed women to serve in the highest ecclesiastical roles. Their theology—with the Holy Spirit being female and women being light- and wisdom-bearers, the manifesta-tion of the Divine in feminine form—carried over into the Gnostics' "real-world" treatment of women. Such views, however, were condemned by the later orthodox Christian church. With such ideas challenged and defeated, teachers of such ideas excommunicated, and writings eliminated, the Gnos-tics would have a tough time remaining a viable branch of anything. Even today, the church is ever-vigilant for ideas that are in error from its position. The following list sets forth ten heresies the proto-orthodox Christian fathers identified and attempted to eliminate.

- **Adoptionism:** Advocates of this heresy believed that God the Father adopted the human child Jesus (either at conception or dur-ing his baptism), and that Jesus then became divine. The tenth-century Bogomils were adoptionists who did not believe Mary was the mother of God nor Jesus part of a Trinity. Some say the French Cathars were adoptionists as well.
- **Apollinarianism:** Followers of Apollinarius espouse a belief that Jesus was neither human nor divine. They asserted that the eternal Logos "overshadowed" his mind but that he possessed a human body and soul.
- **Arianism:** Followers of Arius believed that Jesus Christ had been cre-ated for humanity's salvation. Jesus was not of the same substance as the Father, and, because he was created, was not eternal with the Father. Arianism spread to Africa, Italy, and Spain.

- **Donatism:** This mostly North African group followed Donatus the Great, who emphasized extreme asceticism, including martyrdom.
- **Docetism:** The Docetists believed that Christ was divine and that he only appeared to be human. The crucifixion of his physical body was only an illusion, since he was a divine spirit and could not therefore die.
- **Gnosticism:** One of the most prevalent and serious of the heresies faced by the early Church, continuing into the Middle Ages. Countless sects of Gnostics espoused diverse beliefs but a common belief involved gnosis as the means to salvation.
- **Monophysitism:** The Monophysites held the view that Jesus Christ was two separate beings—human and the divine, eternal Logos fused together into one body during his time on earth.
- **Pelagianism:** This sect did not arise until around the fifth century when Pelagius, an Irish priest, called for the end of baptism, asserting that people could save themselves through individual effort. Followers of this sect did not believe that Adam and Eve passed down original sin.
- **Sabellianism:** The Sabellianists or followers of Sabellius believed that Jesus Christ and the Holy Spirit along with God the Father were just three facets of One Being. They thought that Jesus Christ was not human, but fully divine.
- **Manichaeanism:** Early orthodox fathers considered this a serious heresy because of the way it represented Christian ideas blended with Mithraism, neo-Platonism, Gnosticism, and possibly even Buddhism. Christian Saint Augustine flirted with this doctrine before rejecting it.

Destruction of Writings by Fire and Water

Athough Jesus had admonished all his followers to love one another, make no new law, and judge not, some early leaders, for reasons of self-preservation, were judgmental against the Gnostics. The literalist Christians did not seek out or persecute people who were pagans, magicians, or members of secret societies (as they did the Gnostics) because those people were not calling themselves Christians. Their beliefs were not heresies against Christianity. It is likely, however, that the church would have pronounced disapproval or provided warnings to protect its own flock. Christian heresy, however, from any direction could not be tolerated.

Early church father Irenaeus was among the first to use apostolic succession as a means to refute his opponents' beliefs and also to list the four gospels (now known as the canonical gospels) as divinely inspired. Some scholars suggest that Irenaeus did the latter in response to the Gnostic Marcion severely editing the Gospel of Luke to create his own canon. In fact, Irenaeus believed that the Gnostic writings were unlike the works handed down by the Apostles. The Gnostics found truth in their mystical visions and spiritual insights, less so in the gospel stories of Jesus' life and teachings. This became a source of frustration and anger among the early church fathers, especially Irenaeus.

QUESTION?

What does Jesus mean when he says in the Gospel of Thomas that he reveals his mysteries to those who are worthy of them, and to not let the left hand know what the right is doing?
The esoteric teachings that Jesus gave his disciples are revealed to those ready to learn them, and they are not to be cast about and spread around to anyone other than the chosen ones.

The Gnostic mystics posed a concern to the early Christian fathers. After the Roman Emperor Constantine allowed freedom of religion, the evolving Christian church banished heretics and ordered their tainted texts and materials destroyed by fire or water or other means. One such text, the Gospel of Thomas (a Gnostic text found at Nag Hammadi), preserved a saying in which Jesus told his disciples that he was not their master, but because they had sipped from the "bubbling stream" he had measured out, they had become drunk. In another part of that gospel, Jesus told his followers that those who would drink from his mouth would become like him and that things hidden would be revealed. This gospel is remarkable in that scholars think it might be as old as or older than the Gospels of Matthew, Mark, Luke, and John, the canonical gospels. Some say it may have been a source for those Gospels. Jesus appears to suggest that there are hidden things of which one can obtain knowledge and that it is possible to become like him by drinking from his mouth (taking in his teachings). However, because the the literalist faction of the Christian community found the text heretical, the Gospel of Thomas was condemned and destroyed.

Excommunication

Despite Tertullian's writing that each human should worship according to his own conviction and should never be compelled to follow a particular religion, there were instances when those who believed as he did saw the teaching or activities of some Christians as deeply threatening. The Gnostic Gospel of Philip declares that he who achieves gnosis is no longer a Christian but has become a Christ. What need then would that Christian have for a church, hierachy, creed, canon, or sacramental rites?

The followers of the charismatic teacher Montanus, while under the influence of the Holy Spirit, spoke in tongues and produced new revelations and prophecies. They declared that they were not just inspired by God but spoke in the person of God. Montanus sought to increase the number of sacred texts by adding his own "divinely inspired" works. The orthodox church had other ideas and declared that there was to be no more original revelation through prophecy, that it had ended with the Apostolic Age. That left Christians the option of explaining the Word of God, but they could add nothing new to the body of prophecy and divine revelation that went on during the Apostles' lifetimes. Montanus was excommunicated in circa A.D. 190.

FACT

Excommunication literally means "no longer in communion." Churches use excommunication as a spiritual censure and condemnation of a person or group. After excommunicating someone, the church can also implement a banishment, shunning, or shaming.

Gnosticism took off and flourished in the second century, suggesting that it briefly entered the mainstream of Christianity. The extraordinary Gnostic teacher Valentinus may have been considered a candidate for the position of Bishop of Rome, and history records that he dutifully served the church in the arena of public affairs. He also claimed some apostolic sanctioning as the student of Theudas, a disciple of the Apostle Paul. Still, in his later life his Gnostic thinking (possibly about the lack of need for clergy to obtain salvation) distanced him from the orthodoxy and its emerging apostolic hierarchy. So in A.D. 150 Valentinus, like others before him including Basilides and Marcion, was excommunicated and his writings and sacred texts destroyed.

Excommunication from the church worked to some degree to eliminate heretics, but it didn't completely stamp out the offending sects. Some groups continued to build followings. The orthodox church fathers used the power of the pen and began to write polemics against heresies (mainly Gnostic) that they had identified. Irenaeus wrote his famous *Against Heresies* in circa A.D. 180 and specifically mentioned the Gospel of Truth, believed to have been written by Valentinus. The orthodox fathers revised a baptismal creed into a statement of Christian belief, calling it the Apostles' Creed. The creed's language became extremely important inasmuch as it countered Gnostic heresies. So before the persecution of Christians ended, the patristic fathers had within their spiritual arsenal their written refutations, excommunication and expulsion of heretics from the church, destruction of their offending materials, fiery sermons against the wrong beliefs espoused by their opponents, a creed, and a canon. Once Constantine stopped the persecution of Christians and the orthodoxy had the power of the state to help it push down outbreaks of heresy and heretics, the hunt was on.

The Tragic Fate of the Cathars

In the twelfth century, a religious movement known as Catharism, with distinctly Gnostic elements, emerged in southern France. The people behind the movement were known as Cathars ("pure ones"), although sometimes they were referred to as the Albigensians because they lived near the town of Albi. The Cathars protested against the excesses of the Roman Catholic clergy. Although a few Cathars had been put to death, the group began to flourish under the protection of William, Duke of Aquitaine. No doubt shocking to the orthodox Roman Catholic Church, several priests espoused Cathar beliefs and joined the Cathars. The Cathari elders embraced an ascetic lifestyle and were were known simply as good men or good women. The followers received baptism of the Spirit before death, ensuring that they would become elders or Perfecti.

Beliefs of the Cathars

The Cathars, like Gnostic Christians centuries before them, believed in a divine spark imprisoned in humans. The material or physical realm had been designed and created by an inferior god/Satan/Demiurge. The God of orthodox Christians was not the true God but rather an imposter, and his church was corrupt. Humans, through their individual efforts, had to free themselves from the material existence to obtain enlightenment and liberation. Otherwise, they were destined to have to repeat life in the material realm through reincarnation.

The Cathars rejected the Trinity, the Hebrew scriptures, and the sacrament of the Holy Eucharist. They also rejected the idea of purgatory and hell. To the Cathars, the entrapment of the divine spark in the physical human envelope made this world the real hell. They were pacifists whose nonviolent beliefs extended toward animals. They eschewed meat and dairy products. The Cathars believed that the spirit was found in the soul that was itself contained within the human body. Keeping their spirit pure so that it could return the the realm of Light (God) was the most important task in life.

Hierarchy of Structure

The Cathar hierarchy contained two tiers: *Perfecti* (perfect ones or elders) and *Credentes* (believers). Both women and men could become *Perfecti*, and both practiced extreme asceticism. It was not imposed upon the *Credentes*. The *Perfecti* wore black robes and lived their lives as Jesus had, depending upon alms for food, doing penance and prayer, serving others, and teaching. To become a *Perfecti*, one had to undergo the ritual *consolamentum*, a baptism by the Holy Spirit and an ordination into the ascetic element of the group. The *Perfecti* stood as spiritual exemplars to the community.

The *Credentes* led a lifestyle more worldly than the *Perfecti*. They could even marry. But they had to swear oaths not to take a life or kill animals. If death approached, a *Credente* could accept the rite of *consolamentum* and stop eating and drinking to hasten death. The Cathars worshipped the God of Love rather than the deity of the Hebrew scriptures.

Suppression by Massacre

Pope Eugene III decided that church had to put an end to the Cathars. He sought and received help from Bernard of Clairvaux, Cardinal Peter of St. Chrysogonus, and others, but wiping out the movement proved futile. The Roman Catholic Church issued edicts against the Cathars, but this didn't suppress them either. The Church tried other tactics as well, but without success. Noblemen protecting the Cathars were excommunicated and put to death. In A.D. 1208, the Pope ordered a crusade against them and a papal decree proclaiming that all Cathar lands would be confiscated. The result was the Albigensian Crusade, which took place over the next forty years, during which northern French landowners took up the fight in the south against the Cathars.

The Cathars espoused Gnostic beliefs in the divine feminine and practiced gender equality. They venerated Mary Magdalene, and her legends, myths, and stories are kept alive in oral traditions that are especially strong in southern France where the Cathars once flourished.

The community of Béziers fell on July 22, 1209, the feast day of Mary Magdalene. The Cistercian abbot Arnaud-Amaury, who commanded the siege, was asked how he could distinguish Catholics from Cathars in the battle. He supposedly said that he killed them all, for God would recognize his own. The Church of Saint Mary Magdalene housed 7,000 people and they were all slaughtered. Thousands of other townspeople were killed as well. Some scholars say the figure for the dead could have been as high as 20,000 people, including women and children. Still, Catharism did not die.

The Crusades and Inquisition

By the middle of the thirteenth century, the bishops under Pope Innocent met to again deal with the Cathar "problem." Catharism had become entrenched in the French towns of Albi, Toulouse, and Carcassonne and was spreading its Gnostic heresies. The Pope and his bishops decided to establish the Inquisition for the purpose of permanently exterminating the Cathars, their ideas, and their movement. The Roman Catholic Church set up inquests in various districts, making it easier to find, try, and punish heretics. Another massacre of Cathars took place in Monteségur when two hundred Perfecti were burned in a massive bonfire near the base of the castle located there. The Church also meted out severe punishments for noblemen and anyone suspected of being a Cathari sympathizer. The Cathars who eluded detection went into hiding and scattered far and wide. The Inquisition maintained records of those it executed and so historians know that the last Cathar Perfecti was put to death in A.D. 1321.

Crusades were always announced by a session of preaching after which the "soldier" had to swear a vow. Then the pope or one of his representatives presented the "soldier" with a cross. In this way, the church "inducted" individuals into its army of Christian soldiers to do battle on its behalf.

Some historians refer to the massacre of Cathars as the Albigensian Crusade. The Crusades normally were thought of as military expeditions (holy wars) launched during the eleventh, twelfth, and thirteenth centuries to reclaim sacred places such as Jerusalem and the Holy Land from Muslim tyranny. But since that time the term, according to the dictionary, has broadened to encompass a vigorous, aggressive movement to defend an idea or cause.

Chapter 10

The Nag Hammadi Treasures

Roughly a dozen years after the ascension of Jesus, Mark, the author of the earliest of the New Testament Gospels, traveled to the city of Alexandria, Egypt. He shared the stories of Jesus' life, death, resurrection, and ministry with the people he met. Mark's teachings gave rise to the Coptic Christian Church. Christianity flourished in Egypt, and within fifty years spread throughout the region and beyond. From diverse religious sects, myriad theological texts emerged, including apocalyptic, Gnostic, and monastic.

10

Strange Story of Discovery

The Egyptian Coptic Church also played an important role in infant Christianity as a defender of the faith against Gnostic heresies. The church points out that the Nicene Creed was developed while its own Athanasius served as a deacon and then bishop of Alexandria in A.D. 327 to 373. In fact, Athanasius became known by the title of "the Father of Orthodoxy." During the first three centuries A.D., there were many diverse Christian sects from which certain "secret" and sacred writings emerged. But increasingly, as the emerging literalist church (or what was evolving into the orthodox faction) grew stronger and its suppression and destruction of texts continued against "unorthodox" beliefs, fewer writings to reveal the alternative views of early Christianity could be found.

Modern scholars knew that such texts once existed because of references to them in the writings of orthodox fathers seeking to eliminate heresy. Those heresiologists asserted that some Gnostic sects (in the first few centuries) claimed to possess texts with secret teachings of Jesus. The orthodox clerics argued that the Gnostics' texts were full of fantastical ideas and that the Gnostics were heretics who had misinterpreted Jesus' words. But the discovery of the Dead Sea Scrolls (though technically not considered Gnostic) at Qumrum, and, more recently, the Nag Hammadi find in Upper Egypt, yielded actual copies of some of those controversial works that many of the orthodox early fathers found so offensive.

FACT

The Gospel of Thomas found at Nag Hammadi preserves wisdom sayings, parables, eschatological sayings about the destiny of humankind and the world, prophecy, and Christian community rules. Scholars note that the original Greek version of this gospel was in use in early second-century Egypt. The gospel was among the fifty-two texts discovered in the earthenware jar.

Today, several books and Internet sites present the story of the Nag Hammadi discovery, but a brief synopsis of it is warranted here. Sometime in December of 1945, Muhammad Ali, an Egyptian peasant belonging to the al-Sammān clan, was with his younger brother Abu al-Magd and some other fellahin (peasants) on camelback near a cliff known as Jabal al-Tārif (a mountain honeycombed in caves) near Nag Hammadi. The group sought a natural fertilizer, *sabakh*, that had built up in the dry desert sands among the boulders near the base of the cliff. The peasants needed the fertilizer for their fields.

With their camels hobbled, the peasants launched into digging. Abu al-Magd hit upon an ancient earthenware storage jar. The red jar stood approximately three feet tall and was sealed with a large bowl. Initially, no one removed the bowl for fear that the jar held a bad spirit or jinn inside.

The Contents of an Ancient Jar

Muhammad Ali eventually broke open the jar and found a stash of old codices, or leather-bound books. The twelve codices and eight separate leaves that he discovered were not all later classified as Gnostic writings. Some were categorized as philosophical works while others were distinctly Hermetic texts that fit better into the category of Egyptian tales. A total of fifty-two tractates were found.

Muhammad Ali ripped apart some of the books to share with others, but his companions didn't want them. So he removed his turban and used the cloth to transport the books to his home. His mother started a fire with pages from the some of the books.

Muhammad Ali clearly remembered the date of the discovery because he had been involved in a blood feud with a man from a village near the Jabal al-Tārif mountain. His enemy had murdered Muhammad Ali's father, who had been a night watchman, in retaliation for the watchman shooting an intruder. Many months after the death of their father, Muhammad Ali and his brother took revenge. They sought out, killed, and dismembered their father's attacker, according to Gnostic scholar Marvin Meyer, writing in *The Gnostic Discoveries*. That book states that the brothers cut out the man's heart and immediately devoured it.

Who was Didymos Judas Thomas?
The Syrian Christians identified Judas Thomas as the brother of Jesus. Didymos in Greek means "twin," as does Thomas in Aramaic. He founded many Christian communities in the East and eventually went to India. He was the "Doubting Thomas" of the canonical scriptures (John 20:24–25).

At some point after finding the codices, Muhammad Ali gave a few of the texts to a local history teacher. The teacher sent one of the books to an associate in Cairo. He hoped to find out whether or not the codex had monetary value. It did. The later purchase of the texts by antiquities dealers piqued the interest of representatives of the Egyptian government. They acquired one copy and seized ten and a half of the thirteen books. They placed them for safekeeping in the Coptic Museum in Cairo. But someone smuggled out one of the books—the thirteenth codex with five separate texts—and offered it for sale. The codex contained five unique texts but some of the pages were missing. The late religious historian and Gnostic scholar Gilles Quispel in the Netherlands heard about it and convinced the Jung Foundation to buy it. Unfortunately, the manuscript was missing pages. Quispel then went to the Coptic Museum, where he borrowed photos of the appropriate pages and began translating the material. He suddenly realized that he possessed a "secret" Gospel of Thomas, a Gnostic text whose author declared he was Didymos Judas Thomas the twin and that the text contained the "hidden" or secret sayings of Jesus.

Translation from the Greek into Coptic

The texts found at Nag Hammadi had been translated into Coptic from the original Greek. Scholars say the translations were not always elegant, and the scribes who did the translating and copying certainly missed subtle nuance and profundity. As Christianity took hold and flourished, it brought an end to the use of other Egyptian scripts and gave rise to the Coptic. Some experts say that the Christians did not want to use the ancient hieroglyphs and other scripts of the Egyptian civilization, in order to avoid any connection to Egypt's pagan past. The Coptic script took twenty-four letters from the Greek and added six new characters for sounds required that did not exist in Greek.

The texts found at Nag Hammadi were translations into Coptic made some 1,500 years earlier. Those copies were made from originals that were much older and written in Greek. Scholars and scientists can date the manuscripts found at Nag Hammadi through their Coptic script and the papyri on which they are written, but the dates of the originals provoke sharp disagreement.

Why Bury the Texts in a Jar?

Who buried the texts at the base of the Jabal al-Tārif mountain? And why? Several religious historians have pointed out that a Christian monastery stood not far from Nag Hammadi. The monastery took its name from a man named Pachomius, who became a Christian after being forced to serve in the Roman army. He sought to live the life of a hermit, but decided that solitary life was inferior to community asceticism and ended up establishing six or seven cenobitic religious communities (monasteries and nunneries) overseen by an abbot/abbess where men and women lived monastic lives, sharing their possessions instead of living alone as hermits. He never became a priest, nor did his monks, but his cenobitic communities became popular and eventually housed thousands of spiritual seekers.

QUESTION?

Who was Saint Pachomius?
Pachomius, also called Abba Pachomius, was an Egyptian Coptic Christian founder of cenobitic monasticism. He was born in circa A.D. 292. With an old hermit named Palemon, he built a monastery in the second century that attracted monks to an ascetic life. Tradition states that he established a rule to govern the monastery that was given to him by an angel. He died of plague in A.D. 348.

Some experts theorize that the monks at St. Pachomius buried the jar containing the books, possibly to preserve them from destruction from the orthodoxy. Those monks perhaps felt a special connection with the books or simply did not want that part of their library destroyed in the event that one day the books could be returned. But the truth is that no one knows for certain who buried the books or why. What is known is that the desert sand acted like a drying agent. If someone had attempted to preserve them, it seems that they considered the possible hazard of insects and the elements.

Other Sacred Texts Buried in Jars

The Judean Desert is home to historical sites like Qumran, Ein Gedi, Hebron, and Masada and holds the promise of perhaps more discoveries like those already found at Qumran and Masada. The desert runs from Jerusalem at the northernmost part south to the Negev Desert and then extends west of the Dead Sea.

The Dead Sea Scrolls, which are not considered Gnostic but more correctly Jewish texts, were found near Wadi Qumran and the Dead Sea. They represent another spectacular cache of biblical and non-biblical texts found amid pottery shards and in earthenware jars. Someone had hidden the scrolls in eleven caves. The discovery of the scrolls between 1947 and 1956 yielded over 800 documents. Scholars speculated that the scrolls were hidden at a time when the Romans targeted Jewish and Christian writings for destruction. The scrolls included a diversity of writings but most date from 250 B.C. to A.D. 68. Unlike the Nag Hammadi codices, the Dead Sea Scrolls unfortunately were poorly preserved. A shepherd discovered the first of the scrolls in a cave located near the northern end of the Dead Sea. The mostly intact and moderately well-preserved book of Isaiah turned up in the first group of seven scrolls. Experts dated it to before 100 B.C., making it the oldest surviving copy of a biblical book from the Hebrew scriptures.

The Essenes at Qumran

Subsequent expeditions and surveys made of the eleven caves turned up more pottery shards and scroll fragments, enough to reveal a working theory (which later proved to be true) that the settlement at Qumran was most likely an Essene community. Perhaps it was known to John the Baptist, relative of Jesus, whom some considered to have been an Essene because of the many parallels between John's life and the Essenes.

The Essenes, a Jewish sect observant of the Torah, had split from the type of Judaism associated with the Jerusalem Temple. They took refuge in the desert at Wadi Qumran to live their lives in alignment with their mystical beliefs. Experts like James Robinson, previously mentioned as a Gnostic scholar of the New Testament and early Christianity and editor of the *The Nag Hammadi Library*, expressed the notion that the discovery facilitated scholarly understanding of not only that separatist sect but also the pluralistic ways Judaism was expressed in the ancient world. The Dead Scrolls do not mention Jesus or Christianity. The authors were copyists and commentators. Their writings raised the question about whether or not the Essenes were a Jewish Gnostic sect. Robinson noted how the Essenes embraced ideas that seemed more in keeping with dualism and Gnosticism—and, moreover, that the codices found at Nag Hammadi picked up where the Dead Sea Scrolls left off.

The Essenes—or Essenoi, as ancient Jewish historian Josephus called them—led a simple communal life but one that included celibacy. They chose a leader whom they obeyed, practiced collective ownership and strict vegetarianism (fruits, roots, and bread), refrained from swearing oaths, did not sacrifice animals, and carried weapons only for self-protection. They shunned immoral activities and believed their souls were immortal.

The Essenes held Messianic and apocalyptic beliefs. Baptism was an important ritual. They called themselves "Sons of Light" and the "Holy Ones" (because they believed the Holy Spirit was present and dwelt with them) and referred to their leader as "Teacher of Righteousness." They broke away from Temple Judaism because they thought people were becoming too worldly; they believed that the "end-times" were near and that they were the chosen ones to prepare the way for the coming of the Lord. Some say Jesus may have either been an Essene or had contact with them.

Writings from Masada

Other writings of antiquity have been found at Masada and other nearby sites. Masada was a great fortress that housed two palaces of Herod the Great. The fortress sits above the Judean Desert and the Dead Sea on a flat mesa. It was the site of a battle between the Romans and a sect of the Jewish people revolting against them. The Jews held off the Romans for three years and then, when capture seemed imminent, all 967 committed suicide rather than be taken. In 1963 to 1965, several large-scale excavations were conducted on the Masada site in a joint venture of the Hebrew University, the Israel Exploration Society, and Israel's Department of Antiquities. Archeologists discovered many fragments from twelve first-century scrolls. Some contained writings from certain books of the Hebrew scriptures, including Genesis and Leviticus. Also found were fragments from other biblical and apocryphal books.

Writings from Nag Hammadi, the Dead Sea Scrolls, Masada, and elsewhere represent discoveries in the land of the Nile, but through the centuries many other manuscripts have been found. Such finds of antiquities aid tremendously in the scholarship of the ancient world and its beliefs.

Papyrus, Parchment, and Jars

The ancients used papyrus and parchment for writing surfaces. The papyrus was a common type of reed growing in the Nile Valley. The long-stemmed, bulbous reed was valued for its high durability. After the reed was cut into several long strips and placed flush together in rows, other strips were placed across the rows. The papyrus "page," after being wetted with water and weighted down, was put in the sun to dry. Once dried, the page was burnished with shells to make the surface solid enough for writing.

Parchment was the dried skin of any number of animals found in ancient times, including calves, donkeys, goats, and sheep. By the end of the third century, parchment was preferred over papyrus among scribes intending to make books. Folding the parchment into two, they could cut the folds and get four writing pages. A book consisted of a grouping of these pages, or leaves, into quires.

The Dead Sea Scroll book of Isaiah that heralds the prophecy of John was found in a jar that stood a little under two feet tall and nine inches in diameter. This type of jar has only been found in the caves at Qumran; thus the jar represents a piece of linkage between the Dead Sea Scrolls and possibly the Essene library.

The voice of him that crieth out in the wilderness, Prepare ye the way of the Lord, make straight in the desert a highway for our God. Every valley shall be exalted, and every mountain and hill shall be made low: and the crooked shall be made straight, and the rough places plain . . . the Lord hath spoken it.—Isaiah 40:3–5

The Baffling Copper Scroll

The Copper Scroll found in 1952 and designated as 3Q15 was among the Dead Sea Scrolls' most curious finds. It had nothing to do with religious ideas or doctrine, but may have described the Temple treasure, and huge quantities of it at that. The scroll was found in Cave 3 at Khirbet Qumran. While many of the Dead Sea Scrolls were found by the Bedoin, the Copper Scroll was discovered by archeologists. The oxidized metal scroll was too brittle to be unrolled, and it took scholars roughly five years to figure out how to manipulate the copper to be able to decipher it. Experts finally agreed to cut it into twenty-three strips, each forming a circle. Reading and translating the text proved difficult, since the script was in ancient Hebrew and scholars did not know many of the vocabulary words found on the scroll. In addition, the experts could not decipher the directions (although they were fairly precise and specific) to the treasure's location. According to scholarly commentary, some of the places had different names and some places no longer existed. Opinion is divided between whether the treasure belonged to the Jerusalem Temple (prior to its destruction) or to the Essenes at Qumran. Finally, there are those who think the scroll's description of treasure was nothing more than a work of fiction.

The Obscure Texts Scrutinized

When Quispel produced the photograph of the first page of the Gospel of Thomas and the translation in 1956, his pronouncements generated intense excitement and interest in ancient Christianity and the Gnostics. He asserted that the Gospel of Thomas might have been written quite early in the first century. Other scholars say that some of the sayings found in that Gnostic gospel may actually predate the canonical gospels and belong in even earlier traditions, perhaps within twenty or so years after the ascension of Jesus, or roughly A.D. 50 to A.D. 100.

The translations and commentaries on the Gnostic scriptures discovered at Nag Hammadi are a result of intense academic scrutiny and dedication to the work. In their wide diversity, those texts shed light for the modern world on those who collected the library—they were early Christians involved in a radical movement. Their obscure texts often contained meanings that were obvious and at the same time secret. Scholars scrutinizing the texts and writing commentaries are careful to place the Nag Hammadi library in its ancient philosophical and religious traditions and settings. For out of that world arose the belief in transcendence central to Christianity.

The Search Goes On

While the scholarly work on the Nag Hammadi texts continues, archeologists and religious scholars hope that there are still more writings to be found in Upper Egypt. Robinson and his institute have begun excavating the basilica of St. Pachomius. Those fourth-century ruins are located near where the Nag Hammadi materials were found. And some experts have conjectured that the monks at St. Pachomius may have been the ones to have copied and bound the Nag Hammadi manuscripts.

Relationship of Gnostic Writings to the Canon

Did the New Testament borrow from Gnosticism? The Gnostic writings reveal that a canon existed in the second century that was nearly identical to the formal New Testament canon adopted at various Christian councils, including Laodicea, Carthage, and Hippo. Some modern scholars have attempted to show that some of the canon is indebted to Gnostic texts while others argue that the canon was a response against Gnostic ideas. An example of the former is the Gospel of John, and examples of the latter include the Gospel of Luke, Act of the Apostles, the pastoral Epistles, and Paul's letters to the Corinthians and Ephesians.

It is well known that other gospels existed alongside those deemed acceptable to the orthodox church. Some of those texts may have been earlier versions; others were thought to have been edited, redacted, or otherwise distorted and therefore unacceptable. The consensus is still out as to whether or not any of them actually are earlier versions of those found in the canon. Some of those texts include the Gospel of Cerinthus, Gospel of Mani, Gospel of Appelles, Gospel of Bardesanes, Gospel of Balisides, and Gospel of Marcion, which was Marcion's version of the Gospel of Luke that he claimed was the original. The early church fathers branded them all heretical, and specific information about them only exists in the attacks on the texts by the orthodox heresiologists.

Other texts include the Gospel of Thomas, which current scholarship suggests belongs to a "sayings" tradition that preceded the canonical gospels and from which the canon texts may have borrowed. However, it is impossible, according to some experts, to say for certain that the sayings tradition was either Gnostic or non-Gnostic. Another piece of writing is the Gospel of Philip, which also includes some sayings that may have bearing on the four New Testament Gospels, but linkage remains to be seen.

FACT

The books of the New Testament were originally composed in Greek and translated into Syriac and Latin probably around A.D. 150. The Egyptian translation was likely done around A.D. 200. The copies that scholars used today of these texts are simply lineal descendants of the originals.

Expanding on What Is Known

After the Council of Nicaea in A.D. 325 made the divinity of Jesus official dogma in a vote of 217 to 3 and responded to the Arian heresy, subsequent councils were called to further refine Christian dogma and law. By the time the Council at Laodicea convened at Phrygia in A.D. 364, an approved list of scriptures was already in use. But some were books in dispute. The Council at Laodicea enacted sixty rules that further codified church doctrine. Forty-one sacred texts were banned from the canon and additional rules or church laws were also laid down. Many of the decrees had to do with Christians avoiding contact with heretics (presumably including Gnostics). Other subsequent councils enacted rules that further refined the core Christian ideal, while also strengthening the power and unity of the church. The modern archeological discovery of ancient texts places a new lens upon what scholars know about the birth and evolution of early Christianity and the development and refinement of its canon of sacred writings.

New Source Material for Scholars

After the magnificent discovery at Nag Hammadi, scholars can only hope that the archeological excavations that are going on in the world, the manuscripts that continue to be sold on the antiquities market, and the serendipitous discoveries that have brought other ancient materials to light will uncover new materials to shed light on the birth of Christianity and the world of the Gnostics.

QUESTION?

Were the Dead Sea Scrolls discovered accidentally?
Yes. As the story goes, a Bedouin shepherd whom some sources identify as Mohammed Ahmed el-Hamed discovered the first of the scrolls in 1947 when he tossed a rock into a cave to frighten out his missing animal and heard pottery shattering. Inside were several jars with linen-wrapped scrolls.

These recovered materials from antiquity are invaluable to scholars in whose lifetime the materials were first discovered, and to subsequent generations of scholars who will study them with new questions and theories. With archeological excavations continuing throughout the ancient world, scholars hope to find new source materials that will teach modern people about the origins and influences of the sacred and religious thinking of the ancients.

Chapter 11

The Gospel of Mary

The Gospel of Mary is the only gospel named after a woman. Popular and scholarly opinion assigns that gospel to Mary Magdalene, although the gospel itself does not say. Mary Magdalene's importance to Christianity is well established. She was one of Jesus' loyal followers, stood vigil at his cross, was eyewitness to his resurrection, and received the first commission to preach (declaring the "good news" to other disciples that Jesus had risen).

No Complete Copy

The Apostle John considered Mary Magdalene (or Miriam, as John would have called her) the founder of Christianity (John 20:1–31), asserted Jean-Yves LeLoup in his book, *The Gospel of Mary Magdalene*. The Gospel of Mary exists in three fragmentary texts. To date, there is no complete copy; in fact, only about half of the entire gospel (eight of eighteen pages) survives. The Coptic version portrays Mary Magdalene differently than the two fragments preserved in original Greek. Scholar Karen King, author of *The Gospel of Mary of Magdala, Jesus and the First Woman Apostle*, pointed out that the Greek fragments are written in the original language and are dated earlier in church history while the more complete Coptic version features language and theology that places it in a later time and different milieu.

QUESTION?

Who translated the Gospel of Mary from the original Greek?
Most likely Christian scribes in Egypt during the second century translated the Gospel of Mary into the Coptic Egyptian script. Today, that language is still used for liturgical purposes by the Coptic Church and its parishioners known as Copts (Egyptian Christians).

The longest version of the Gospel of Mary is the fifth-century Coptic translation published in 1955 and known to scholars as the Berlin Codex 8502,1 (*Berolinensis Gnosticus* 8502,1). After being discovered at a burial site in Akhmim, in central Egypt, the Berlin Codex was sold to German scholar Carl Reinhardt, who took it from Cairo to Berlin in 1896. Although Reinhardt knew the manuscript was ancient, neither he nor the manuscript dealer from whom he acquired it knew what the codex contained. The Berlin Codex consisted of leaves stitched together and placed inside leather-bound boards. The book held a fragmentary copy of The Gospel of Mary in Sahidic Coptic (with some faulty translation errors) along with three other texts—The Apocryphon of John, The Sophia of Jesus Christ, and The Act of Peter. The amazing discovery in 1945 of the Nag Hammadi texts generated public interest in the Gospel of Mary, due in part to the Gnostic and Coptic linkage it shared with many of the Nag Hammadi writings.

The Other Fragments

The two Greek fragments of the Gospel of Mary date to the third century. They are called, respectively, Papyrus Rylands 463 and Papyrus Oxyrhynchus 3525. The former was translated and published in 1938 and the latter in 1983. Experts say the existence of the Gospel of Mary was already known as early as the third century because of references to it by early church fathers; however, the original gospel likely dates to the second century. Scholar Karen King believes it belongs in the first half of that century.

In the gospel, Mary Magdalene is exalted. Peter, leader of the disciples, even acknowledges her stature when he tells her that the disciples know their Teacher loved her differently from other women. This Mary Magdalene is not represented as the penitent prostitute depicted for centuries by the church and in popular culture, but rather as a worthy woman loved by the Savior. She possesses knowledge that the Savior Jesus has not shared with the others. She appears to have a legitimate claim to leadership in the Christian circle.

Differences Between the Coptic and Greek Versions

The third-century Greek fragments have theological differences with the Coptic version. The Greek fragments seem to find no issue with a woman's right to teach or lead, but the Coptic version, two centuries later, suggests patriarchal challenges to female leadership. Taken together, the versions elucidate a historical shift toward increasing exclusion of women as leaders in the early Christian churches and communities. The conflict between Mary and Peter illustrated in the Gospel of Mary has resonance in the Pistis Sophia, the Gospel of Thomas, and the Gospel of the Egyptians and may have been indicative of tension within the church during the second century.

Mary's Special Revelation

Some early Gnostic Christian circles revered Mary Magdalene as the worthy repository of divine revelation and wisdom. They quite possibly saw her as Jesus' Sophia, perhaps even his spiritual heir. She was the Apostle to the Apostles, an honorific title bestowed upon her after she faithfully carried out the risen Jesus' commission to tell the other disciples the "good news" of his resurrection. In the third century, Hippolytus, a Christian bishop (circa A.D. 170–236), wrote of female apostles charged to rectify ancient Eve's sin through their obedience. His noting of female apostles suggests that at least in earliest Christianity, apostles were of both genders.

The Gospel of Mary reveals that Mary Magdalene was an authority figure who comforted her fellow disciples and turned their minds from the dark fog of grief and suffering back toward the "Good" after Jesus left them. The writer of that gospel provides a unique lens through which to view women disciples of Jesus in the infant early church that is exemplified in Mary Magdalene. Yet the wider culture, still patriarchal, held a view of women as inferior. By the end of the second century, Jesus' example of egalitarian and respectful treatment of women shifted back to the patriarchal status quo. A female authority figure with a message had to be defended. It was no longer assumed that she could speak with any real power. In the Gospel of Mary, Mary Magdalene represents the Gnostic Christian position in which women served as leaders, visionaries, prophetesses, preachers, and interpreters while Peter and Andrew represent the orthodoxy.

The Savior's Discourse and Departure

The Gospel of Mary opens on page seven (pages one through six are missing) in a scene after the Resurrection in which the disciples are having discourse with Jesus about matter and its nature and if it will last forever. Jesus explains that each thing born is interconnected but one day must return to its own root. Peter asks about sin and Jesus explains that there is no sin. The attachment humans have for things of matter is what deceives them. It is the improper mingling of the spirit with matter that causes disharmony and imbalance and that, in turn, brings about sickness and death.

Scholar LeLoup pronounces this teaching as both liberating and demanding. It basically says that people cannot blame others or their circumstances for their woes; instead, they must understand that they alone are responsible for their own actions and thoughts and attitudes. Even sickness and death are a result of their own actions. Blaming is a waste of time and energy.

The Gospel of Mary says that before Jesus departs, he warns the disciples against establishing rules or laws. If they make such laws or rules, then they will necessarily be constrained by them. Jesus commands them to go forth into the world and share the good news. He reminds them that the Son of Man is within each of them. This portion of the Gospel of Mary is known as the "Savior's Farewell."

After Jesus leaves them, the disciples are overcome with grief and they weep. Their hearts were deeply attached to their teacher. They fear that Jesus' unfortunate fate of being crucified will become theirs. Who will lead them now? Mary Magdalene stands and greets, comforts, and consoles them. She emphasizes the Savior's greatness. Mary, the gospel notes, turned the disciples' hearts away from the heaviness of sorrow and suffering back toward "the Good."

Several sources on the Web feature English translations of the Gospel of Mary. One is The Gnostic Society Library, located at *www.gnosis.org/library/marygosp.htm*. Another site is at *www.thenazareneway.com/the_gospel_of_mary_magdalene.htm*. Excerpts from the gospel are at *www.sacred-texts.com/chr/apo/marym.htm*.

Seeing with the Mind's Eye

As they begin talking again about Jesus' words, perhaps about the best way to go forth and spread the gospel teachings, Peter tells Mary Magdalene that everyone knows that Jesus loved her more than all the other women. Peter asks her to share some of the Savior's words. He wants her to tell the disciples something that Jesus had not already shared with them. Mary Magdalene agrees. She tells him a vision she had of the Lord and how he called her blessed and praised her for not "wavering" at the sight of him.

Then she says that she asked Jesus how it was she could see him, whether it was with the soul or the spirit (*pneuma*), and he told her that it was through neither soul nor spirit but the mind between them. Then Mary recounts the part of the vision Jesus gave her about how the soul must move through seven wrathful powers in order to ascend to the place where it rests in silence.

Mary Magdalene's Vision

Mary Magdalene explains that the soul is questioned by seven cosmic powers as she (soul is most often referred to in the feminine gender in ancient literature) ascends from matter through ever-higher realms toward her final place of rest. As she passes successfully through each of the seven powers that bind her to matter, the fetters become loosened. The seven powers she must pass through are darkness, desire or craving, ignorance, death wish, enslavement to the flesh, foolish fleshly wisdom, and guileful wisdom (wrath). Having successfully moved beyond them, the soul becomes free and rests in eternal peace and silence.

The idea of being able to direct the mind inward and to merge it with divine cosmic consciousness, thereby forever freeing the soul from its karmic bonds, has resonance with ancient eastern philosophies of Buddhism and Hinduism. Buddhists call the resting place of the enlightened *Nirvana* (meaning "extinguishing or unbinding"), while the Hindus call it *Maha Samadhi* (meaning "establish"). Dualism is transcended and the soul rests in an effortless and continual state of perfection, in silence, beyond all thought.

Importance of Mary's Secret Vision

In the absence of the Savior, Mary Magdalene stepped up as the voice of calm, reason, and authority. When the disciples were overcome with fear about their own safety in going forth to preach the "good news," Mary reminded them that they had everything they needed. When Peter asked her to share some words of the Savior, his overture suggested a legitimacy that she possessed, perhaps as Jesus' favorite or most astute student who possessed secret words or teachings that the Lord had not shared with others. Peter made the overture toward her with at least a show of respect. He would have known that she was a visionary with a quick and insightful mind and that she had understood Jesus' teachings as perhaps he and the others had not. Peter's request suggests that he was seeking comfort in her revelation of Jesus' words and that those words necessarily had value and importance.

Mary Magdalene held the pre-eminent position of Jesus' leading female disciple, and was also his friend, companion, and confidante. She, too, must have felt the pains of grief. Yet she showed a spiritual maturity by stepping into the void left by their departed teacher. Mary Magdalene complied with Peter's request and articulated the complex ideas that Jesus had revealed to her in her vision, and she did it with eloquence and clarity. You might think that the response from Peter, his brother Andrew, and the others assembled would have been to thank her. But quite the opposite happened.

Why Peter Disbelieves

The first response to Mary Magdalene's vision came not from Peter but from his brother Andrew, who didn't believe her. In an indirect challenge to her, he asked the other disciples what they thought of the things she had told them. He said that Jesus would not have spoken such things, as they were simply too different. Then Peter agreed with Andrew and opposed Mary Magdalene as well, asking rhetorically how it could be possible that Jesus would talk in such a way with a woman of secret things about which he (Peter, the chief disciple) and the others remained ignorant. Then he asked incredulously if they were to change their ways and listen to her. He wondered aloud if Jesus really chose her or preferred her to them, the male disciples.

Some scholars say that this scene shows the disharmony that existed within the core group of disciples that was also symptomatic of the tensions in the ancient world during the time when this gospel was written. Mary Magdalene, as you learned in previous chapters, had just given the disciples a teaching about how the powers of darkness, desire, ignorance, and such things keep the soul imprisoned. The emotions of anger and rivalry, along with the lack of respect toward Mary Magdalene by Andrew and Peter, do not seem like acceptable behavior from disciples of Jesus but rather appear to be in keeping more with the dark imprisoning powers in Mary Magdalene's vision. Peter and Andrew perhaps do not understand the teaching. Maybe they resent the fact that Jesus gave Mary Magdalene a special blessing that he did not give to them. Possibly they resented her ability to have visions. Or perhaps they felt threatened by their lack of understanding of the teaching.

Peter's Bullying

The Gospel of Mary reveals that Mary Magdalene wept and challenged Peter, asking him if he thought she just imagined the vision, made it up, and lied about Jesus. While Jesus was alive, she had expressed her fear of Peter. In other Gnostic texts, Jesus rebuked Peter for bullying Mary Magdalene. Peter was known to be volatile, dense, and at times even disbelieving of what Jesus said (Matthew 16:22–23). Like many of Jesus' other disciples, he probably had a rudimentary education (although two epistles ascribed to him were most likely written by secretaries and display a knowledge of Greek higher education). While he was tenderhearted and courageous on some occasions, at other times he seemed uncomprehending and obtuse, trying Jesus' patience. He could be hot-headed, as demonstrated in the canonical Gospel of John.

Following the confrontation between Peter and Mary Magdalene in the Gospel of Mary, Levi steps in to calm the situation. He tells Peter that because of his hot temper he has stooped to treating Mary Magdalene like their adversaries do. Levi reminds Peter that if Jesus found Mary Magdalene worthy, who was he, Peter, to put her aside. Levi also reminds Peter that Jesus had loved her the most of all and that they should go forth, as Jesus had told them, to spread the gospel. The Gospel of Mary ends with the disciples going out to do the spiritual work Jesus had instructed them to do.

Then Simon Peter having a sword drew it, and smote the high priest's servant, and cut off his right ear. The servant's name was Malchus. Then said Jesus unto Peter, Put up thy sword into the sheath: the cup which my Father hath given me, shall I not drink it?—John 18:10–11

Articulating Jesus' Ideas and Words

The Gospel of Mary implies that Peter and Andrew seemingly have a desire to dominate her when they reject the precious teaching that Peter had requested from Mary Magdalene. In this way, the gospel illuminates a picture much bigger than Andrew and Peter in conflict with Mary Magdalene. The gospel delineates two distinct groups of people who followed Jesus. The Peter and Andrew types display what seems to be spiritual immaturity or ignorance, not only in devaluing Mary Magdalene's vision but in rejecting her as a woman with special knowledge that she willingly shared after they had asked her for it. This lack of consideration reflects the patriarchal view of a woman having no real power in her own right beyond the male who heads her family. A woman's words are only to be believed or considered worthy if a man says they are so. In Jesus' time, women could not give testimony, were not educated, and had little value beyond running a household, preparing meals, and providing their husbands with children (preferably boys). Peter and Andrew represented the conservative and patriarchal branch of earliest Christianity.

FACT

Peter and Andrew were the sons of Jonah. Peter (also called Simeon bar Jona) was born in Bethsaida (John 1:44) and with his brother Andrew operated a fishing business with two other disciples of Jesus, James and John, the sons of Zebedee. After Jesus' death, Peter gave testimony to his young scribe Mark for the Gospel of Mark.

Mary Magdalene represented the non-orthodox branch. In standing up to Peter and Andrew, she gave a voice to women visionaries, prophetesses, and preachers, and those resisting injustice. She dealt with Peter's bullying much as the soul in her vision dealt with the cosmic powers, refusing further entrapment, enslavement, and domination. She perhaps understood better than her brethren Jesus' teaching in her vision about the dark powers, and that the ignorance displayed by Peter and Andrew was, as LeLoup classified it, a sickness of the mind and heart.

Elevated Status of Mary

Several scholars assert that after Jesus' death Mary Magdalene stood out in the Gnostic texts—in particular, the Gospel of Mary—as an example of perfect discipleship and spiritual leadership. People likely gravitated to those closest to those Apostles for whom they felt a kinship or respect for correctly conveying Jesus' original teachings. Some chose to follow Peter, James the Just, or Paul. But others preferred Mary Magdalene—the Thirteenth Apostle, as the Gnostics referred to her.

Leader of a Gnostic Branch

Mary Magdalene might have been the leader of a Gnostic branch of the Jesus movement. Scholars say that Mary Magdalene was well qualified to serve because she had proven her worthiness and because her grasp of Jesus' spiritual teachings far exceeded any other disciple's. Loyal to Jesus throughout his ministry, she followed him to the cross where, in spite of concern for her own safety, she stood fearless under the watchful gaze of Jewish priests and Roman soldiers, according to the Gospel of John. After his death, instead of hiding out and giving in to despair, she took decisive action, showing everyone that she possessed a steady, confident heart. She ran to the empty tomb, was eyewitness to the risen transcendent Savior, and faithfully carried his message to the others. The Romans knew that killing the head of a movement made the movement likely to die as well, and were probably counting on that for the Jesus movement. But Mary Magdalene stepped into the void and became the cement that held the followers together. Peter and Andrew spoke of going back to their pre-Jesus lives as fishermen in Capernaum. All the disciples grieved. But Mary Magdalene remembered the "Good," according to the Gospel of Mary, and helped the others to remember it as well.

Author of the Gospel of John?

Catholic author Ramon Jusino has theorized that Mary Magdalene may have been the Beloved Disciple of Jesus mentioned in the Gospel of John. In fact, he suggests that Mary Magdalene might have been the author of or source for that canonical gospel. He points out that if she were the author of the Gospel of John, that in no way diminishes the gospel's apostolic origin. She was most likely recognized as an apostolic authority within her community. The Roman Catholic Church has called her *apostola apostolorum*, the Apostle to the Apostles.

Other Sacred Texts Mention Mary Magdalene

The canonical gospels mention Mary Magdalene in the briefest way. All four of the New Testament gospels mention her central role in Jesus' resurrection. Also, she appears in several lists where a clue to her status can be found in her position (usually first) in a group of names. Some academics of ancient Christianity have theorized that references to her may have been largely edited from the New Testament but that her role in the Resurrection story was too well known for it to be completely eliminated. The canonical Gospel of John noted that three Marys stood vigil by Jesus' cross; one was Mary Magdalene.

Now there stood by the cross of Jesus his mother, and his mother's sister, Mary the wife of Cleophas, and Mary Magdalene. When Jesus therefore saw his mother, and the disciple standing by, whom he loved, he saith unto his mother, Woman, behold thy son!—John 19:25–26

In spite of the reference to "thy son" in John 19:26, and using Ramon Jusino's theory that Mary Magdalene might have been the Beloved Disciple, the quote presents the puzzling but interesting possibility that Jesus might have been entrusting his mother into the care of Mary Magdalene. Elsewhere in the canonical gospels, it says that Mary Magdalene and the other women provided for Jesus out of their means (their own finances). Some sources say she may have been a wealthy woman and that she and other women may have financed the earliest beginnings of Christianity.

Gospel of Philip's Revelation

The Gospel of Philip agrees with the canonical accounts that there were three Marys who always walked with the Lord. They included his mother,

her sister, and Mary Magdalene. That Gnostic gospel also suggests a relationship between Mary Magdalene and Jesus that goes beyond teacher and disciple. Seeing his display of affection toward her causes the other disciples to question his love for them. The modern best-selling book *The Da Vinci Code* makes a case for a marriage between Mary Magdalene and Jesus, based in part on the Gospel of Philip. However, a modern Gnostic *hierophant* (the equivalent of bishop) and spiritual successor to the Mary Magdalene tradition asserted that it would have been unlikely that Jesus and Mary Magdalene would have been married, since in those times marriage was about a form of ownership, something neither of them would have wanted.

The Pistis Sophia Shines a Spotlight on Her

The Pistis Sophia (the text of a Gnostic myth important to the Valentinian belief system) details Sophia's mistake, her repentance, redemption, and restoration. After Jesus discusses Sophia's remarkable and complex journey through the cosmos and his mission as Savior, Mary Magdalene requests permission from him to speak "in boldness." Jesus seems delighted and tells her that he will complete her in all that she lacks in knowledge of the divine mysteries because her heart exerts toward heaven more than those of her brother disciples. Mary Magdalene dazzles as the chief questioner of Jesus. She elaborates upon his comments. Of the forty-six questions asked in the Pistis Sophia, Mary Magdalene poses thirty-nine. Peter becomes upset that she dominates the discourse and complains to Jesus that he and the other disciples can no longer bear her because she won't let them speak. Jesus replies to Peter that anyone inspired should speak without hesitation. As if in an effort to placate Peter, Jesus gives him a hymn to decipher.

The Byzantine liturgy of Eastern Orthodox Churches allows for the intonation of Sophia's name before passages from the Gospels are read. Byzantine music such as sacred chant plays an important role in rites and ritual in the Greek-speaking world.

Mary Magdalene, the protagonist of several of the Gnostic texts, continues to be venerated by the Eastern Orthodox, the Catholic, and the Anglican churches as a saint. Her feast day is July 22. In the Eastern Orthodox tradition, Mary Magdalene went to Ephesus with Jesus' mother. After Mary Magdalene passed away, her relics were taken to Constantinople during the reign of Emperor Leo VI in A.D. 899, and they remain there today.

There is also a tradition of Mary Magdalene in southern France where her relics are venerated by the faithful at her sepulcher in the basilica of St. Maximin. The abbey of Vézelay also claims to have her relics. Finally, the grotto at Sainte Baume, where Mary Magdalene did penance for decades before her death, continues to be a popular pilgrimage site.

Chapter 12

The Gospel of Thomas

The Gospel of Thomas is what is known as a "sayings gospel." It is a text of hidden or secret sayings of Jesus as recorded by Didymos Judas Thomas the Twin. The gospel makes a bold proclamation: if the interpretations of the sayings are properly understood, they provide salvation. This gospel, unlike others in the New Testament canon and apocrypha, does not narrate incidents in Jesus' life and ministry, culminating in his death and resurrection, but instead provides 114 loosely grouped sayings attributed to Jesus.

Wisdom Interpretation of Jesus' Sayings

The Gospel of Thomas, containing the sayings of the "living" Jesus and found at Nag Hammadi (Codex II, 2, which is the second document in the second book), is a complete and well-preserved papyrus manuscript written in Egyptian Coptic script that dates to about A.D. 340. There are earlier Greek fragments that date to about A.D. 200. The Coptic version, scholars believe, was translated from the original Greek. Three other fragments of this gospel were previously discovered in 1898 at Oxyrhynchus, Egypt.

The sayings may be interpreted with Gnostic meaning and context, but because the term "Gnostic" is being hotly debated, some scholars hesitate to call the Gospel of Thomas a Gnostic text. However, since it was found with other Gnostic texts and was also written in the Coptic Egyptian script, it may be judged Gnostic because of that association. Some say that since the Greek fragments of the Gospel of Thomas are much older than the copy found at Nag Hammadi, the Gnostic labeling of the gospel should be removed. Another reason for removing the Gnostic classification is that the Gospel of Thomas does not contain the complex mythology of Gnosticism that modern scholars now associate with Gnostic texts. Nevertheless, it is included in James Robinson's *The Nag Hammadi Library: The Definitive Translation of the Gnostic Scriptures Complete in One Volume*. Scholar Helmut Koester raised an issue of concern about the Gospel of Thomas in the introduction to the gospel in *The Nag Hammadi Library*, namely, that the Greek fragments and the Coptic version seemingly have not preserved the Gospel of Thomas in its oldest form. In other words, the text may have changed with subsequent copying.

The Book of Thomas the Contender, another sacred text bearing the name of Thomas, details the missionary experiences of the Apostle Thomas (Didymos Judas Thomas) in the literary traditions belonging to the ancient people of Edessa, Syria. The writing dates to the first half of the third century. The Gospel of Thomas was composed between A.D. 50 and A.D. 125. The Acts of Thomas was written in A.D. 225.

Many of the wisdom sayings in the Gospel of Thomas are similar to those contained in the New Testament gospels, although some seem to differ, even conflict. There is no narrative structure to this gospel. Spiritual seekers most likely interpreted the sayings or used the sayings as points of contemplation or departure into meditation in order that gnosis—true knowledge—might come. The Gnostics believed that instead of becoming a Christian, through gnosis you became a Christ. Indeed, the sayings may be yeast for the gnosis. Some of the wisdom sayings contained in the gospel point to the Gnostic belief in dualism, the heavenly realm of light and goodness with the dark realm of material existence that is imperfect and evil. Some of the wisdom sayings in the Gospel of Thomas do not depend on the New Testament gospels and may have been in existence before the canonical versions of them were written. Marvin Meyer, in his book *The Gospel of Thomas: The Hidden Sayings of Jesus*, suggests that this might be true for the saying commonly known as the Parable of the Sower, which also appears in Matthew, Mark, and Luke. In the Parable of the Sower, Jesus talks about a farmer who sows his seed. In one instance, some seeds fall by the wayside; in the second instance, some fall upon a rock. Seeds also fell among thorns, and some landed on good ground and bore fruit. In the New Testament Gospels, an explanation or interpretation follows the parable itself, applying the meaning to church experience. Here's the interpretation found in the New Testament Gospel of Luke that follows Luke's Parable of the Sower (Luke 8:5–8). Jesus speaks the parable and then gives the interpretation.

. . . The seed is the word of God. Those by the way side are they that hear; then cometh the devil, and taketh away the word . . . They on the rock . . . receive the word with joy; and . . . fall away. And that which fell among thorns are they, which . . . bring no fruit to perfection. But . . . they . . . having heard the word, keep it, and bring forth fruit . . . .—Luke 8:11–15

The Gospel of Thomas does not contain interpretations. The presence of interpretations after the sayings means that interpretations were added later in the canonical versions of the sayings, asserted Meyer. He also pointed out that the Gospel of Thomas and the other sayings gospel, Q, create a paradigm for glimpsing and studying the historical Jesus.

Myriad Literary Forms

The ancient world made use of wisdom sayings in its oral traditions and in its sacred written texts. The Gospel of Thomas reflects that tradition. Collected into the Gospel of Thomas are traditional wisdom sayings, including some of the canonical gospels' oldest sayings circulated first in Aramaic, Jesus' mother tongue. Experts do not think the Gospel of Thomas derives from the New Testament Gospels but rather may have preceded the canonical gospels, because many of the sayings are in a more original and traditional version and are forged into several literary forms.

Five literary forms were commonly used in ancient oral and written traditions:

- **Parable:** A simple narrative story containing a religious idea or spiritual point. Often the story will be realistic and involve setting, action, character's dilemma (moral or spiritual), character's decision, and consequences.
- **Prophecy:** The foretelling or predicting of something, often through divine inspiration. Some prophecies found in the Old Testament were fulfilled in the New Testament.
- **Proverb:** A short wise saying or precept, often of an unknown or ancient origin. Proverbs are found in the Bible in both the Old Testament and the New Testament.
- **Rules for the Community:** The rules for right behavior in ethical and moral conduct.
- **Aphorism:** A succinct or terse saying that embodies a general truth.

The wisdom of the Hebrews has been preserved for centuries in parables, proverbs, and aphorisms that have been passed down. The Gospel of Thomas preserves some sayings that were not only known to Jews during Jesus' lifetime and also spoken by him but also recorded in the canonical gospels.

Early church fathers certainly knew about the Gospel of Thomas, for they mention it (usually in a negative context) in their polemics, homilies, and histories. Those fathers included Hippolytus of Rome (*Refutation of All Heresies*), Origen (Homily on Luke), Eusebius of Caesarea (early church historian and author of *Historia Ecclesiae*), and Philip of Side (another church historian who relied, in part, on writings of Eusebius).

Who Was the Source for the Gospel of Thomas?

Jesus was the source for the Gospel of Thomas inasmuch as the document itself claims to be a preservation of the sayings of the living Jesus. As already noted, many of the sayings found in the Gospel of Thomas have parallels in the Gospels of Matthew, Mark, Luke, and, especially, John. But the sayings also have some parallels in the Gospel of the Hebrews and the Gospel of the Egyptians. In addition, the Gospel of Thomas has some sayings of Jesus that are not found in other texts.

The literary genre of the Gospel of Thomas resembles the hypothetical sayings gospel known as the Synoptic Sayings Source or the Sayings Gospel Q. Writers of the Gospel of Mathew and the Gospel of Luke likely relied on Q as a source. Many scholars believe that the Gospel of Thomas dates to the first century and, unlike Mathew and Luke, is completely separate and independent of Q. The Sayings Gospel Q is most often dated to the middle of the first century.

Was Didymos Judas Thomas Jesus' Twin?

The Syrian Christians believed Judas Didymos Thomas was the twin brother of Jesus. In the Book of Thomas the Contender, a text detailing the dialogue between the risen Jesus and Judas Thomas before Jesus' ascension, Jesus calls him "brother," "twin," and "friend." But for Didymos Judas Thomas to be Jesus' identical or fraternal twin when Jesus, according to the scriptures, is born of God and the Blessed Virgin Mary seems problematic, at least from an orthodox theological point of view. In the birth narrative of

Jesus, no mention is made anywhere in the New Testament that Mary gave birth to twins. Possibly there is another meaning. Consider that Didymos Judas Thomas was a member of Jesus' inner circle, that he adopted Jesus' ways and teachings to become a highly evolved spiritual being akin to being Jesus' "twin."

Didymos Judas Thomas was one of the twelve disciples and was present at the Last Supper, witnessed the miraculous catch of fish, ate breakfast with Jesus after the Resurrection, was present for the Great Commission (when Jesus sent his disciples into the world to spread the good news), and saw Jesus ascending into heaven. He also doubted that Jesus rose from the dead and declared that he would have to touch the wounds of Jesus' body in order to believe; hence he became known as "Doubting Thomas." As mentioned previously, the name Thomas in Aramaic (*Tau'ma*) means twin and the name Didymos in Greek also means twin. Matthew (10:1–3) named him as an Apostle, as did Mark (3:14–18) and Luke (6:13–15).

. . . he called unto him his disciples: and of them he chose twelve, whom also he named apostles; Simon (whom he also named Peter) and Andrew his brother, James and John, Philip and Bartholomew, Matthew and Thomas, James the son of Alpheus, and Simon called Zelotes, and Judas the brother of James, and Judas Iscariot, which also was the traitor.—Luke 6:13–16

Doubting Thomas

Didymos Judas Thomas doubted that Jesus rose from the dead until he was able to put his fingers into the wounds on Jesus' body. In John 20:29, Jesus said to him, "Thomas, because thou hast seen me, thou hast believed: blessed are they that have not seen, and yet have believed." Could it be that the point of the story of Thomas doubting in the Gospel of John was directed at those who might be in doubt over the resurrection of Jesus? It certainly seems likely. Perhaps the author of the Gospel of John thought that others might be convinced of the Resurrection by the testimony of Thomas who had doubted it and then became a believer.

The Gospel of John reveals many of the qualities that Thomas possessed. For example, Thomas appears inquisitive in John 14:5, doubtful in John 20:24–25, courageous in John 11:16, and faithful in John 20:26–29.

Thomas Takes the Gospel to the East

Didymos Judas Thomas the twin is mentioned in all the canonical gospels. In the Gospel of John when Jesus learns that his friend Lazarus, brother of Mary and Martha of Bethany, is gravely ill and perhaps dying, he announces his desire to return to Judea to see Lazarus. Thomas declares to the other disciples, "Let us also go, that we may die with him" (John 11:16). The Gospel of John references Thomas again when he is part of the group discussion at the table during the Last Supper. In what has come to be known as Christ's Farewell Sermon, Jesus tells those gathered that they should not let their hearts be troubled because his Father's house has many mansions and he is going to prepare a place for each of them. Jesus says, "And whither I go ye know, and the way ye know" (John 14:4). But Thomas says, "Lord, we know not whither thou goest; and how can we know the way?" (John 14:5) Jesus reassures them with his famous saying, "I am the way, the truth, and the life: no man cometh unto the Father, but by me" (John 14:6). In the canonical gospels, the other disciples respect Thomas for his honesty and viewpoint. He doubted the resurrection of Jesus, but once convinced, his belief was unshakable. His faith in Jesus as Lord and God is affirmed in John 20:28.

QUESTION?

Who was Bardesanes?
He was a Christian Syrian writer, philosopher, astrologer, and Edessan poet and possibly the author of the Acts of Thomas, a story of Thomas's exploits in India that promotes the idea that Christians must be chaste even though married. The Apostle Thomas and the Gnostics may have embraced that idea. The early church fathers rejected the Acts of Thomas as fanciful fiction.

The Apostle Peter took Christianity to Rome, Paul spread the good news to Greece, Mark Christianized Egypt, and Judas Didymos Thomas brought Christianity to Syria and India. As a result, many Christian churches were built in those lands. Both the Eastern Orthodox Church and the Roman Catholic Church honor Thomas as a saint, celebrating his feast day on the Sunday following Easter. The day bears his name as St. Thomas Sunday. For centuries, the Syrian Christians have venerated his relics at the Church of Edessa. Many sources on the Internet discuss the missionary travels of the Apostles.

The Gospel Is Excluded from the Canon

The Gospel of Thomas did not make it into the New Testament canon. Although it was likely one of the earliest texts (other than the canonical gospels) that offered teachings of Jesus, it might have been rejected because the "canonizers" thought it contained heresy. It is also possible that it was put aside because it lacked any mention of the death and resurrection of Jesus, information that the other four chosen gospels did include. However, the Epistles and the book of Revelation do not mention stories of Jesus' demise but they are included, so the reason the Gospel of Thomas was excluded remains a point of debate among biblical scholars.

The Infancy Gospel of Thomas is a text of the second century, most likely composed in Syria, that attributes its authority to the Apostle Thomas. That work chronicles miraculous occurrences in Jesus' childhood and reveals incidents of his precociousness.

The Gospel of Thomas does not mention many terms associated with other Gnostic texts. For example, Demiurges, the Aeons, and the Pleroma do not appear in that text. As previously mentioned, the Gnostics loved their mythology, but the Gospel of Thomas contains no myths. Some historians feel that the Gospel of Thomas should not be labeled a Gnostic text—yet some elements of the manuscript certainly seem to have Gnostic shadings, so others disagree. If versions of Gnostic thought existed in pre-Christian Judaism, perhaps Thomas, a Jew, may have been aware of it. Or perhaps some of the more Gnostic of the sayings were added to the Gospel. Among scholars, the discussion about whether or not it is truly a Gnostic text continues.

The Gospel's Parallels in the New Testament

The Gospel of Thomas stresses the importance of each individual looking inward and finding gnosis of the Self. It is that process that bestows right understanding of Jesus' sayings. Strip away everything that binds you to the world, become a solitary one, seek gnosis: the gospel suggests that this is how to find eternal life.

There are numerous parallels between the sayings found in the Gospel of Thomas and the canonical gospels. Some are almost word for word while others seem thematically linked. An example of the way these sayings have resonance can be seen in the following examples. The Gospel of Thomas saying number 31 states that a village won't accept its own prophet and a doctor doesn't heal people he knows. The canonical gospels each have a version of that saying.

"And they were offended in him. But Jesus said unto them, A prophet is not without honor, save in his own country, and in his own house. And he did not many mighty works there because of their unbelief" (Matthew 13:57–58).

"But Jesus said unto them, A prophet is not without honor, but in his own country, and among his own kin, and in his own house. And he could there do no mighty work, save that he laid his hands upon a few sick folk, and healed them" (Mark 6:4–5).

"And he said unto them, Ye will surely say unto me this proverb, Physician, heal thyself: whatsoever we have heard done in Capernaum, do also here in thy country" (Luke 4:23).

"For Jesus himself testified, that a prophet hath no honor in his own country" (John 4:44).

Another saying found in the Gospel of Thomas has to do with the important stone that has been rejected by the builders, which is identified as the "cornerstone." See the Gospel of Thomas saying number 66. The parallel in the New Testament Gospel can be found in Matthew, Mark, and Luke.

"Jesus saith unto them, Did ye never read in the scriptures, The stone which the builders rejected, the same is become the head of the corner: this is the Lord's doing, and it is marvelous in our eyes?" (Matthew 21:42)

"And have ye not read this scripture; The stone which the builders rejected is become the head of the corner: This was the Lord's doing, and it is marvelous in our eyes?" (Mark 12:10–11).

"And he beheld them, and said, What is this then that is written, The stone which the builders rejected, the same is become the head of the corner?" (Luke 20:17).

QUESTION?

Why did the Apostle Thomas not emphasize Jesus' life and ministry in his gospel?
Thomas emphasized the "secret sayings" of the "living Jesus." The sayings become the point of his gospel because if the sayings are rightly understood, through gnosis, the reader becomes like Jesus' twin or the Christ (instead of a Christian), thereby achieving salvation.

In the parable of the yeast in saying number 96 from the Gospel of Thomas, Jesus compares heaven or the father's kingdom to a woman with some yeast hidden in bread dough that yields large loaves. The parallel is found in the Gospel of Matthew 13:33, "Another parable spake he unto them: The kingdom of heaven is like unto leaven, which a woman took, and hid in three measures of meal, till the whole was leavened;" and also in the Gospel of Luke 13:20–21, "And again he said, Whereunto shall I liken the kingdom of God? It is like leaven, which a woman took and hid in three measures of meal, till the whole was leavened."

The sayings found in the Gospel of Thomas have parallels not only in the synoptic Gospels but also in the Sayings Gospel Q, as well as in several other Gnostic texts and ancient writings. Some are repeated or offered with variations in Paul's New Testament Epistles.

Thomas was a Jew and possibly also a Galilean. Some sources say his name Thomas is Syriac and Didymos is the Greek equivalent. In Syriac legends, he is often called Judas Thomas. According to one tradition, Thomas and the other disciples after Pentecost divided up the countries of the world and drew lots to see where each of them would go. India fell to Judas Thomas.

Jesus Responds to Peter

In the last saying of the Gospel of Thomas, number 114, Peter complains to Jesus that he wants Mary to leave because women aren't worthy of life. Peter, by his own words (in the Gospel of Thomas, the Gospel of Mary, and other texts), shows that he is a man who is intolerant of women in general and Mary Magdalene in particular. He is truly a man of patriarchal times. In spite of having a wife, Peter has little patience for women in a man's discourse with other men. He doesn't hide his feelings toward Mary Magdalene. Peter seems to be saying that women cannot receive salvation and eternal life because they are not worthy. But could he really mean that? Could not women, like men, become spiritually mature? Could not women also become solitary sojourners on the path to renunciation of the world of flesh and matter? Jesus seemed to think they could, because he admitted them to his inner circle. He healed them, trusted them, and taught them. He knew Peter's heart and also his impulsiveness. Jesus did not banish Mary Magdalene as Peter had demanded.

Making Mary Male

Jesus responds to Peter's objection to Mary Magdalene by saying he will lead her himself in order to transform her into male. In that way she will be like Peter and the others, because women who become male enter the kingdom of heaven. This saying from the Gospel of Thomas has prompted various insights from scholarly commentators. Some say it is a polemic against marriage and procreation and bondage to flesh. Others assert that it means

that Jesus will help her to spiritually develop even more, so that gender iden-
tification falls away, leaving Mary Magdalene as an androgynous spirit. Still
others say that male and female are metaphors for higher and lower spiritual natures. By making Mary Magdalene male, Jesus makes her more conscious of her higher spiritual self. She will leave behind her earthbound,
passionate, emotional nature for a heavenly spiritual nature. The Naassenes believed that when one ascended to God's house, only spiritual beings
could enter, and when they went in they necessarily shed their garments
(maleness and femaleness). Could becoming more male mean becoming
more like the bridegroom ready to enter the wedding chamber for the rite of
sacred marriage, *the hieros gamos*, of the Gnostics?

The Gnostic sacred texts reflected, in many ways, an egalitarian view
toward gender. Their holy teachings were often communicated through
a divine female voice such as Luminous Epinoia or Sophia, or an earthly
woman's voice such as Mary Magdalene. In some Gnostic sects, men
and women equally functioned as teachers, prophets, and leaders.

In the male-dominated society of first-century Palestine where the place
of the female was inferior to the male, it was an honor for a woman to be considered the equal of a man in spiritual matters. As men and women became
ascetics, taking upon themselves the life of renunciation, detaching themselves
from the world in order to study all things of the spirit, women became less
female and more male (referring possibly to a spiritual state of androgyny).

Scholarly debate continues as to whether or not the Gospel of Thomas
is dependent upon or independent of the synoptic Gospels. The gospel's
text shares similarities with the canonical gospels, to be sure, but also offers
some esoteric keys (through the sayings of the "living Jesus") for inner awakening. This gospel's Jesus is a wisdom teacher, a Jewish sage, calling others to knowledge rather than faith, according to scholars Marvin Meyer
and Harold Bloom in *The Gospel of Thomas, The Hidden Sayings of Jesus*.
Meyer translated the text and Bloom wrote a Gnostic sermon based on the
translation.

Chapter 13

The Gospel of Philip

Some Gnostic scholars and experts on early Christianity have called the Gospel of Philip a text of Valentinian theology or simply a Valentinian anthology of sayings and excerpts. The gospel also has been referred to as a sayings gospel, with wisdom sayings attributed to Jesus, but in addition it includes information about the sacraments, especially the sacrament of marriage. The literary forms found in the Gospel of Philip include some parables and aphorisms, an interpretation of Genesis, some narrative dialogue, paraenesis, analogy, and a smattering of polemics.

What Is Found in This Gospel?

The Gospel of Philip expounds upon the Valentinian notion that the separation of the sexes brought error into the world. When Adam and Eve were together, death did not exist. But when Eve became separate from Adam, their androgyny ceased. Christ had to come in order to reunite Adam and Eve. The gospel reveals that two thus united in the "bridal chamber" no longer will be separated. Such were the beliefs of the followers of Valentinus, the great Gnostic teacher who almost became pope (he was a candidate but narrowly lost the election). They called themselves the "spiritual ones" or "the elect" or "disciples of God."

What was the gospel tradition? It encompassed the oral teaching about Jesus' ministry, death, and resurrection. The Christian church initially began and evolved through public preaching (not with the use of texts). The Apostles traveled throughout the ancient world, sharing a core message that Jesus died for the sins of humankind. However, their retelling of the stories of his life most likely meant that many gospels accounts circulated.

The Gospel of Philip dates to roughly the third century. Scholars are still debating whether the original was written in Syriac or Greek. The gospel was lost until a copy was found in the Nag Hammadi cache of ancient texts that were buried perhaps in the fourth century, when the official church was burning texts deemed heretical.

Philip, the Third Man Jesus Called

The Gnostics had high regard for Jesus' apostle Philip and believed he was the authority for the gospel named after him. Unlike the Gospel of Thomas that declares Thomas to be the author of that account, the Gospel of Philip makes no such declaration. The Philip of the Gospel of Philip is not to be confused with the evangelist (whose name appears in the Acts of the Apostles). Like the Apostles Peter and Andrew, Philip was born in

Bethsaida. Originally a follower of John the Baptist, Philip became the third disciple that Jesus called. He was knowledgeable about the scripture and may have spoken Greek. The book of John reveals that Philip was both practical and helpful.

Philip's Family

Philip was married, according to the writings of early church father Clement. Like the other Apostles, after Jesus' resurrection Philip went to work, performing miracles, preaching, and traveling to Greece, Azota, Phrygia (modern Turkey), Galilee, and Syria (some sources also say Gaul) in connection with his Christian missionary tasks. Tradition teaches that Philip also may have lived and worked in Scythia, which today is the Ukraine. At least one of his daughters was married. Other daughters of Philip remained unmarried, for church historian Eusebius stated that Polycrates, bishop in Ephesus in the second century, wrote that one of Philip's daughters was buried in Ephesus while Philip was interred at Hieropolis.

Exploits and Demise

One story of Philip's exploits during Emperor Domitian's rule, circa A.D. 80, occurs in Hieropolis where Philip had gone in the company of the Apostles John and Bartholomew (also called Nathanael) and Marian, Philip's sister (not Mary Magdalene). There, while preaching, Philip killed a giant snake through prayer. The local pagans worshipped the snake and its death so outraged them that they crucified Philip upside down. Another version of the story says that the pagans crucified both Philip and Bartholomew, but when the earth opened up and swallowed the judge (who had ordered their deaths) along with a number of pagan people, others rushed to remove the men from their crosses. Unfortunately, Philip had already passed away.

FACT

Sayings attributed to Jesus and used in the New Testament Gospels are known as *logia* (from the Greek *logia*, meaning "divine utterances or sayings"). The Sayings Gospel Q and the Gospel of Thomas may have served as the sources for the logia contained in the canonical gospels.

Philip's virgin daughters were buried with him at Hieropolis, although one of his daughters was buried at Ephesus. At some point later, Philip's relics were taken from Hieropolis to Constantinople and then to Rome, where they were placed in the Basilica of the Twelve Apostles. The Roman Catholic Church now celebrates Philip's feast day on May 3 (from the sixth century, it was celebrated on May 1); the Greek Orthodox Church celebrates it on November 14.

The Holiest of Holy

The Gospel of Philip declares that the means of attaining Christhood is in the sacrament of the Bridal Chamber. That Gnostic sacrament was also mentioned in other noncanonical texts—for example, the Gospel of Thomas (saying number 75) and the Exegesis on the Soul, in which the Soul waits for the true bridegroom in the bridal chamber that she has filled with perfume and in which she has cleansed herself. The Gospel of Philip, however, discusses the value of the sacraments but places special emphasis on that particular sacrament, raising questions for modern scholars. For example, what did the Gnostics mean by the sacrament of the Bridal Chamber? Should the meaning be taken as allegorical, as the merging of two beings or energies, or the sense of separateness from the wholeness of the Divine back into oneness? Or could the sacrament refer to the physical sexual union between a man and a woman? Could it have been a single initiation that included five steps: baptism, chrism, Eucharist, redemption, and bridal chamber all in one?

Consecrated Sex?

Another theory suggests that the Bridal Chamber might simply be a single sacramental rite, perhaps involving an entirely spiritual sexual act performed in a controlled manner rather than through inflamed passions. If so, was it a fertility rite? Could it have been a sacred sexual act to create spiritually-evolved offspring? Could the Gnostics have seen it as the "correct, conscious" way to have intercourse because of a belief they may have had about the spiritual pitfalls or consquences of an unconsecrated sex act? If, as some Gnostics believed, that improper mixing of the spirit with the flesh (as in the sexual act) was the reason for humanity's downfall from grace, then the idea of procreating physical offspring in order to have spiritually advanced children would have had little appeal. The higher path would have been to abstain and have no children.

Some Christian sects embracing Gnostic ideas saw the body as filthy and the world of matter as evil. Many practiced celibacy, lived an ascetic lifestyle, fasted, and gave little attention to the demands of the flesh. Hoping to be freed from passions of the flesh and sexuality altogether, they sought to clothe themselves in the "light" through gnosis of the divine truths.

The Valentinians sought in union with the Divine the kind of love that would reestablish wholeness, fill the longing of the empty heart, restore the soul, and heal the fractiousness found in the human condition. Their sacrament of the Bridal Chamber represented their hearts straining toward that transcendant love.

The Gospel of Philip states that the bridal chamber cannot be entered by defiled women (prostitutes, adulteresses), slaves, and animals. It states who can enter: free men and virgins. It also declares that those clothed in the "perfect light" cannot be seen by the powers and that in the sacramental union, one clothes oneself in that light.

Free men do not love the flesh and are not enslaved by it. But archons by nature seek to entrap free men and imprison them in fleshly ignorance. Slaves are those unknowing about their inner lives and what entraps them as well as what frees them.

The gospel also differentiates between sons of man who create and sons of man who beget. Those who create (or have the ability to do so) are creators and their progeny are humans ensnared in matter, but those who beget do so in private and their offspring are children of light. No one knows when the husband and wife have intercourse because it is pure and in the light and no one can see them. The Gospel of Philip states that for those who have received the light of the bridal chamber, none can torment them for they cannot be seen and they cannot be detained or enslaved.

Sex with an Angel

The Gnostics saw the Sophia's fall from the Pleroma as the beginning of the imperfect physical universe and all the suffering that accompanied material creation. You'll recall from previous chapters how she tried to create without her male counterpart and the result was the Demiurge. Early church father Tertullian's polemic *Against Valentinians* explains the fantastic theology and complexities of the Valentinian doctrine.

In chapter seventeen of *Against Valentinians*, Tertullian examines the Valentinian idea that Achamoth (the fallen Sophia) harbored a carnal desire for angelic luminaries (Tertullian saw this kind of thinking, in particular, as lascivious) and during her emotionally inflamed, passionate phase became pregnant. In due time, she birthed an offspring, the Demiurge, that had three natures—material, animal, and spiritual. The Demiurge then created humans. The Redeemer, Christ the Savior, came to the aid of humanity and into the world, not by virtue of being born of a virgin, but using the virgin as a passageway or channel. Tertullian wrote that the Valentinians strangely believed that Jesus and Christ were not the same. He noted that the Valentinians "engrafted Jesus," inserting a spiritual seed into him through animal "inflatus." Indeed, Tertullian addresses rather condescendingly the studying that the Valentinians did in their theology. He noted that they believed Jesus was not human, that Soter (seeded) Jesus entered Christ but left again when Christ was examined by Pilate. In fact, Tertullian claimed that the Valentinians reduced everything to images and imaginery beings.

Who Was Valentinus?

Egyptian-born Valentinus was among the Christian mystics who had visions of the risen Lord. Born in Upper Egypt circa A.D. 100, he received his education in Alexandria. He studied Greek philosophy, Christianity, and techniques for interpreting Jewish scripture. He may also have had some knowledge of Sethnian Gnostic teachings and integrated Gnostic principles into his own philosophy. He became a disciple of Theudas, who was himself a disciple of the Apostle Paul. Valentinus said that Theudas taught him the same the secret knowledge that Paul had taught his core of disciples. From his vision of the risen Christ, Valentinus felt inspired to become a Christian teacher. He developed a following in his homeland and also in Syria. Eventually he went to Rome and there established a reputation as an eloquent and persuasive speaker. The Roman Church must have held him in high esteem, because he was considered for the candidacy of bishop. Some reports say an election took place and he failed by a narrow margin. Others say he refused the position. What is known is that Valentinus continued to preach in Rome for another decade. After his death, his followers continued to evolve his ideas, further developing and spreading them throughout the ancient world.

Shades of Valentinian Ideas

Early orthodox father Tertullian pointed out that the Valentinians, whether advocating a particular point of view or negating it, had disagreements not only among themselves but with their own founder's ideas on how to interpret their doctrines. The Gnostics considered all spiritual doctrines as only paths or approaches to the truth manifested in the realm of Light. They emphasized that gnosis was the means to that enlightenment. The early church fathers, conversely, came to believe that their orthodox doctrine was itself the truth. They taught that one had to have faith that the church's teachings were the right interpretations of the gospel. Their doctrine represented the truth, or so they believed, whereas the unorthodox doctrines like those of the Gnostics encouraged a constant questioning but never achieved the truth.

QUESTION?

What did the Valentinian teacher Theodotus teach about gnosis?
He taught that "saving" knowledge can be summarized as understanding who we were; where we were (came from); where we have been, where we have come to, and where we are hastening; from what we are redeemed; and what is birth and rebirth.

Gnostic scholar Elaine Pagels suggests that the "radical" Gnostics and the orthodox Christians were aligned on opposite poles and the followers of Valentinus, who saw themselves not as outsiders, but inside the Christian church, assumed a middle position. But like a pot of water simmering until it reached the boiling point, the Valentinians began discoursing among themselves about who constituted the body of Christ until the debate became a conflict that ultimately split the Valentinians into two groups. One group said that the church (the body of Christ) was made up only by those completed in gnosis while the other group believed that the church was split between the spiritual ones with gnosis (Gnostics) and those who had not yet received gnosis (the unspiritual Christians).

Gnostic Masters in Disagreement

Gnostic teachers holding viewpoints at variance with each other were Theodotus (espousing the view that only the eastern Valentinians were spiritual ones with gnosis) and Ptolemy and Heracleon (representing the western Valentinians), who taught that the church was made up of both those Christians with and without gnosis. The former was to teach and lead the latter, or so they thought. The Gnostic view that many orthodox Christians did not have gnosis and therefore were unspiritual beings to be led by Gnostics with gnosis outraged the orthodox leadership. Modern scholars know about Ptolemy from mentions of a letter he sent to Flora, a wealthy woman who some sources say was not a Gnostic. He was definitely a follower of Valentinus, but was active in southern Gaul (modern France) and Italy. Heracleon was a second-century Gnostic and perhaps one of the most well-regarded teachers in Valentinian tradition at Rome. His commentary on the Gospel of John exists in fragments that were written about by early church father Origen in his own commentary on John. Heracleon also wrote about the Gospels of Matthew and Luke and some of his beliefs have been preserved in the writings of Clement of Alexandria.

Conservative Church Outraged

The bishops were intent on guiding the church in a direction of universal acceptance of converts of varying degrees of knowledge and understanding and would not tolerate challenges to their doctrine, hierarchy, or ritual. As Pagel noted in her book, *The Gnostic Gospels,* the Gnostics challenged them all. Consquently, the Gnostic teachings were suppressed and Gnostic texts destroyed, and the Gnostic churches died out within a few centuries.

Revealing Statements

There are seventeen sayings in the Gospel of Philip, of which about half have resonance in the canonical Gospels. These sayings and citations suggest a connection (however loose) between the Gnostic Gospel of Philip and the canon gospels.

The Gospel of Philip states that Jesus would not have prayed or referred to the father in heaven unless he also had an earthly father (presumably because he was differentiating between the two when he identified the one in heaven).

He saith unto them, But whom say ye that I am? And Simon Peter answered and said, Thou art the Christ, the Son of the living God. And Jesus answered and said unto him, Blessed art thou, Simon Barjona: for flesh and blood hath not revealed it unto thee, but my Father which is in heaven.—Matthew 16:15–17

The Gospel of Philip saying number 57:5 iterates a saying about the celebration of the Eucharist. A similar version of the saying is found in the Gospel of John 6:53: "Then Jesus said unto them, Verily, verily, I say unto you, Except ye eat the flesh of the Son of man, and drink his blood, ye have no life in you."

Also in Philip's Gospel is found the statement about praying in secret that has a parallel in the canonical Gospel of Matthew: "And when thou prayest, thou shalt not be as the hypocrites are: for they love to pray standing in the synagogues and in the corners of the streets, that they may be seen of men. Verily, I say unto you, They have their reward. But thou, when thou prayest, enter into thy closet, and when thou has shut thy door, pray to thy Father which is in secret; and thy Father which seeth in secret shall reward thee openly."—Matthew 6:5–6

Finally, saying number 84 in the Gospel of Philip iterates the well-known saying that truth will make you free. Its parallel is found in John 8:32: "And ye shall know the truth, and the truth shall make you free" (John 8:32).

Some of the sayings or statements must be interepreted in purely Gnostic context. For example, the Gospel of Philip states in 55:33–34 that those who say that the conception of Jesus in Mary (the Blessed Virgin) was due to the Holy Spirit were wrong because no power ever defiled Mary. The Valentinians saw the Holy Spirit as female, and the author of the Gospel of Philip poses the question: How is it possible for a female to conceive by a woman? Another excellent question might be: How is it possible for a human female to conceive by something that is not a human male (i.e., the Holy Spirit)? Both of these conceptions require a leap of logic.

Much Ado about a Kiss

The Gospel of Philip suggests a close relationship between Mary Magdalene and Jesus. In fact, it has often been cited as a source for the belief in popular culture that the two may have been married. The gospel states that Jesus' mother, her sister, and Mary Magdalene always walked with him and further states that Mary Magdalene was his companion (sometimes also translated as consort). In Chapter Seven, you learned that the Gospel of Philip contains the now famous phrase that Jesus loved Mary Magdalene more than the other disciples and kissed her often on the . . .—then there is a lacuna (hole) in the manuscript.

In ancient times, texts often bore the names of an individual or individuals seen as authorities for the work so that the author could further a particular point of view. Materials might thus be linked to an individual such as an apostle of Jesus, a disciple of an important apostle, or student of a famous teacher where no linkage could actually be made.

The point is that Jesus kissed a woman who was not his mother or his sister and he kissed her often, to the consternation of the other disciples. They struggled to understand why. The gospel states that they asked Jesus why did he love her more than he loved them. He responded by asking them why he doesn't love them as her, then he tells them a parable about how when a sighted and a blind person are together in darkness, they are not different, yet when the light comes, the sighted one sees and the blind individual does not see.

Was Jesus Married to Mary Magdalene?

The Gospel of Philip mentions Mary Magdalene in saying number 63:35 as the companion that Jesus often kissed. This has led to much modern speculation about the relationship between Jesus and Mary Magdalene. The Gospel of Philip does not reveal whether or not the two were married and neither do the canonical gospels. In fact, there is no historical proof whatsoever of the two being married. There is, however, a lot of speculation. Some assert that Jesus was a Jewish rabbi, and in his time Jewish men were expected to marry and bear children. In fact, his mother Mary's own father Joachim was ostracized for being barren until he and his wife Ann prayed for the birth of a child. Tradition says that God heard and granted their prayer, allowing them to bring forth Mary. Some modern Gnostics take the opposite view—that is, that Jesus and Mary Magdalene would not have married because in society in the first century, marriage was about ownership. Women became the property of their husband, and neither Mary Magdalene nor Jesus would have wanted that, according to those believers. So, until some historical document surfaces that proves Jesus and Mary Magdalene were husband and wife, the question remains unanswered.

Handbook of Gnostic Sacramental Rites?

The Gospel of Philip contains many disparate pieces arranged in an illogical, even eccentric manner. The gospel perhaps makes the most sense if thought of as a kind of handbook containing oral religious instruction before baptism—in other words, a book of sacramental catechesis. The word "catechism" derives from the Greek verb *katexein*, which means to teach. Catechism has been used from the fourth century (perhaps even earlier) to teach candidates for church membership about church doctrine, history, beliefs, practices, sacraments, and rites.

The Valentinians most likely instructed their initiates into their Gnostic doctrine before they could particpate in the sacraments. The five Gnostic sacraments, as discussed earlier in this book, included baptism, chrism or rituals of anointing with oil, redemption, bridal chamber, and the Eucharist, which possibly involved readings of scripture or sacred texts (some Valentinian liturgical readings can be found in *The Gnostic Bible* by Willis Barnstone and Marvin Meyer). The Gospel of Philip in saying number 69:11–13 expounds upon the Valentinian belief that followers have to be baptized in the water and the light, and that the light is the chrism. The Gnostic sacrament of the chrism was a sacrament through which they received the Holy Spirit. Its counterpart would be confirmation in the Roman Catholic church.

A final word about Gnostic salvation—it includes individual and also a cosmic redemption. In other words, all things must be returned to what they were before they came into being in the realm of matter. All sparks of light must be set free to return to the divine light. Only then will the flawed and evil material realm that the Gnostics called *Hyle* be destroyed. The Valentinians developed a doctrine that espoused an extremely complicated and elaborate salvation process that involved Aeons who must restore order in the Pleroma after Sophia's fall. An Aeon called Jesus-Soter (also called Jesus Logos and Christ) comes into the material world as a second Savior and unites with Jesus (at Jesus' baptism). This savior comes to show humans the way to return their spirit (*pneuma*) "home" to the Pleroma.

Chapter 14

The Gospel of the Egyptians

The (Coptic) Gospel of the Egyptians is also known as The Holy Book of the Great Invisible Spirit. This text is not to be confused with The Greek Gospel of the Egyptians mentioned by several early church fathers, including Clement of Alexandria, Hippolytus, and Epiphanius. The Gospel of the Egyptians exists in two versions; both versions are in Coptic script translated from the original Greek.

The Unknowable Divine Being

The Great Spirit, the Invisible One, the Unknowable Divine Being, the Unproclaimable Father, and the Father Whose Name Cannot Be Spoken— these are just a few of the ways the author of the Gospel of the Egyptians referred to the Unknowable Being who existed before existence. This Unknowable One is the Light of all lights, the Divine Parent, from whom proceeded the three powers in one: Father/Mother/Son (the Holy Trinity) except that they are not three, but one. Think of the Trinity as the Mother of all powers who is called Barbelo—the three-in-one. But when split into three separate powers as Father, Mother, and Son, each has eight qualities. For example, the Father's qualities are thought, word, eternal life, intellect, incorruptibility, foreknowledge, will, and androgeny.

FACT

Alexander Bohlig and Frederik Wisse, who introduce and translate the gospel in the Nag Hammadi Library (Codex III, 2 and IV, 2), assert that the Gospel of the Egyptians offers a Gnostic salvation history.

The Son's qualities are not listed per se, but the text states that the Son brings forth seven powers, the "light" of seven voices, which, in turn, are manifested as the seven vowels or sounds from which comes the Word. Taken together, the vowels hide the name of God in an unseen symbol.

The Gnostics developed a complicated backstory for God in their Gnostic mythology to explain his emergence into being. But explaining the unexplainable must have proven difficult even for the Gnostics. The construct that the author uses to tell God's creation story in the Gospel of the Egyptians is somewhat difficult to follow. It begs the question of why one should try to explain the unexplainable. The answer is that the ever-questioning Gnostic mind could not simply accept that God was ever-existent and forever would be.

The Eternal Christ Emerges

The self-evolving First Parent (who began as the manifestation of three-in-one from the unknowable, incomprehensible One) began the process of emanating into existence a whole host of beings. Among them is a being called the Christ, but not Jesus the Christ of the New Testament. The Christ in this gospel is an eternal being (also known as a power) that came into existence through the Divine Parent's emanation. The five seals (more on which later) is another being that also emanates into existence. So to recap: The Divine Parent emanates the Christ *through* the Father/Mother/Son trio named Barbelo and the powers associated with them. And as with other emanations, a cycle of praising follows.

Adamas Comes to Annul the Deficiency

From the emanation of Christ, the first human being emerges. His name is Adamas. However, this is no ordinary human man like Adam as in the book of Genesis. This being is a spiritually superior version of the first man. The gospel gets a little confusing in this section because something has gone wrong with the world and Adamas must correct the problem, or, as the gospel says, "annul the deficiency." What could have gone wrong, you might wonder. Well, remember the myth of Sophia from an earlier chapter? The Demiurge, her offspring, created the flawed material universe. Without explicitly revealing it, the Gospel of the Egyptians makes note of that "problem."

In Sethian texts, the word deficiency is often used to mean the lack of knowledge (or divine light). The lack is brought about by the fallen Sophia. Since she is seen as the Wisdom attribute of God, the lack must point to a loss of enlightenment.

In the Gospel of the Egyptians, Ogdoad referred to powers or deities that the Unknowable Father brought forth in silence from Himself. From these came other powers such as the Aeon of the Aeons. The Aeons made up the

Pleroma of heavenly powers, which eventually led to Seth, father and savior of the Gnostics, or the "incorruptible race."

So how does Adamas remedy the problem? Adamas has light as his potent attribute. He merges with the Word and the two form human reason. Unlike Sophia, Adamas asks permission of the Divine Parent to create a being. He emanates a son and names him Seth. The lesson for the Gnostics seemed to be that the highest good comes from work aligned with the Divine Parent rather than against that Heavenly Force.

Divine Characteristics

The Gnostics offered high praise for their unknowable and unnameable God. The Gnostic Apocryphon (or Secret) Book of John proclaims God as the "unknown." Not only the Gnostics revered the unknowable and incomprehensible One and declared his greatness to others, but so did Christians such as Paul. The Apostle preached in the New Testament Acts of the Apostles, "For as I passed by, and beheld your devotions, I found an altar with this inscription, TO THE UNKNOWN GOD [sic]. Whom therefore ye ignorantly worship, him declare I unto you" (Acts 17:23). Paul goes on to refer to God as male, omnipotent, omniscient, and benevolent.

The Gnostics saw themselves as the incorruptible ones, a superior race of beings within humankind who could trace their ancient spiritual lineage to Seth. In the Gospel of the Egyptians, when Seth was emanated so were four luminaries, who together with Seth completed the fullness of the Pleroma. The work of the four luminaries was to oversee the four realms populated by the divine race of beings. Each of the luminaries had a characteristic or attribute called a consort. The consorts, in turn, had an attendant, accompanied by a counterpart expressing a divine quality. This group included:

- **Harmozel**, consort is Grace; attendant is Gamaliel, whose counterpart is Memory.
- **Oroiael**, consort is Perception; attendant is Gabriel, whose counterpart is Love.
- **Davithe**, consort is Understanding; attendant is Samblo, whose counterpart is Peace.

- **Eleleth**, whose consort is Prudence; attendant is Abrasax, whose counterpart is Eternal Life.

In the classic Sethian myth, the Gnostic idea of God was one in which God possessed male and female characteristics. Some experts point out that negative theology (God as unknown, incomprehensible, unproclaimable, etc.) was an important aspect of Gnosticism and continued in the Greek Orthodox Christian tradition. The unknowable God, the Father of the Trinity remains beyond any sexual identity and is even beyond being and beyond the word "God" to define him. The Father/Mother/Son, referred to as Barbelo, allows the Unknowable One to be discussed, so the word "Barbelo" works as a literary device.

All the emanations of Barbelo that populate the Pleroma are attributes of God. The Unknowable God and his Aeons make up the fullness of the Pleroma. This heavenly realm exists in the non-material universe of the Gnostic myth. But the Demiurge threatens the stability of the divine Pleroma.

QUESTION?

Is it possible that the Gnostics borrowed names for their mythical archons from other sources?
There are similarities between the archon names and the words for Babylonian astrological planets. For example, the Gnostic Jaldabaoth is the Babylonian planet Saturn, and the Gnostic Oraios becomes a term for Babylonian Moon.

Genesis Prologue, a Redemption Tale

As the classic myth goes, the Demiurge then creates a shadow world, the material universe, that is a flawed imitation of the Pleroma. To do the work of creation, he must have helpers in the form of archons. Having created the prologue to Genesis, the Gnostic myth now incorporates the story of Adam and Eve found in Genesis.

The Gnostics believed that the Demiurge created the first man, Adam, who received a portion of the light (power) belonging to Sophia, the

Demiurge's mother. In creating Eve from Adam's rib, some sources for the myth say the Demiurge attempted to rape Eve to regain his lost power. But her spirit moved into the Tree of Knowledge. Thereafter the wise serpent tempted the couple and they ate the fruit of that tree, opening their intellectual power and restoring their knowledge. Instead of the myth pointing to the orthodox Christian view of Adam and Eve's act as the original sin, the Gnostics, through the creation of a backstory for Genesis, put forth a redemption story for Adam and Eve.

Rulers for Hades and Chaos

Chaos and Hades surely were present from the beginning of creation in the imperfect world made by the Demiurge. At a certain point in Gospel of the Egyptians myth, the great luminous being Eleleth declared that someone must reign over Hades and chaos. The lower or hylic Sophia, the part of Sophia trapped in the physical universe, suddenly appeared as a "cloud being," prompting the Luminary Gamaliel to address Gabriel (the attendant of the Luminary Oroiael) to say, let an angel do it. In other words, they, the luminaries, had decided to delegate the rulership of chaos and Hades to an angel. And the great angel Sakla (in Aramaic, the name means "fool") emerges, perhaps emanated from Sophia, although the Gospel of the Egyptians is not explicit on this point. Sakla is accompanied by a great demon named Nebruel. These two generated twelve more Aeons to rule over the various realms of Hades and chaos. The twelve angels were identified as Athoth, Harmas, Galila, Yobel, Adonaios, Cain, Abel, Akiressina, Yubel, Hamupiael, Archir-Adonin, and Belias.

Sakla's Arrogance

After he had finished appointing rulers over the regions of the world, Sakla arrogantly declares that he was a jealous god and that nothing could come into being except through him. The declaration has resonance with the righteous and sometimes harsh Jewish Father God of the Old Testament. In fact, Sakla's statement is echoed in the book of Deuteronomy of the Hebrew scriptures.

(For the Lord thy God is a jealous God among you) lest the anger of the Lord thy God be kindled against thee, and destroy thee from off the face of the earth. . . . And the Lord commanded us to do all these statutes, to fear the Lord our God, for our good always, that he might preserve us alive, as it is at this day.—Deuteronomy 6:15–24

Sakla's self-absorption was short-lived because a voice from on high (presumably heaven) called out to him with a reminder of the existence of Adamas and Seth. The voice was accompanied by an image that created a physical body for itself in the form of Adam. Thereafter this being evolved the earthborn race of humans, each of whom contained Seth's seed. As the myth unfolds, two strands of human beings are spawned. Sakla has a son named Cain, and one lineage extends from them while the other group of humans evolve from Adam and Seth. The offspring of Seth had much to endure, including floods, plagues, famines, and false prophets, as Sakla desired to destroy them. This imagery suggests that the author of the myth may have had knowledge or some association with the Jewish scriptures.

Many of the names found in the Gospel of the Egyptians are Jewish names that appear in both the Old and New Testaments. For example, Gamaliel is the name of a Pharisidic Jew in Acts 5:34. Cain and Abel appear in Genesis 4:1–7. Seth shows up in Genesis 5:3. This might suggest that the author of the gospel was familiar with older Hebrew traditions and names.

Seth observed the Devil at work persecuting his children, the incorruptible race, leaving a path of darkness and destruction. He sent an army of angels, 400 of them, to protect and watch over his children. With the blessing of the whole Pleroma, the Invisible Spirit, and the five seals, Seth himself came into the world to battle Sakla. He first had to create a suitable body, so he prepared a special one that was born of a virgin. Seth had to pass through flood, fire, and the judgement of lesser gods belonging to the material realm before he could "put on" the Logos-begotten body that he had prepared. The body that would be his envelope or covering or fleshly garment was Jesus.

At this juncture in the myth, the story begins to take on Christian shading. Seth "puts on" Jesus. Seth/Jesus through the crucifixion, the gospel reveals, "nailed" the thirteen dark powers or rulers, crucifying the ignorance in the law. Seth/Jesus had brought the truth of the incorruptibility of the race and armed them with the knowledge of their incorruptibility. The souls of the elect were thereafter protected.

The Gnostic idea of evil archons tempting, persecuting, leading astray the children of light has some resonance in the canonical Gospel of Matthew. In that text, Satan tempts Jesus with the kingdoms of the world. ". . . the devil taketh him up into an exceeding high mountain, and sheweth him all the kingdoms of the world, and the glory of them; and saith unto him, All these things will I give thee, if thou wilt fall down and worship me." (Matthew 4:8–9). The verse seems to match Gnostic theology in that Satan (an evil archon in Gnosticism) has some kind of ownership or power over the kingdoms of the world in order to be able to offer the world to Christ.

Five Seals and Gnostic Rituals

Baptism and the "renunciations of the five seals" must have been significant to gaining gnosis and the transcendental experience so desired by the Gnostics. The five seals may have been five ritualistic initiation rites. The five seals may correspond with the five sacraments associated with the Gnostics that have been mentioned in previous chapters.

The Gnostics could have intended for the Gospel of the Egyptians to be studied as a preparation for baptism. Baptism was an extremely important, necessary, and desirable Gnostic ritual. The gospel reveals that Seth established a rite of baptism, and it was holier even than heaven. Although a baptismal practice seems straightforward enough, the meaning of the five seals, even used in conjunction with the baptismal information, remains obfuscated, perhaps deliberately veiled in mystery.

Gnosis Through Baptism

Could baptism confer gnosis? Perhaps; the rite was certainly important to the Gnostics. The Mandaeans had a daily baptism ritual. Other cults, including the Christian Gnostics, used some form of baptism with water and a declaration. From the Gospel of the Egyptians, it appears that candidates may have been expected to understand from the myth how the earth was generated and how Seth incarnated as the savior figure Jesus. Engaged in the rite, the baptismal candidate had to sing a hymn as a response to the transcendent vision that was expected as part of the rite. Baptismal candidates might have been expected to learn the hymn with its parts broken by a series of vowels in long sequences that some experts have asserted might be Christian glossolalia or speaking in tongues. The term "glossolalia" derives from the Greek words *glōssa* (tongue) and *lalein* (to babble or talk). The speaking in tongues was mentioned in the Acts of the Apostles as a gift of the Holy Spirit. It was one of the charismas the Holy Spirit bestowed upon the Apostles on the day of Pentecost. The Apostle Paul, however, put forth rules governing Christian use of the gift of tongues in 1 Corinthians 14. Paul counseled churchgoers to pray with the spirit but also with understanding and to use the speaking in tongues to edify the whole church, not to show off.

And the spirits of the prophets are subject to the prophets. For God is not the author of confusion, but of peace, as in all churches of the saints. . . .Wherefore brethren, covet to prophesy, and forbid not to speak with tongues. Let all things be done decently and in order.—1 Corinthians 14:32–40

The baptismal candidates made what seemed to be a profession of faith, declaring that they have commingled their natures with the living water of the Divine, thus they could perceive the Divine within. Also, the new Gnostic apparently was given a glimpse of the path to the Divine that he or she would necessarily have to inwardly traverse.

Magical Incantations, Gnostic Ritual, and Censure

The Gnostic baptismal hymn spelled out sequences of vowels interspersed with praise. They are mixed up and strung out in varying sequences with words like "really truly" interjected throughout the vowels and also with words of praise to the Holy One. You might wonder if the string of vowels might then be magical incantations or some symbolic way of uttering divine praise or addressing the Unknowable Holy One. Both options might be correct. The Gnostics, at least some of them, possessed esoteric knowledge that included symbolism, astrology, and numerology. It is possible that numerologically the vowels added up to some number equating with a symbolic name for God or power.

It is also possible that uttering them might have invoked some kind of magical power that afforded some degree of protection from the archons and enemies of light. A final possible meaning might be that chanting the vowels, if correctly done, induced an ecstatic trance, brought about meditative centering, or invoked contemplation in which a transcendent experience could occur.

Simon Magus (magus means worker or practitioner of magic), who was a contemporary of the Apostles, was credited with establishing Gnosticism and specifically starting a sect known as the Simonians. In his polemic Against Heresies, Irenaeus called Simon Magus the "father of all heretics."

Did the Gnostics even practice magic? Probably. Some sources say Gnostic magic was for medicinal purposes such as healing illnesses and afflictions. The Christian Gnostics certainly would have known about and possibly have had contact with the magic of the Chaldeans, Egyptians, and Hebrews. Many first-century Christians believed that invoking the name of Christ called forth unseen powers that bestowed healing and banished darkness.

However, the early church fathers, notably Irenaeus of Lyons, Hippolytus, and Tertullian, did not think magic and magical incantations had a part in the Christian experience, although in the first-century world many diverse groups worked with magic. In some non-canonical texts, Jesus was called a master magician. Irenaeus had personal experience with the Gnostics, and wrote extensively against what he considered the error of their thinking and their practices. In his writings, he gave detailed accounts of their doctrines, especially focusing on the Barbelo-Gnostics and the Valentinians. Hippolytus thought that the Gnostics' philosophy was rooted in heathenism, and Tertullian spent much of his life writing against Gnostic heresies. These three church fathers, from their positions within the orthodox church, refuted, censured, and documented the Gnostics and their doctrines.

Chapter 15

The Gospel of Judas

The Gospel of Judas provides a radical new version of the story of Judas Iscariot. The text portrays Judas as the only Apostle who truly understood Jesus. It reveals Judas as a hero for carrying out the betrayal that freed the Christ within the garment of Jesus. Those opposing that view undoubtedly destroyed the original text, but farmers in Middle Egypt discovered the Coptic copy of the papyrus codex in the 1970s. Later, antiquities traders bought and sold it. Experts have translated the fragile document from the Coptic into English.

A Divergent View of Jesus' Betrayer

Written sometime in the second century, the Gospel of Judas opens with Jesus' twelve disciples piously offering a prayer over bread. Jesus sees them and laughs. The disciples don't understand why their teacher is laughing. They tell him that they are doing (what they believe) is right. Jesus explains that they aren't performing the prayer through their own will, but by their actions their god receives praise. He tells them that they are praying to the creator god of the physical world. This god is an inferior deity. They still don't understand because they think that they know him and that he is the son of their god. When Jesus tells them that no one among them really knows him, they become angry. He asks them what provoked their anger and tells them that their god, who is within them, has done it. He invites whoever is strong enough to stand before him. The others hold back while Judas alone dares remain. He does not look at Jesus (perhaps out of respect) but says that he knows who Jesus is and from where he has come. Jesus, he says, is from the immortal realm of Barbelo (thereby acknowledging Jesus' divinity).

QUESTION?

How did Jesus know that Judas truly understood who he was?
Judas told Jesus he was from the immortal realm of Barbelo. The gospel writer's Jesus and Judas would have understood that Barbelo was the androgynous Mother-Father. She was the pronoia, or forethought, of the Infinite Father, according to Sethian Gnostic belief. All creation in the divine realm took place because of her co-action with the Father.

This initial image of Judas being the only one of the disciples who recognizes Jesus and who finds the strength to stand before Jesus contrasts with the conservative or Catholic view of Judas as being traitorous and greedy. *The Gospel of Judas*, edited by Rodolphe Kasser, Marvin Meyer, and Gregor Wurst with commentary by Bart D. Ehrman, is an excellent source for the study of this lost gospel; not only is the translation clear and presented with plenty of footnotes, but the book contains the story of the

Codex Tchacos with fascinating commentary by the translators and scholars studying the Gospel of Judas.

The Canonical Version of the Betrayal

At the Last Supper, Jesus announced to his disciples that one of them would betray him. The disciples, of course, became bewildered and asked aloud which one of them would do such a thing. Judas's name was not spoken. Jesus, however, whispered to John that it was the one to whom he would give the honorary morsel (piece of food given to the host of a feast). "When Jesus had thus said, he was troubled in spirit, and testified, and said Verily, verily, I say unto you, that one of you shall betray me. Then the disciples looked one on another, doubting of whom he spake. Now there was leaning on Jesus' bosom one of his disciples, whom Jesus loved. Simon Peter therefore beckoned to him, that he should ask who it should be of whom he spake. He then lying on Jesus' breast saith unto him, Lord, who is it? Jesus answered, He it is, to whom I shall give a sop, when I have dipped it. And when he had dipped the sop, he gave it to Judas Iscariot, the son of Simon" (John 13:21–26).

Judas Iscariot served as the group's treasurer. The New Testament portrays him as greedy, treacherous, and deceitful. He criticized Mary's anointing of Jesus with a pound of expensive spikenard, asking why the ointment was not sold for 300 pence and given to the poor (John 12:4–8). Iscariot is also similar to Sicarii, dagger-bearing assassins who belonged to the Zealots (a Jewish sect advocating violent overthrow of Roman rule).

Judas was responsible for handling the group's moneybox. When the soldiers of the High Priest Caiaphas went looking for Jesus in order to hand him over to the Roman authorities (who would then crucify him), Judas betrayed Jesus with a kiss. For his part, Judas was paid thirty pieces of silver. The orthodox Christian view was that Judas's action was one of free will and that he alone was responsible for what he did. The gospels say that Jesus knew that Judas would betray him and yet still showed him love, patience, and compassion. When Jesus washed the disciples' feet, he also washed Judas's feet.

Jesus saith to him [Simon Peter], He that is washed needeth not save to wash his feet, but is clean every whit: and ye are clean, but not all. For he knew who should betray him; therefore said he, Ye are not all clean.
—John 13:10–11.

The canonical Gospel of Matthew portrays Judas Iscariot as someone whom Jesus condemns. Mark's portrayal of Judas seems more ambiguous because he does not mention the one who betrayed Jesus by name. John said that Satan entered Judas at the Last Supper. How did the early church fathers portray Judas in their writings?

Judas Iscariot's Portrayal in Church Writings

Irenaeus mentions Judas in his writings in conjunction with his polemic against the Gnostic views put forth in a certain Gospel of Judas, which troubled him. The emerging orthodox church believed in one God, so the notion of many gods as revealed in the Gospel of Judas would be troubling for a bishop such as Irenaeus, who believed in the supreme Almighty, the one God, the maker of all that existed. Origen, another early church father, knew about a tradition that acknowledged that a group of Jesus' disciples betrayed him, but did not specifically name Judas. Celsus, a pagan whose written works have not survived but were mentioned in the writings of Origen (who wrote a refutation against Celsus's ideas in the third century), claimed it was unthinkable to believe literally in the betrayal story, since Jesus knew in advance about the act, announced it to all the disciples at the Last Supper, identified his traitor with the morsel, and made no attempt to avert the betrayal. Interestingly, Celsus also believed that Jesus claimed to be a god on the strength of magical abilities that he had acquired in Egypt.

Jesus Reveals Wisdom, Makes a Request

Jesus tells Judas to leave the others. He desires to reveal to Judas the divine mysteries in the kingdom of heaven. But first, Judas must understand that to reach the kingdom, he will have to grieve and be replaced in the circle of disciples. This section of the Gospel of Judas suggests that Jesus already knows that a betrayal must occur as a necessary act that leads to his crucifixion and death, and that the disciples will elect Matthias to replace Judas. As they converse privately, Judas asks Jesus when he plans to reveal all the mysteries of the kingdom of God and when the superior generation of beings will be glorified. No response comes from Jesus as he suddenly departs.

When Jesus returns, the disciples want to know where he went and what he did there. Jesus discourses on visiting a realm of spiritually superior beings whom the disciples will never see and with whom mortals can never associate. He reminds the disciples that they themselves are of a generation of human beings who are mortal. Perhaps he meant for them to understand that the other generation of beings he visited were immortal or incorruptible as opposed to humans. Again, the disciples felt disconcerted and stopped talking.

The Disciples' Vision

In the next section of the Gospel of Judas, the disciples discuss with Jesus a troubling vision they have had in which they visit the Jerusalem Temple. They tell Jesus that in the vision they see a house with a large altar where twelve men who are the priests invoke "your name." They tell Jesus that they are kept waiting by the priests. At that juncture of the story the Gnostic bias against the orthodox point of view starts to seep in, for the disciples tell Jesus that priests are sinful and lawless.

FACT

King Solomon built a magnificent temple in Jerusalem during his reign, and when he inaugurated it, he offered prayer and sacrifice. Four hundred years later in 586 B.C., the Babylonians destroyed the temple, but within seventy years the temple was rebuilt. During Herod's reign, the temple was enlarged. Sacrifices were again offered.

Jesus reveals that the individuals that the disciples saw accepting offers at the altar are the disciples themselves. They serve the same god as the Temple priests in their vision. This must have been difficult for the disciples to hear, but the text does not say how the disciples reacted. Jesus expounds further upon the vision, telling the disciples to stop sacrificing. The sacrificial cattle, he tells them, are the people that have been led astray by those (the orthodox priests) invoking Jesus' name. Just as the cattle die, so, too, will those led by the emerging dominant church leaders experience spiritual death. Those priests, Jesus tells them, are working with the creator god of the material world. The text continues in that vein with Jesus suggesting that the priests' time will end and they will have to answer for their actions.

Meaning of Judas's Vision

Judas inquires about the fruit produced by the human generation. Jesus answers Judas by saying that all the souls of humans perish whereas the souls of the spiritual generation remain alive and are taken up once their bodies die. Jesus explains that seeds cast upon rocks do not grow (the result of Sophia's fall from grace). This passage is similar to the Parable of the Sower found in Matthew 13:1–23. Jesus again departs.

The Gospel of Judas picks up once more with Judas recounting a vision in which the other disciples were stoning him. Jesus laughs and calls him the thirteenth (spirit or demon). The translators put the word in as "spirit" but in the footnote they also offer the word "demon" and explain it is because the Coptic word they have translated is from the Greek *daimōn*. Jesus tells Judas that he will ascend to the realm of the spiritual generation. Judas will be exalted and will rule over the other disciples, but they will curse him.

Sethian Gnostic Teaching

The gospel states that Jesus invited Judas to receive a secret teaching about the generation of the cosmos, the great invisible Spirit, and the emergence of the Divine "Self-Generated." Jesus discussed with Judas how the Self-Generated emerged first from a cloud and how, later, four angels also emerged to be the Supreme Being's attendants. Numerous other angels came into being. Finally, Adamas (an enlightened being, the exalted alternate version of the human Adam, also comes forth to begat the incorruptible race of Seth. Adamas emanates seventy-two luminaries and they bring forth 360 more of the incorruptible race. Many more beings are emanated along with heavens for the luminaries. At this point in the narrative, Judas perceives the world of the immortals, the cosmos, and the underworld. The rulers include Seth (also referred to as Christ), Harmathoth, Galila, Yobel, and Adonaios. Judas learns that the angels or luminaries are the ones who created humans and he desires to know if humans have immortal spirits. Jesus' reply seems to suggest that the "breath" of life that animates humans comes through the angel Michael as a loan (so humans can offer service) but for others, "the great generation," the spirit and soul come as gifts through the angel Gabriel.

What Jesus Saw in the Stars

The text of the Gospel of Judas breaks and then resumes with Jesus discussing what will happen to the irredeemable generations of humanity. Jesus laughs and answers that the stars will guide them and their rulers to their completion and ultimate destruction. Jesus refers to the stars as "wandering," which may mean the planets that the ancients saw moving through the heavens. They believed the planets exerted influence over human life. Astrology was studied in the Greek-speaking world and showed up in Platonic, Stoic, and other traditions. The ancients studied the heavens and knew about astronomy and astrology; they performed calculations, making predictions based on their findings. As mentioned in Chapter 14, the Gnostics may have named some of their archons after planets bearing Babylonian names.

After Jesus' discussion about the stars, Judas asks him what the Christians (those baptized in the name of Christ) will do. The Gospel of Judas text is then missing about nine lines but continues when Jesus declares that Judas will be exalted above all of them because Judas will sacrifice the body that clothes the Christ. In other words, Judas will enable Christ to discard what he has put on (the fleshly body that is Jesus) and the Christ, the Divine Self, will live on.

Jesus instructs Judas to look up at a cloud that had light with stars around it. Judas did as he was told and entered the cloud. Afterwards, a voice speaks from the cloud but the text becomes again corrupted by a lacuna, so no one knows what the voice said.

QUESTION?

What heavenly images did the Babylonian astrologers observe to make their divinations?
Although the two brightest objects in the sky—the sun and moon—were most important, the Babylonian astrologers also considered the phases of the moon, stormy or clear skies, a halo around the moon, any eclipses, and even strikes of lightning and eruptions of thunder. They also used known cycles and seasons to make their divinations.

The Gospel of Judas concludes with the high priests speaking in hushed tones while Judas retreats to pray in the guest room, possibly the same guest room where the Last Supper was taking place. Judas, the text says, was being watched by scribes desiring to arrest him. When they asked him why he was there, declaring him Jesus' disciple, Judas tells them what they want to know. Judas then takes the money and betrays Jesus. There is no mention of the torture, crucifixion, death, and resurrection, since that is not the point of this Gnostic text.

Gnosis Is the Point

As with other Gnostic texts, the Gospel of Judas shows how the Gnostics developed their own traditions and stories that often conflicted with the more familiar material. Their gospels and other sacred texts offered a distinctly different lens from orthodox Christianity for viewing the events and people in the life of Jesus as well as his teachings. The Gnostics taught their followers that God could be directly accessed in the most intimate way, within themselves, and without the need of an intermediary such as an authoritative member of the clergy. They affirmed transcendence through gnosis from a world that they perceived as dark, evil, and impermanent. That belief permeated Gnostic writings.

The Gospel of Judas suggests that those with knowledge of God are the "seeds" of Seth, the Beings of Light, the Incorruptible Ones. After Adam and Eve's firstborn son Cain murdered his younger brother Abel (Genesis 4:1–8), God marked Cain and banished him from Eden. Adam and Eve conceived again and the child was called Seth.

And Adam knew his wife again; and she bare a son, and called his name Seth: For God, said she, hath appointed me another seed instead of Abel, whom Cain slew. And to Seth, to him also, there was born a son; and he called his name Enos: then began men to call upon the name of the Lord.—Genesis 4:25–26

Seth appears in many Gnostic texts as the father of a new race of humans, those that "call upon the name of the Lord," or, in other words, those who are spiritual beings. Jesus in the Gospel of Judas does not say he comes to die for the sins of humanity, but rather comes as a bringer of knowledge, someone to point the way out of ignorance and erroneous thought.

A Brief History of This Gospel

In circa A.D. 180, Irenaeus mentioned in his work Against Heresies a Gospel of Judas as a fictitious account that involved the mystery of Judas's betrayal of Christ. Scholars, therefore, set a possible date for the original composition of the gospel between A.D. 130 and A.D. 170. It remains to be seen, however, whether or not scholars can definitively declare that the early church father was referring to this particular gospel. The Gospel of Judas contains a Gnostic polemic against the orthodox leaders of its time. The priests that the disciples described to Jesus engaged in all kinds of unsavory, immoral, and impious activities. The gospel declares that the solution to rectifying the problem of ignorance (not sin) that humanity faces is to replace ignorance with knowledge.

The Coptic copy of the incomplete Gospel of Judas dates to roughly the end of the third century and was discovered as the third text in an ancient book called the Codex Tchacos. Scholar Rodolphe Kasser writes in *The Gospel of Judas* that he first saw the papyrus Codex on the evening of July 24, 2001. He describes in heart-wrenching detail the condition of the fragile book that had been brought to him for examination. The Maecenas Foundation for Ancient Art currently owns the codex; they engaged an individual named Herb Krosney to try and reconstruct the history of the codex, which he did. Krosney subsequently wrote a book about his findings in *The Lost Gospel*. The short explanation of why the codex was in such terrible condition is this: before it ended up in the possession of the Maecenas Foundation, it endured the temperature variations of a safe-deposit box in a New York bank, including numerous humid summers and an episode of being frozen that caused the pages to darken. Plans are for the codex to be permanently placed in the Coptic Museum of Cairo.

Within its sixty-six pages, the codex contains three other tractates in addition to the Gospel of Judas. They include a Letter of Peter to Philip (pages 1 through 9). Another copy of this letter also was found in Codex VIII of the Nag Hammadi materials. A manuscript with the title of James supplements the version of the First Revelation of James in Codex V in the Nag Hammadi texts. Finally, The Book of Allogenes, a previously unknown manuscript, was the fourth tractate in Codex Tchacos.

Radical Departure from Orthodox Christianity's Judas

Gnostic theological interpretation veered sharply away from the conventional orthodox tale of Judas's betrayal of Jesus after the Last Supper. The Gnostics seemed to have asserted that Jesus knew about the betrayal beforehand and that Jesus worked with Judas to carry it out at the right time. But even in the canonical Gospel of John 13:27, Jesus tells Judas to quickly do that which he had to do. While the orthodox version paints a picture of a despicable and treacherous act, the Gnostics treat it as the loving act of the only disciple who truly knew Jesus, the friend who helped his Master throw off his human body and thereby release the eternal Divine Spirit of Christ.

Of course, to the orthodox Christians, that act of a friend assisting in a death wish would have been reprehensible.

In the Gospel of Matthew, Judas tries to give back the silver, but the priests consider it tainted money and decide that it cannot be placed in the Temple Treasury. They use the money to purchase the Potter's Field, which will become a burial ground for strangers.

And the chief priests took the silver pieces, and said, It is not lawful for to put them into the treasury, because it is the price of blood. And they took counsel, and bought with them the potter's field, to bury strangers in. Wherefore that field was called, the field of blood, unto this day.—Matthew 27:6–8

The purchase by the priests of the Potter's Field is said to fulfill prophecy of Zechariah found in the Hebrew scriptures, "And I said unto them, If ye think good, give me my price; and if not, forbear. So they weighed for my price thirty pieces of silver. And the Lord said unto me, Cast it unto the potter: a goodly price that I was prised at of them. And I took the thirty pieces of silver, and cast them to the potter in the house of the Lord" (Zechariah 11:12–13). So the prophecy in Zechariah was fulfilled. Judas, overcome with guilt, commits suicide by hanging himself from a tree, according to Christian tradition. After the Savior's Passion and ascension into heaven, the disciples meet to select a replacement for Judas. The fate of Judas is thus revealed. "Men and brethren, this scripture must needs have been fulfilled, which the Holy Ghost by the mouth of David spake before concerning Judas, which was guide to them that took Jesus. For he was numbered with us, and had obtained part of this ministry. Now this man purchased a field with the reward of iniquity; and falling headlong, he burst asunder in the midst, and all his bowels gushed out. And it was known unto all the dwellers at Jerusalem; insomuch as that field is called in their proper tongue, Aceldama, that is to say, the Field of Blood." (Acts of the Apostles 1:16–19).

The hanging of Judas appeared as a suicide, but the gut-bursting mess seems more in keeping with a divine act of retribution. Interestingly, Mark,

Luke, and John do not mention Judas's death. The canonical scriptures do show Judas to be a treacherous character who loved money and that, in the end, was his undoing. Judas, from the orthodox viewpoint, could have seen Jesus as a political leader in a Jewish holy war to bring down Roman occupation. It was known that Zealots (members of a Jewish political sect advocating militaristic overthrow of Roman rule) were among Jesus' followers. Perhaps this worldly-minded Judas desired a role in the government of Jesus. When he finally realized that Jesus had come to liberate the spirit rather than the Hebrew race of people, Judas sold out for thirty pieces of silver.

Troubling Questions about the Orthodox View of Judas

The Romans, Jewish priests, and elders were aware of Jesus and his ministry. They almost assuredly knew not only who he was but also what he looked like. So why was Judas paid thirty pieces of silver to reveal Jesus' identity? The betrayal and arrest story of Jesus in the Gospel of Matthew makes note that many people not only knew Jesus but had seen him in the temple.

In the same hour said Jesus to the multitudes, Are ye come out as against a thief with swords and staves for to take me? I sat daily with you teaching in the temple, and ye laid no hold on me.—Matthew 26:55

If Judas was such a villain (as bad as the devil himself, some would say), why did he not receive any mention in the writings of first-century Jewish historian Flavius Josephus? Or, for that matter, in the writings of Philo Judaeus, or other historians of the period? Why did his name and wicked deed not appear in the earliest New Testament writings of Paul, the Didache (sometimes called The Teachings of the Twelve Apostles and considered one of the oldest surviving pieces of non-canonical literature), the Sayings Gospel Q, or the Gospel of Thomas?

The Gospel of Matthew says that Judas was overcome with remorse and shame and hanged himself, but Acts states that his guts exploded. The discrepancy between the two canonical texts begs the question of which version of Judas's death was correct.

Who Was Missing at the Gathering?

One final question bears asking about Judas. After the death and resurrection of Jesus, the disciples gathered behind closed doors on the first day of the week. At the gathering, one disciple was missing; the obvious conclusion is that it was Judas. However, it appears to have been Thomas, not Judas, so wouldn't that suggest that if both Judas and Thomas were absent, there would have been ten disciples present, not eleven? Was Judas still alive, among the twelve, and still participating? According to scriptural accounts, Judas was alive after Jesus had risen.

Then said Jesus to them again, Peace be unto you. . . . And when he had said this, he breathed on them, and saith unto them, Receive ye the Holy Ghost: Whose soever sins ye remit, they are remitted unto them; and whose soever sins ye retain, they are retained. But Thomas, one of the twelve, called Didymus, was not with them when Jesus came.—John 20:21–24

The Gospel of John does not clearly say that Judas and Thomas were absent. The Gospel of Luke does not shed any light either, except to say that the disciples had gathered together and there were eleven of them.

And they rose up the same hour, and returned to Jerusalem, and found the eleven gathered together, and them that were with them, saying, The Lord is risen indeed, and hath appeared to Simon. And they told what things were done in the way, and how he was known of them in breaking of bread. And as they thus spake, Jesus himself stood in the midst of them, and saith unto them, Peace be unto you (Luke 24:33–36).

The Gospel of Judas does not answer these questions either, but it treats Judas differently, showing him to be a worthy disciple of Jesus who carried out an important role as the life of Jesus came to its prophetic end. The secrets contained in that Gnostic gospel, condemned as heresy, would have remained secret if not for the Egyptian farmers finding the only surviving copy. It adds to the body of knowledge that scholars have pieced together about the diversity of ideas, opinions, and theology that developed during the earliest beginnings of Christianity.

Chapter 16

The Gospel of Truth

The original text of the Gospel of Truth was composed in Greek sometime between A.D. 140 and A.D. 180. The Coptic translation of that gospel was one of two copies found at Nag Hammadi. Labeled Codex I, 3, it survived in better shape than the second copy, Codex XII, 2, which was fragmentary. Not a gospel in the classic sense, the work does provide glimpses of Gnostic mystical doctrine interspersed with paraenesis, or an exhortation against impending evil. The text offers a Gnostic interpretation of the salvation work of Jesus.

Could Valentinus Have Written This Text?

The Gospel of Truth does not reveal its author, although scholars say it seems to have an affinity with the Valentinian school of Gnosticism. Whether or not Valentinus, himself, wrote it, remains a point of scholarly debate. In Against Heresies, Irenaeus mentioned a Gospel of Truth. Irenaeus complained that the followers of Valentinus claimed that they had more gospels than really existed, among them the Gospel of Truth. Irenaeus found the Gnostic content of the Gospel of Truth objectionable. He branded it heresy and declared that a disciple of Valentinus composed it. Many modern scholars are inclined to agree because of the similarity of the gospel with other writings of the Valentinians; some even suggest that Valentinus may have written the piece, which has been described as being written in an intricate and bombastic, though at times poetic, style.

FACT

Valentinus was born in circa A.D. 100 in Phrebonis, Egypt and died in circa A.D. 175. After having a vision of the Christ child, Valentinus established a school in Alexandria. His most notable follower in Egypt was Theodotus. Later, in Rome, his students included Ptolemy and Secundus. In A.D. 143, Valentinus was a candidate for the ecclesiastical position of bishop of Rome.

Valentinus had the benefit of an excellent Greek education in Alexandria, Egypt. Possibly he had been influenced by a Christian philosopher named Balisides. He definitely had knowledge of Plato, though it's been suggested that he picked that up through a study of the Jewish method of interpretation of the scriptures. He began a teaching career in circa A.D. 117 in Alexandria. Valentinus claimed having received Christian religious teachings from Theudas, a disciple of the Apostle Paul. The Gnostics had an affinity for the Apostle Paul and claimed, in some cases, that their secret wisdom came from Paul. Valentinus, too, inferred a kind of apostolic connection by claiming that he had studied under the tutelage of Theudas.

Irenaeus mentions the Gnostic claim upon apostolic sanction for their teachings in his *Against Heresies* book three, chapter two, verse one. Gnostic Christians most likely participated in the growing Christian community in Rome and served in various ecclesiastical capacities within the church at Rome, at least initially. Only later, under attack by the literalist Christians, did the Valentinian Gnostic Christians separate.

Valentinus, the Teacher

Valentinus was a powerful thinker who started a movement with his mystical ideas and esoteric teachings. Valentinus found a receptive audience among his followers in Egypt. When he left Alexandria and moved to Rome, he became involved in the Christian church and also taught privately. No doubt, there were many who felt that studying with Valentinus would deepen their inner spiritual lives. In was not uncommon around the Mediterranean region during that period in history for a community of faithful followers to group around a charismatic teacher, just as they once did around Jesus, the Apostles, and disciples of the Apostles. Hippolytus asserted that Valentinus had many followers in both the Oriental and Italian branch of his school.

Other Writings of Valentinus

He wrote homilies and letters (some of which Clement of Alexandria possessed) as well as sermons, treatises, and myths. His cosmic myth, Summer Harvest, told in a linear story, garnered for Valentinus the reputation of a mystical poet. Valentinus espoused a doctrine of early Christianity that differed from that held by the traditional church leaders. At one point (presumably before fully developing a Gnostic doctrine), Valentinus had been considered as a candidate for the office of bishop of Rome; however, he was not elected. The Early Christian Writings site on the Internet states that the Roman church adopted doctrines more in keeping with those of Justin Martyr, who may have even played a role in Valentinus never becoming a bishop. For more information, see *www.earlychristianwritings.com/valentinus.html*. Also, Tertullian, writing in *Against Valentinians* IV, noted that Valentinus had indeed been considered for bishop but that another, a "confessor for the faith," was chosen instead.

Audience for the Gospel of Truth

The Valentinians were intellectuals, although they came from mostly middle and lower classes. They were Christians who understood the various mystical theologies of their teacher Valentinus as being allegorical interpretations of Christian and Hebrew scriptures. The Gnostic worldview claimed that rebellious angels created the "evil" world in which to trap *Ennoia* (Perception). *Ennoia* was originally paired with *Nous* (Mind), but they divided into two separate entities. The Valentinians revered Jesus as the Word or Logos incarnate. Because humankind had forgotten the truth of the Father, the truth of themselves as sparks of the Divine, and the true path of the return home, Christ came as a savior through the dark powers of an imperfect world to lead the way back to the Divine.

But to the traditional Christians, the Father created all things, including this universe. He sent Jesus into the world of humanity to bring redemption and salvation. He sacrificed his only begotten Son on the cross so that believers could have everlasting life.

For God so loved the world, that he gave his only begotten Son, that whosoever believeth in him should not perish, but have everlasting life. For God sent not his Son into the world to condemn the world; but that the world through him might be saved.—John 3:16–17

The Gospel of Truth has been called a homily or sermon, deftly crafted, to communicate a spiritual message for those who were receptive. Perhaps the gospel's author intended to bridge the growing gap between traditional Christians and the Gnostic Valentinians. Whoever wrote it may have had in mind an audience that included the spiritual ones, who by their very nature were the Gnostics or Pneumatics and the "psychics," or those with free will to become spiritually-aware humans.

Central Ideas and Concepts of the Gospel of Truth

The main theme of the Gospel of Truth reveals that knowledge of the Father breaks down ignorance and makes possible revelation so that the return to the divine realm becomes possible. The gospel discusses how Error came into the world, and stresses that fear is a fog suffered by ignorant beings. In that fog, Error takes hold and grows in power. Jesus came from the Father to erase ignorance, prompting Error (now personified) to become inflamed with hostility and anger and to nail Jesus to the cross.

QUESTION?

Does the figure of Error in the Gospel of Truth signify Sophia or the Demiurge of Gnostic myth?
Some have theorized that a mythological figure underlies the gospel's "creation story" but others assert that Error is tied to Jesus' crucifixion and linked with destruction, putting the gospel at variance with known myths about Sophia. Still others say that Error is simply a synonym for the Valentinian idea of "lack" or "deficiency."

The Gospel of Truth holds that ignorance of the Divine is what brings about fear and terror. The gospel reveals that the way of coming to know the Father is through mystical experience (gnosis), for the lamp of divine knowledge dispels the darkness of ignorance. Another idea, not as easily understood so that it remains a bit of Gnostic mystery, is that error and ignorance are found in the Pleroma; since the Pleroma or heavenly realm resides in the Father, those things (error and ignorance) come forth from the Father—but they are neither created by him nor take away from his power. The gospel's description of Error (which appears in the first section) probably is underscored by the myth of Sophia's fall. The mythological references to her error can be found in such Gnostic texts as the Hypostasis of the Archons and On the Origin of the World.

Hypostasis of the Archons is an anonymous text found in the Nag Hammadi discovery. It features two characters, a questioner and an angel, whose discourse about Genesis provides a purely esoteric interpretation. The text has been classified as a Gnostic Christian work. On the Origin of the World is a fourth-century Gnostic text written in a scholarly fashion. It was also found at Nag Hammadi and bore no title or author's name. It deals with the cosmology of the universe and the end-time.

The Valentinians believed that error of thought, perception, and understanding represented humanity's downfall but salvation was available through interior mystical knowledge. Because of forgetfulness, many humans fall into darkness, fear, and terror. The Gospel of Truth declares that Jesus revealed aspects of the face of the Father to those who appeared like children and became spiritually strong. The gospel states that for those living in the fog of ignorance, Jesus embodied perfection and knowledge and revealed to them that which remains hidden in the Father's heart. The Gospel touches upon troubling nightmares and how a spiritual aspirant achieves clear vision and awakens to gnosis. It offers a parable of the good shepherd and another about anointing before concluding with a discussion about the relationship between the Father and Son.

Admonitions to Share Knowledge of Salvation

The Gospel of Truth interprets the death of Jesus as the supreme act of revelation. Jesus reveals the truth to humanity, the truth not only of its own origin and divine destiny but also of the very essence of the Father. Those who remain trapped in ignorance or deficiency, the gospel warns, are doomed to perish. Through narrative exposition the gospel advocates and extols the benefits of knowing the truth. For example, Christians experience joy, a personal discovery of the Pleroma, and unity with the Father. The process of returning to the Father is described as a sweet and joyful process that leads to ultimate repose within the primordial source of all things. The Father is perfection itself and when individuals ascend to the Father, they then can claim their divine birthright and the things that are theirs. The text says that blessings belong to those who share the knowledge of the truth, who do the work of the Father, and who do work among others.

Meanings Hidden and Revealed

The writer of the Gospel of Truth made frequent use of analogies. For example, those who return to sobriety from drunkness is a reference to returning to knowledge from a state of ignorance. Likewise, the gospel states that the person who has awakened is happy, meaning that the individual who is cognizant of the Father or who has a clear vision of the Divine is happy, as opposed to the one who is asleep in ignorance. For the one in ignorance, like one asleep, is susceptible to troubled dreams. The gospel goes on to describe various types of nightmares that disappear upon awakening.

Envy and strife sprout in an environment of incompleteness, the text states, but where there is no strife, unity prevails, completeness is restored. Completeness means "no lack" or "no deficiency," terms often used in Valentinian Gnostic rhetoric. Those who believe that they are not separate from the Father are incorruptible. All that exists does so within the Father, hence all physical space and things are emanations of Him. There is nothing that is not the Father. Those people who know they are of the Father will have eternal life. Such individuals are not "lacking" nor are they in any way "deficient." They are complete. But those who do not know the Father and think that they exist apart from him will perish. This particular section of the Valentinian homily seems to be saying that just as the dream world is not real, neither is the material world once you awaken. Separation from God is not possible once you know the truth—that you and God are one and that the separation exists only in the mind.

A Parable Used to Reveal Truth

The Gnostics were adepts at syncretizing existing sacred stories of other traditions and putting them upon a Christian framework. They also could reinterpret those stories spoken by Jesus to fit their own meanings. The Parable of the Good Shepherd, from the canonical Gospel of John, also appears in the Gospel of Truth. In the Gospel of John, the parable reveals how the good shepherd guards the sheep with his life, lest they fall prey to wolves.

I am the good shepherd: the good shepherd giveth his life for the sheep. But he that is an hireling, and not the shepherd, whose own the sheep are not, seeth the wolf coming, and leaveth the sheep, and fleeth: and the wolf catcheth them, and scattereth the sheep. The hireling fleeth, because he is an hireling, and careth not for the sheep.—John 10:11–13

Jesus articulates the parable in John. He explains that he is the good shepherd. He knows his sheep and will lay down his life for them. He knows the Father and the Father knows him. He reiterates that he will lay down his life that he might take it again and that no man takes his life from him but that he lays it down of his own accord.

In the Gospel of Truth, the Son is the shepherd who left behind ninety-nine sheep to seek out the lost one. The text details how ninety-nine could be expressed on the left hand but add one more number and the counting shifts to the right hand. The ancients had a way of counting up to ninety-nine on one hand before shifting to the other hand, so this was simply a real-world connection that the author of the Gospel of Truth used to express his meaning. Basically he was trying to convey the idea that the incompleteness represented by the lost sheep was restored to completion once the lost sheep was found. *The Gnostic Bible* states that the Valentinians believed that the right represented people who were psychical (or with free will, so could choose to know the Father) while the left represented the hylics (or people of the physical/material world).

Ptolemy's Letter to Flora

This is another document, not part of the Gospel of Truth, but illustrative of the Valentianin effort to convert others. Ptolemy was a student of Valentinus and Flora was presumably a traditional Christian. In his letter to Flora, Ptolemy makes a case for the necessity of reading and understanding the

Hebrew scriptures. He explains to Flora that the God of the Hebrew scriptures and creator of the Law of Moses is just, but imperfect.

According to Ptolemy, people have neither understood the Law nor him who ordained it. Ptolemy considers whether Mosaic Law is from God, the Father (who some believe to have created the universe), or the Devil (set upon destruction) and surmises that it is neither. He draws upon the gospels of Matthew and John to make a case for a just God who stands against evil. Having made the point, he explains that it is his job to reveal to her the truth and he can do that because of his understanding of the Hebrew scriptures as well as the words of the Savior. He explained that the teachings of the Hebrew scriptures necessarily had a threefold division of contributions—those from God, those from Moses, and the rest from Jewish elders.

The Law of Moses consisted of three parts or codes: the Commandments (Exodus 20:1–17), the Ordinances (a Christology and a doctrine of salvation; this section contained the spiritual code), and the Judgments (a social code that had revelance to daily life). Issues involving purity laws, taxation, divorce, and slavery were covered in the Judgments.

He credits the Savior's teachings for his understanding of the imperfection within the Hebrew scriptures. In the case of divorce, Ptolemy noted that scriptures prohibited the divorce,but a law of Moses permitted it in a case of hard-heartedness. So the Law of Moses created legislation contrary to the law of God. Ptolemy imparts to Flora a belief that the God of the Hebrews and the God that the Savior revealed were not the same. He then embarks upon an esoteric explanation of how the Savior completed the incompleteness and weakness in the law, which was misunderstood and misinterpreted.

Ptolemy offers to send Flora another letter in which he would delve into the topics more deeply. He tells Flora that he has purposefully kept his statements brief but also assures her that he has given her sufficient information so that the seeds may bear fruit (an allusion to the Parable of the Sower). He may have intended to send her a series of letters that explained the Valentinian Gnostic doctrine.

Ptolemy's letter shows his straightforward approach to the subject and the clear and linear flow of logic to his conclusions. The letter is preserved in its entirety by fourth-century church father Epiphanius of Salamis, who quoted it word for word. Epiphanius, who was born a Jew but later converted to Christianity, earned a reputation as a heresiologist who tracked down deviant teachings (teachings at variance with the orthodox doctrine). He spent a period of time in Egypt as a monk and there became aware of popular Valentinian ideas. He founded a monastery in Judea in A.D. 333 and served as the superior for thirty years before becoming the Bishop of Salamis. Ptolemy's Letter to Flora is preserved in his work *Panarion* (also known as *Adversus Haereses*).

Chapter 17

A Sampling of Other Gnostic Literature

There are many fascinating texts beyond those already described in this book that experts call "Gnostic." They are products of various ancient and medieval sects and include Valentinian, Sethian, and Syrian writings; early wisdom gospels; Manichaean, Mandaean, and Hermetic literature; and Catheri writings, among others. This chapter highlights a sampling of a few of those texts. For a fuller offering of Gnostic texts, see *The Gnostic Bible* or *The Nag Hammadi Library*, or search myriad Internet libraries for early Christian writings.

The Acts of Peter and the Twelve Apostles

This document, like so many of the Gnostic texts, relies heavily on allegory for its account of a pearl hawker who does not possess the gem he offers, but instead directs those interested in it to his city. Experts date the first part of the text to roughly the middle of the second century with the remainder dating to the end of the second or beginning of the third century. The beginning of this tractate (in Codex VI, 1 of the Nag Hammadi materials) is missing.

When the story commences, Peter and the Apostles are on a trip to spread the gospel. After finding a ship to transport them upon the sea, they sailed a day and night. They arrived at a small city called Habitation. The Apostles sought lodging and met a man carrying a book cover in one hand and a wooden staff in the other. He began hawking pearls. Peter asked him about lodging but the man said he, too, was a stranger. The man called out the word "pearls," and the rich men of the city looked at him, but not seeing a pouch or bag upon his body to contain valuables, they turned away from the hawker. The poor and the beggars heard the hawker's call, and they asked to see the pearl. The man told them that if they would go to his city they could not only see the treasure but he would give it to them for nothing.

Peter asked the man his name and was told Lithargoel, meaning the "glistening stone." The hawker told Peter that only those who have forsaken everything and who have fasted daily can embark upon the trip to his city because of the robbers and wild beasts who attack travelers to the city in order to steal from them bread, costly garments, water, meat, and green vegetables.

. . . the kingdom of heaven is like unto treasure hid in a field; the which when a man hath found, he hideth . . . selleth all . . . and buyeth that field. Again, the kingdom of heaven is like unto a merchant man, seeking goodly pearls: Who, when he had found one pearl of great price, went and sold all that he had, and bought it.—Matthew 13:44–46

Peter sighed while reflecting on the possible hardships. He thought aloud that they could do it if only Jesus would empower them. The man asked Peter why he sighed if he truly knew and believed in Jesus, adding, that he, himself, believed in Jesus and also the Father who sent Jesus. When Peter asked the man what his city's name was, the man told him Nine Gates and to remember that the head is the tenth.

The story shifts a little awkwardly to the next section where Peter and the others embark upon the journey to the city of the hawker. Peter was told that the inhabitants of the city were people who had endured. Lithargoel now appeared as a physician carrying an unguent box. A disciple followed with a bag of medicines. Peter asked the physician how to get to Lithargoel's house and was shocked when the man called Peter by his name. Jesus then disclosed his identity to Peter. The disciples fell on the ground and prostrated themselves before the Lord. The text says that they comprised eleven disciples (the title states twelve), but does not reveal the identity of the one absent.

Jesus presented the box and pouch to Peter and told the Apostles to go back to the city of Habitation and give the poor what they required to live. Peter did not understand how they could possibly find food to feed all the poor. Jesus reminded Peter of the power of his name, telling him that the invocation of his name and the wisdom of God surpassed all riches. Jesus gave them the medicine pouch and told them to heal the sick. Peter feared questioning Jesus again, so he pushed John into speaking for the group. John asked Jesus how they could heal bodies since they had not been trained. Jesus said to heal the bodies of the people who believed in him—when you heal bodies without medicines, you can later heal the hearts because they will trust you. Jesus admonished them to stay away from the rich men.

It seems odd that the journey to Jesus' island village of Nine Gates is undertaken on foot. Another oddity is that the number of disciples in the text contradicts the number in the title. Finally, there are several awkward transitions in the piece, which suggests that it is a composite work that might be Gnostic in some sense but with little in it to offend traditional Christians.

Certainly, early Christians could see the message here that the wealthy are so preoccupied with appearances (or lack of appearance, in the case of the hawker and the treasure that they could not see) that they would not hear Jesus' message nor know the great treasure that he offered to give them for free. The text also dispels doubt about the power of prayer and of invoking the names of the Father and Son.

The Secret Book of John

The Apocryphon (Secret Book) of John offers a Gnostic mythological story of the creation, fall, and salvation of humankind. The text exists in three versions translated from the original Greek into Coptic—two similar versions plus a shorter text found at Nag Hammadi. Another Coptic version from the original Greek was part of the Berlin Codex 8502.

The story is told from the point of view of the risen Christ to John, son of Zebedee. The cosmology is similar to Gnostic teachings known to early church fathers. As with other versions of the Gnostic creation myth, error occurs when Sophia, a light being, attempts to create without permission of the supreme deity or her consort. Sophia brings forth a creature known as Yaldabaoth, the creator of the material universe who has some of his mother's light/power. He then creates rulers for his world (angels). He and his attendants create man in the image of God with characteristics that each of them contribute. When Yaldabaoth is tricked into infusing man with some of his light/power, the man, Adam, comes alive.

QUESTION?

Who was John, son of Zebedee?
John was the "Beloved Disciple" of the canonical New Testament, the authority for the Gospel of John, and author of Revelation. John, son of Zebedee and Salome and brother to James, was called "Boanerges," meaning "Son of Thunder." He was one of three disciples in Jesus' core group.

The manuscript declares that the struggle for the trapped light in humans is the catalyst for the ensuing struggle of the forces of light and dark, good and evil, which is the whole point of the text—the origin of evil and the means of escaping it. When woman is created, and man knows woman in sexual desire through their physical bodies, the light is kept trapped and escape becomes difficult, but not impossible. Christ comes into the world to broadcast the news that humans have forgotten their divinity. Those who renounce the material world and live ascetic lives return to the heavenly realm of perfection, but those who do not reincarnate.

FACT

The Apocryphon of John existed prior to A.D. 185 because Irenaeus referred to it in Against Heresies as among the writings possessed by unorthodox teachers. There are four versions of the text—three are Coptic versions from the ancient Greek found at Nag Hammadi and another version survives as part of the Berlin Codex 8502 found in Akhmim, Egypt.

John writes that at the temple one day, he encountered Arimanius, a Pharisee, who castigated him, telling him that Jesus was a deceptive Nazarene who had turned John away from his ancient Jewish traditions. John retreated to a solitary place where he grieved and prayed for answers to his questions about the Father God, Jesus the Savior, the realm of the imperishable ones, and the future.

He found himself suddenly in the middle of a divine visitation. Heaven opened and the world below could be seen. John observed a boy who changed into a man who then became like a servant. John explained it was a single being showing likenesses in three different forms. The being asked John why he had doubt and fear and explained that he was the undefiled and incorruptible Father, Mother, and Son who was going to teach John hidden mysteries about the immortal ones. John then received a detailed description of the Monad, the Invisible Spirit, as majestic Perfection that bestows knowledge, grace, life, blessedness, goodness, mercy, and redemption.

John was told that the Forethought of All, the first power of the Invisible Spirit, emerged as Barbelo (the Mother/Father, First Man, and Holy Spirit). From the Invisible Spirit and Barbelo, emerged Forethought, Foreknowledge, Indestructibility, Eternal Life, and Truth.

QUESTION?

What is a visionary gospel?
Narrative accounts in ancient times evolved into the Christian gospel as a means for declaring their faith. Often they included visions, post-resurrection stories, and miracles, such as healings. Other types of gospels are the sayings gospels, like Thomas and Q, which contain the sayings of Jesus.

The Apocryphon of John describes the five powers that emerged from the Invisible Spirit and Barbelo as androgynous emanations (although each is made up of a masculine and feminine Aeon). Therefore, ten Aeons make up the unknowable Divine Parent. From this beginning all others emerged, including Christ and Sophia.

Here again, the myth of the Gnostics stays true to the storyline of Sophia trying to create on her own without permission of the Invisible Spirit or her own consort, thus bringing forth Yaldabaoth, the arrogant one. He created many Aeons and then proclaimed himself ruler over them. His mother Sophia wept and repented and everyone in the Pleroma heard her. The Invisible Spirit allowed for Sophia to return to the ninth level, one above the Demiurge that she had created, until she could correct the deficiency her act had caused. In the meantime, the Secret Gospel of John states that Yaldabaoth called upon his powers to create a human being, Adam, starting with a variety of souls: bone soul, sinew soul, skin soul, blood soul, and so forth. In mind-numbing detail, the gospel lists every power involved in the creation of man's body parts as well as the seven powers in charge of the senses, and the demons of the whole body.

In great detail, the Apocryphon of John describes how Adam came into being and received the gift of light/life. Actually, it was three men (psychic, pneumatic, and hylic) that came into being in the body of one man who remained lifeless. Adam was imperfectly made, so the angels of the first archon told the Demiurge Yaldabaoth to breathe out the power of his own pneuma (the light power of his mother Sophia) into the Adam's face. When he did, Adam moved with life. But he was so strong and bright that the rulers became fearful and they cast him into the darkest regions of the physical realm. The pneuma seeds remained in Adam, but the powers of darkness no longer had complete control over them. Thereafter, the struggle ensued between the powers of light and the powers of darkness.

The most exalted deity found in the Apocryphon of John is synonymous with the Greek abstract idea or concept of perfection. From this impersonal being, who has no involvement in the material world, beings of light, including Christ and Sophia, emerge.

The risen Savior instructs John to write down the revelation about the mystery of the immovable race. John must keep it safe, for anyone trying to exchange the revelation for food, drink, or clothing will be cursed. Then John declares that he goes to the other disciples to tell them what has been revealed to him.

The beginning of the text explains how Christ emerged when the Invisible Spirit "gazed" upon Barbelo, who became impregnated with the pure light of the spark of the Invisible Spirit. The Invisible Spirit then anointed the Christ with "goodness."

The Apocryphon of John seems to emphasize the importance of Barbelo and Christ asking and receiving permission from the First Parent before emanating others. Afterwards, the First Parent is praised. In contrast, Sophia did not seek permission or create with her consort (the established protocol) and, therefore her offspring was a monster created in error, and he, in turn, created an imperfect shadow world of the heavenly realm.

FACT

Christianity takes its name from the word "Christ." The Greek word is Christos, which means "anointed one." The ancient Hebrews anointed their sacred objects, such as vessels, and also their priests as an act of consecration. References to anointing of the high priest is found in Exodus 29:29 and Leviticus 4:3. The canonical gospels share accounts of the anointing of Jesus.

The Dialogue of the Savior

The Dialogue of the Savior, a fragmented manuscript with many lacunae in the first part of it, details a dialogue that the Savior has with his disciples Mary Magdalene, Matthew, and Judas, although further along the text refers to twelve disciples. Nowhere in the manuscript is the speaker ever called Jesus or the Christ; rather, he is referred to as the Lord or Savior. Many of the questions that the disciples ask and the Savior answers parallel the traditional sayings found in the canonical gospels as well as in the Gospel of Thomas. Some of the sayings, which may have been part of an older tradition and certainly were circulating prior to the writing of the gospels, were elaborated upon and reinterpreted upon the framework of Gnosticism. However, it is important to remember that the Gnostic sects did not all hold the same beliefs, were fiercely independent, and did not establish a hierarchy of leadership like that of the emerging orthodox Christian church. The disciples of Jesus, the author reveals, still had work to do while they were in the flesh, but the time of rest was coming, just as it had come for the Savior. Their work was also the work of their Lord while he was enveloped in a garment of flesh—to save souls and extol the greatness of the "revealer."

The greater part of the Dialogue of the Savior consists of sayings that address redemption, rest, work of the Christian life, and the passage of the Gnostic soul through the powers to its final resting place (the latter topic also was addressed in the Gospel of Mary (Magdalene). Other literary pieces have been woven into the manuscript, including some baptismal theology, apocalyptic revelation, cosmological wisdom, and creation mythology based on Genesis. A redactor has tacked onto the beginning a prayer along with some Gnostic teaching about the ascension of the soul through the dark powers to heaven. There are no mentions of the Dialogue of the Savior in other sources that could help establish the date of the composition, but experts think the most likely date for the original source for the material could be the end of the first century. Others assert that the final redaction of the work could have been around A.D. 150.

The Dialogue of the Savior describes Mary Magdalene as the "woman who had understood completely." Scholars Helmut Koester and Elaine Pagels write in their introduction to the *Nag Hammadi Library* that it addresses, among other things, the theme of continuation in the human race through the process of childbirth.

At the beginning of the text, the Savior tells his disciples that they must abandon their work, for the time has come to rest. The text seems to offer an exhortation to baptism, saying that those who seek unceasingly until they find then have rest and rule. In baptism, you symbolically die, casting off your old self to be born anew in a life in Christ.

After telling his disciples how to offer a prayer of praise, the Savior discusses how their souls, when the fleshly body is discarded, will ascend through the powers in the physical realm. He warns the disciples that they will be afraid, but to remember to be of a "single" mind or focus. He reminds them that the lamp of the body, which illuminates and therefore dispels darkness, is the mind. Luminosity comes when hearts are not dark and the thoughts of the mind are not scattered. Matthew tells the Savior that he wants to see the place of light where there is no wickedness. This suggests a saying found in Matthew.

The Savior tells that Matthew cannot see that place of light as long as he wears his fleshly body. So was the Savior saying that Matthew had to die before seeing the place of light where wickedness is not found? The Gnostics believed that they did not have to die in order to gain new life. Perhaps the text is suggesting a baptism by light, the inner light of gnosis. Once baptized in that inner mystical knowledge, conferred in or by holy light, Matthew and the others could remain in their bodies and do the work of the Savior, revealing the "Revealer" and saving souls, confident of their future in heaven where their rest and rule was assured. In fact, the translators of the text suggest that the baptismal initiation discussion pertains to the conflict over eschatology (the last days or final events in the world and human destiny).

The light of the body is the eye: if therefore thine eye be single, thy whole body shall be full of light. But if thine eye be evil, thy whole body shall be full of darkness. If therefore the light that is in thee be darkness, how great is that darkness!—Matthew 6:22–23

The Savior tells them that whatever is born of truth (the place where the Lord is present) never dies but that which is born of a woman does. Mary asks the Savior why she has come to the world she is in, whether it is for gain or to give up something. The Savior tells her it is to make clear the revealer's abundance. This leads into a section about the dissolution of the works of womanhood.

The admonishment from the Savior to find a place to pray where there is no woman should not be taken as a command to negate the value of women or withdraw from the world to become an ascetic. Rather, it is a command to understand birth in a different context—that is, through the one (issuing forth from the Father) born in Christ. In fact, the Dialogue of the Savior showcases to a degree Mary's vital role in the discussion with the Savior through her meaningful and insightful comments, even to the point of claiming that she had "understood completely."

The first-century followers of Jesus believed that the end of the world would come in their lifetime. Church leader Justin Martyr believed that the end-time had not come in circa A.D. 130 because God desired for Christianity to spread worldwide. Some modern Christians prophesied that the end-time is near.

The Sophia of Jesus Christ

A pair of documents discovered among the Nag Hammadi treasures contained such similarities that one appeared to be based upon the other. Scholars assert that the Eugnostos the Blessed tractate was directed at one audience and the Sophia of Jesus Christ was aimed at a different group, possibly non-Christian Gnostics who were already familiar with Eugnostos but for whom Christianity was something new. In the *Nag Hammadi Library*, side-by-side texts show how the non-Christian document (Eugnostos) could be transformed into the Gnostic Christian text of the Sophia of Jesus Christ. Some words are taken verbatim from Eugnostos into the other text and placed upon Jesus' lips. This raises the question of whether writers in antiquity borrowed from other texts to attribute sayings and words of explanation to Jesus in the works they were creating.

The process of drawing upon one document to modify or create another was possibly used on other Gnostic texts, such as the Apocryphon of John and the Gospel of the Egyptians, according to Douglas M. Parrot's introduction to the Sophia of Jesus Christ in the *Nag Hammadi Library*. Scholars have referred to Eugnostos the Blessed and the Sophia of Jesus Christ (also called the Wisdom of Jesus Christ) as a revelation discourse in which the risen Christ answers his disciples' questions. Two different versions of both the Sophia of Jesus Christ and Eugnostos the Blessed were discovered at Nag Hammadi. The dating of the Sophia of Jesus Christ seems to be near the end of the first century. Eugnostos may have been composed during Jesus' lifetime or thereafter.

Eugnostos the Blessed opens as a letter with a formal greeting and goes on to proclaim that even the wisest philosophers have not understood the truth about the "ordering" of the world and that they have spoken three opinions, not agreeing. The Sophia of Jesus Christ opens after Jesus has risen and his twelve disciples and some women go up on a mountain called Divination and Joy. There the Savior appears and tells them that their speculation about the world order has not reached the truth, nor has it been reached by the three ways the philosophers (who don't agree) have put forth. Right away, it is easy to see the close association of the two texts.

The similarity continues with the way both texts describe the Supreme Being as "ineffable." Jesus says the word in response, however, to a question from Matthew. And so the two texts move along, with the Eugnostos the Blessed revealing how the universe emerged out of the "ineffable" Father. A series of Aeons (male and female) emanated from him. They, in turn, along with their assorted attendants, fill various heavenly realms. Eventually humans emerge. Their realm is called the realm of Immortal Man. In the Sophia of Jesus Christ, much of the same information unfolds in Jesus' answers to his disciples' questions.

FACT

The Syrian and Egyptian schools of Gnosticism often featured in their doctrines an unknowable Supreme Being who emanated lesser beings called Aeons in pairs (male and female). These Aeons came forth in sequential order with the lowest of them being the Christ and Sophia pair. All together, they were seen as symbolizing the abstract nature of the Divine.

The Father of the Universe, according to Eugnostos the Blessed, is more correctly referred to *not* as Father but as Forefather. The text discusses how that which comes from the imperishable will never perish but that which emerges from the perishable will die. These sections of the two texts are almost identical. Both texts conclude with the revelation that the Son of Man and his consort Sophia together show forth a light that is both great and androgynous—this light is the Savior. His masculine name is Savior, Begetter of All Things; his feminine name is Sophia, All Begetress.

The Apocalypse of Peter

Peter has three visions or revelations and the Savior interprets them for him in the Apocalypse of Peter. The visions reveal hostility toward the Gnostics and their persecution by the various factions of the emerging Christian church. The Gnostics look like traditional Christians on the outside but inwardly they know they are different because of their immortal essence. The apocalyptic part comes in when the Gnostics yearn for the Son of Man to return (Second Coming) to judge the aggressors and oppressors and prove right the beliefs of the Gnostics.

The Apocalypse of Peter has been dated to roughly the third century. Although not accepted into the canon of the New Testament, Clement of Alexandria regarded the Apocalypse of Peter as a sacred scripture, and it may have been once widely circulated in the ancient world. Today, the text remains in the New Testament apocrypha. Two quite different versions from the original Greek survive, one in Greek that was discovered in an excavation of a monk's grave at Akhmim, Upper Egypt, in 1886 to 1887, and the other in an Ethiopic script found in 1910. The author of the tractate uses Peter as the authority for its content. At least three other ancient texts possess parallel passages, suggesting a reliance on a previously existing but unknown source of apocalyptic literature. The Apocalypse of Peter was likely written for a popular audience.

QUESTION?

What are tractates?
The literature found at Nag Hammadi included tractates (religious piece of writing) and codices (leather-bound books with pages made from papyrus). The codices are the physical makeup of the texts, while the tractates refer to essays or type of writings. The tractates were bound into the codices.

The Apocalypse of Peter opens with the Savior in the temple praising Peter. While the Savior was speaking, telling Peter to be strong (with emphasis on spiritual authority and leadership), Peter sees a mob of priests and others with stones who seem intent on assaulting him. The Savior explains that there are blind people. He tells Peter to cover his eyes and see for himself. Told to do it a second time, Peter then saw light, and in it the Savior with the priests praising Jesus. Peter is made to understand that there are deaf and blind people and that he had to be careful about revealing things to others. Some, who do not understand or have no knowledge, will blaspheme. Some will believe him when he speaks about the Savior, but then later will fall away from their beliefs. The immortal ones who mingle with them become their prisoners. Clinging to the name of a dead man, thinking it will make them pure, the deaf and blind ones fall into error and become defiled. Peter is assured that the blind will be judged. In the conclusion to the Apocalypse of Peter, Jesus gives Peter a pep talk and tells him that his enemies will not prevail. After that, Peter "awoke" from his vision.

It is obvious that the apocalyptic text is referencing the schism between the Gnostics and the orthodox Christians, which by the third century was very much in the open. Differences between the literalist Christian and Gnostic interpretations of Jesus' life and teachings resulted in accusations of Gnostic heresy by the church. It is interesting that the Gnostic writer of the Apocalypse of Peter chose Peter to star in his account, since Peter was seen as Jesus' chief disciple and was venerated by the traditional Christian community. In fact, the emerging orthodox hierarchy saw Peter as its human spiritual anchor, referring to him as its first bishop or pope.

Chapter 18

Gnostic Texts and Early Christianity

With the discovery and translation of each new manuscript of antiquity, biblical scholars, religious historians, theologians, archeologists, and others have a new lens through which to view our ancient ancestors and their beliefs. Whether the modern mind finds their spiritual stories of creation and salvation delightful or disturbing matters less than what their stories tell us about the thinking and interpretations of those humans who were also reaching back in time to understand their world and to find meaning in it.

A Complex, Vibrant Movement

Many Christians might be surprised to learn that the birth of Christianity was anything but smooth. The polytheistic Romans ruled the world into which Christianity was born. They held political, cultural, and religious beliefs different from those of the Jews living in ancient Palestine. The Hebrew people would have had contact with myriad ideas from Roman and non-Roman influences from around the Mediterranean region and eastward into Africa and even India. Hellenistic philosophers, magicians, prophets, charismatic teachers of various belief systems, itinerant preachers, and self-proclaimed messiah figures of the Jewish tradition populated the lands around the Mediterranean. Some established schools, movements, and offshoots of existing religions. In fact, the world of Jesus was a hotbed of complex religious ideology, and the Romans enabled the spread of all the radical new ideas by making travel easier through their engineering of a vast network of roads and bridges throughout the empire.

FACT

Jesus did not found Christianity, per se. He was a Jew and his twelve disciples were all Jews, so the earliest Jesus movement was seen as a Jewish sect, albeit a reformed one. The first few centuries bore witness to the embryonic Christian religion redefining itself, not as a variant Jewish religion, but as a new movement with roots in the older faith.

As Christianity evolved, it grew increasingly diverse in both converts and various branches that soon developed. The branch of the church that remained close to the traditional Apostolic teachings and was patriarchal in its view toward women emerged as the dominant arm of the church. Eventually, its ecclesiastical hierarchy gained imperial power and authority to safeguard its doctrine. But like a vibrantly healthy plant, the church developed new branches that espoused different interpretations of the life and death of Jesus and the core teachings of the Apostles. The leaders in the dominant branch of the faith had to vigorously defend their beliefs against these new ideas and interpretations of Christianity.

Conflict, Misunderstanding, and Rising Tensions

A reading of the Acts of the Apostles and Paul's letters to various infant Christian churches he had established shows that he had to clarify misunderstandings about the teachings of Jesus and the moral conduct becoming Christians. But even before Paul dealt with the issue of proselytizing Gentiles and bringing them into the Jesus movement, conflict had been brewing among the disciples. The tension between Mary Magdalene and Peter, in particular, surfaced before Jesus' death and did not abate after the Resurrection, or so we are told in some of the Gnostic writings composed after Jesus' lifetime. The canonical gospels do not address the conflict between Mary Magdalene and Peter, but, as you already have discovered in previous chapters, several of the Gnostic texts do. The disciples had their differences. And there were also differences in texts and their interpretations by the various groups of Christians.

The Gospel According to Hebrews, which has not survived but is known through the writings of Origen and Saint Jerome, attributes to Jesus a quote about his mother, the Holy Spirit, taking him to the Mountain of Tabor. Jesus' linkage between mother and Holy Spirit also occurs in the Gnostic Gospel of Thomas saying 101.

Peter also had conflicts with Paul. After Jesus' death, Peter became the spokesman for the Jewish Christian community and was credited for its growth, while Paul spread the teachings of Jesus all over Asia Minor and converted many Gentiles. But Paul refused to impose Mosaic Law upon the Gentile converts. Initially, that was a source of contention between Paul, Peter, and James. The Jewish Christians, who saw the swelling numbers of Gentile converts as a threat to their cultural heritage, became outraged. Paul was seen in the company of Trophimus the Ephesian (a non-Jew) and was arrested for a charge of bringing a Gentile into the Jerusalem Temple, thus defiling it, something he didn't actually do. The Jews vowed to kill him. He only managed to escape through Roman intervention (Acts 21:17–40). Paul, by his own admission, was by birth a Jew and a Roman citizen. The preceding represents a few instances of conflicts and misunderstandings that triggered rising tensions among the disciples themselves and the people to whom they ministered.

Differences in interpretations of the various teachings of Jesus, as you have already learned, accounted for tensions and conflicts. As various interpretations of his teachings came to be transcribed into texts, new points of contention necessarily had to be addressed by the fathers of the faith.

Spreading the Good News

After the Resurrection and Pentecost, the Apostles traveled to lands around the Mediterranean eastward to Egypt, Africa, and India and westward to Gaul and Rome to spread the gospel. As they did, they came into contact with people of varying cultures, languages, and belief systems.

QUESTION?

How does knowledge of the Gnostic material benefit modern spiritual seekers?
It affords modern readers new ways to study and discuss the complex diversity at the heart of early Christianity. Such study also encourages open discourse about beliefs of inclusion and exclusion, tolerance and intolerance, and the power of tradition versus individual interpretation.

Since the Apostles believed the apocalypse would come within their lifetimes, they did not immediately write down their recollections of the Lord's life, events, or teachings. They had received Jesus' teachings through oral tradition. Most likely, they endeavored to avoid corrupting the teachings in their recounting of the stories of Jesus' life, ministry, death, and resurrection. By the end of the Apostles' lifetimes, gospels, accounts of acts of the Apostles, hymns, prayers, dialogues with the Savior, catechesis texts, poems, and other religious writings were circulating in various Christian churches throughout the world. It is easy to imagine a tiny community of Christians in some far flung corner of the Roman empire possessing a letter or perhaps a copy of some sayings or gospel that they treasured. In time, such materials surely helped to keep the gospel message alive and spread the teachings of Jesus. The Gnostics, too, had some textual materials. Those that have survived continue to be studied by modern scholars.

Many Gnostic texts that were circulating revealed differences with the traditional four gospel accounts, Matthew, Mark, Luke, and John. These four were considered by church fathers to be legitimately written by the Apostles and their followers, while other accounts (especially those of the Gnostics) were suspect and without authority or authenticity. In short, various Gnostic texts were thought to be works of fiction and fantasy.

The Gnostic Variants

Some of the ancient Gnostic communities listened to voices from their past such as Pythagoras and Plato. The former argued that humans were of three kinds: lovers of gain, lovers of honor, and lovers of wisdom. The Gnostics most likely fell into the last category. They liked Plato's ideas as well and incorporated his argument for a lesser god (demiurge) into their spiritual cosmology. Other ancient influences resonated as well, not surprisingly, since theirs was a syncretistic approach to spiritual belief.

FACT

The Tripartite Tractate, Codex I, 5 in the Nag Hammadi library almost appears to be an apology for Western Valentinianism. It emphasizes that the Psychics, the second division of humans in the Gnostic hierarchy, have a choice about their ultimate destiny of whether or not to return to the Pleroma. It goes beyond the elitism of other Gnostic texts that favor the Pneumatics for such a return.

In antiquity, the Mandaeans were a sect of Gnostics who revered John the Baptist as their last great holy teacher and believed that the first Mandaean was Adam, who communed directly with God. They did not believe in Moses or Jesus and had differences with later Gnostic sects while also sharing some of the same beliefs, including the dualistic ideas of a divine Mother and Father, male-female pairs of Aeons in divine and lower realms, light and dark, right and left, etc. They engaged in public worship and baptismal rites, adhered to strict dietary rules, and rested on Sunday, their holy day.

The Gnostic Christians placed upon the framework of Christianity diverse ideas that set them apart from traditional Christians and also other Gnostic sects. But Gnostic ideas, because they necessarily relied on personal visions and revelation of spiritual truths, posed the biggest threat to the dominant branch of the early church. The early church fathers accused the Gnostics of perpetually changing their opinions and viewpoints in contradiction of their own doctrines. Those fathers believed that the Gnostics were innovators and their various schools of thought formed no part of Jesus' original teachings. The Gnostic claims of possessing secret teachings of Jesus brought about vigorous refutations by the orthodox fathers. However, there must have been some truth that Jesus imparted secret teachings or gnosis, because even the canonical gospels refer to them.

And he said . . . Unto you it is given to know the mystery of the kingdom of God: but unto them that are without, all these things are done in parables: that seeing they may see, and not perceive; and hearing they may hear, and not understand; lest at any time they should be converted, and their sins should be forgiven them.—Mark 4:11–12

A similar saying appears in the Gospel of Matthew. "He answered and said unto them, Because it is given unto you to know the mysteries of the kingdom of heaven, but to them it is not given . . . Therefore speak I to them in parables: because they seeing see not; and hearing they hear not, neither do they understand" (Matthew 13:11–13).

The Gnostics Speak Through Their Writings

Christian heresiologists—Ignatius of Antioch, Polycarp of Smyrna, Irenaeus of Lyons, Hippolytus of Rome, Tertullian of Carthage, and others—used their rhetorical, reasoning, and writing skills to wage a rigorous campaign against false teachers and their Jewish, Gnostic, pagan, and otherwise heretical ideas that polluted the Christian doctrine, at least as the traditional Christian fathers understood it. After Emperor Constantine stopped religious persecution and allowed Christians to worship freely, the church leadership was able to police its own congregations, label individuals as heretics, and excommunicate offenders. Once the offenders were cast out of the church, their writings were destroyed, often burned. But modern scholars were able to learn about them through the writings of the heresiologists, who, in their defense of traditional Christianity, wrote polemics against the opposition and often quoted the offensive works, sometimes in totality.

The loss of Gnostic texts was irreversible. Modern scholars have known about secret texts, but many such writings did not survive the destruction by the Church. Modern excavations, mainly in Egypt, have turned up spectacular discoveries of Gnostic materials. Of course, there have been amazing accidental discoveries of manuscripts by peasants. Insightful scholars who kept a vigilant eye on the antiquities trade have also recovered some ancient sacred texts having to do with the origins of early Christianity. In these ways, many of the Gnostic writings that were once thought forever lost to humankind have been found (and in some cases, purchased for a great deal of money).

QUESTION?

What is a creed?
A creed is a doctrine of faith that includes a statement of belief to live by. Ancient creeds included the Apostles' Creed, the Nicene Creed, and the Athanasian Creed. Modern creeds in Christianity are found in branches including Baptist, Episcopal, Lutheran, Mennonite, Reformed, Orthodox, Puritan, Quaker, Roman Catholic, and others. The Creed of Apelles is a Gnostic creed from the second century.

Through the diligent efforts of scholars, the voices of ancient Gnostics and early Christians reveal that Christianity did not come about through one being founding a movement, but rather by a group effort during a tumultuous time in history. Christianity survived to become a major world religion, with Roman Catholic and Eastern Orthodox churches representing the dominant traditional branches and numerous divisions splitting off to establish reformed congregations.

The Orthodoxy's Fear of Gnostic Views

Assuredly, the emerging dominant branch of the Christian church viewed the Gnostic doctrine as a threat for various reasons, among them the Gnostic belief in a feminine aspect of God (as opposed to the God of Israel who did not share his authority and power with a female), an elaborate cosmology with androgynous male-female Aeons, a belief that the creator God is the Demiurge and that the physical world he created was evil, the role of women in Gnostic religious services, an emphasis on salvation through gnosis, and a refusal to submit to the leadership and authority of the church through its priests and bishops. Despite the suppression of their texts and teachings, some Gnostic sects remained popular until between the fourth and fifth centuries, eventually dying out only to resurface and flourish again at different points in history and in various parts of the world.

Today there are two main branches of Gnosticism, the French and the English. France, formerly called Gaul, was home to Irenaeus, Bishop of Lyons. The Gnostics in France trace their lineage back to those whose ancestors lived during the lifetime of Irenaeus. Of the various sects of French Gnostics, the medieval Cathars, also known as the Albigensians, are perhaps best known. Their movement rivaled the popularity of Marcion and Arian in the early centuries of Christianity, and that worried the church. Pope Innocent III, in concert with the French King and crusaders, made a bold attempt to eradicate Gnostic and Arian heresy entrenched in the south of France, first through peaceful means and then, when that didn't work, through a massacre of the Cathars on Mary Magdalene's feast day (July 22). The Inquisition followed.

Gnostics Reinterpreted Orthodox Views

Traditional early church fathers scoffed at the claims of some Gnostic sects to possess teachings of Jesus so sacred as to be guarded and kept secret from the masses and imparted only to those souls "ready and mature enough" to receive them. The early church fathers welcomed people of all races and social strata if they were willing to say the creeds, be baptized, partake of communion, and promise to live a Christian life. The Gnostics, on the other hand, were more selective and welcomed into their groups only those who would adhere to the sect's teaching with a strict devotion and high level of self-discipline. This necessarily eliminated a lot of people. Gnostic Christians sought deeper insights and meanings from the gospels, whether or not the texts were "authorized" versions. They honored those who derived understanding from Jesus' teachings for their spiritual maturity. Those who received inspired revelation were not criticized for indulging in flights of fancy or accused of lying, as Peter had inferred with Mary Magdalene's vision, but instead were considered blessed.

Secret Teachings

The Gnostics welcomed the gifts of Spirit in whatever form they took— that is, whether through inner visions, revelations, the charismatic speaking in tongues, or prophecies. They were in some ways elitist in that they believed that not everyone who practiced religion was spiritually evolved or could ever be among the "chosen ones." Only their most spiritually advanced received secret teachings. In the Gnostic Secret Book of James, in the midst of the twelve disciples, Christ appears and chooses only James and Peter from all the others to whom to impart some secret knowledge. The orthodox fathers rejected the notion that Jesus imparted secret teachings that the Gnostics possessed, and also found offensive the implied superiority of those receiving such knowledge. Irenaeus accused the Gnostics of claiming to have discovered more knowledge through their gnosis than what the Apostles knew. He wrote that the Gnostics thought the Apostles had preached a gospel influenced by Jewish opinion.

The discovery of numerous Gnostic writings unearthed at Nag Hammadi that were copies of original texts, some of which may date to the Apostolic Age, suggests that perhaps the Gnostics did possess some secret teachings.

The Gospel of Thomas contains sayings (on which that gospel was based) that may even predate the New Testament gospels of Matthew, Mark, Luke, and John, according to some academics.

Howbeit we speak wisdom among them that are perfect: yet not the wisdom of this world, nor of the princes of this world, that come to nought: But we speak the wisdom of God in a mystery, even the hidden wisdom, which God ordained before the world unto our glory.—1 Corinthians 2:6–7

The early orthodox leaders stressed unity of their churches in the doctrine taught and obedience to the church's growing power and authority. They saw any deviation as a threat that could erode the church's growing power and authority. The Gnostic emphasis on individual effort to gain spiritual knowledge and salvation ran counter to the orthodox position. Despite their popularity, many Gnostic sects lacked a strong organization. That worked against them and helped the dominant branch of early Christianity suppress the various Gnostic doctrines and sects. The Gnostic systems flourished from the second century to roughly the middle of the fifth century. Their numbers continued a steady decline, and they were eventually eradicated as heretics—that is, except for isolated secret underground movements. Some say the Gnostic sects disappeared because of political and social reasons, a lack of hierarchy, no organized means for holding the sects together, and doctrines that appealed to those who were intellectually and philosophically inclined rather than to the masses.

It is possible that on some library shelf in a monastery somewhere, a research scholar might still discover an unknown Gnostic manuscript, or that another earthenware jar in Egypt will be unearthed and found to hold priceless ancient Gnostic writings. After all, no one knew about the texts at Nag Hammadi until a peasant looking for fertilizer happened upon them. The world might just get lucky again and find some ancient Gnostic text that a versatile scribe copied and a well-meaning monk hid for future generations. Archeologists are still digging in Egypt and elsewhere.

Chapter 19

Modern Scholars Examine Ancient Texts

It is remarkable that many of the ancient Christian and Gnostic writings have survived centuries of assault from weather (temperature fluctuations and humidity), mishandling, and deterioration from exposure to insects, mildew, and rot. A few survived in decent shape and relative completeness while others exist in only fragments. Scholars have reconstructed some texts using a variety of methods, including sorting and reassembling fragments, making educated guesses about missing words, and cross-referencing against other copies or translations. Their monumental efforts have contributed greatly to the scholarship on early Christianity.

The Original Sacred Documents

Biblical scholars who worked on the Nag Hammadi library have mentioned in their commentaries the language used to write each copy of the sacred manuscripts. Most often the work was a Coptic translation from the original Greek. That raises the obvious question: if the discovery was of copies, where are the originals? Many things could have happened to them. Not only ancient writings of the Gnostics, but writings of philosophers and religious texts were lost, destroyed, or fell into disuse and, therefore, were no longer copied, circulated, or passed down. Some ancient manuscripts written in Greek only exist today as fragile bits of papyri or scroll.

Today, the Nag Hammadi treasures are safely protected in the Coptic Museum in Cairo, Egypt, after spending centuries tucked away in a jar buried in the Egyptian desert. The Berlin Codex (also known as the Akhmim Codex or *Berolinensis Gnosticus* 8502), which included a fragmentary copy of The Gospel of Mary as well as The Apocryphon of John, The Sophia of Jesus Christ, and an epitome of The Act of Peter, had been wrapped, according to one story, in feathers until it was discovered at a Christian burial site in a wall niche in 1896. The Dead Sea Scrolls dating to the first century B.C. were stashed in an earthenware jar in the valley of Qumran near the Dead Sea where there once stood a settlement of the Essenes. Today four scrolls are housed in The Shrine of the Book in Jerusalem.

Interestingly, the book of Jeremiah, found in the Hebrew scriptures in a passage about deeds of purchase for land, told the ancients how to store such important documents—in earthenware jars.

Thus saith the Lord of hosts, the God of Israel; Take these evidences, this evidence of the purchase, both which is sealed, and this evidence which is open; and put them in an earthen vessel, that they may continue many days.—Jeremiah 32:14

Many of the Gnostic works are copies from the Greek, translated into the Egyptian Coptic script. With regard to the Nag Hammadi texts, the monks living in St. Pachomius Monastery near Nag Hammadi possibly copied and later hid the codices in the desert at a time when such writings were denounced as heresy. But no one really knows for certain who copied the texts. Scholars can only make educated guesses based on clues. James Robinson, editor of *The Nag Hammadi Library*, asserts that the Nag Hammadi texts have a resonance with ascetics of all times. Robinson also states that Christians composed many of the works in their original forms and that the individuals who collected the Nag Hammadi library were also Christians. So putting the two comments together, it would appear that Christian ascetics are the most likely persons to have copied and buried the texts. This again suggests the monks.

Manipulation of the Copies and Translations

How can modern readers be sure that the works they are reading have remained faithful to the original composition when numerous translators and copyists likely participated in the creation of new transmissions of the texts? That question seems particularly significant in respect to works of antiquity, especially the Bible. To answer the question, it may be helpful to first know that the Hebrew scriptures or books of the Old Testament were composed in Hebrew, with some portions in Aramaic. The New Testament was written in Greek.

FACT

Pope Damasus commissioned a standardized version of the Bible known as the Latin Vulgate when he became totally exasperated by Latin versions of biblical texts that were rife with errors. The word "Bible" derives from the Greek word *biblia*, meaning books. Jerome, a highly regarded scholar, did the work on the Latin Vulgate version.

Modern translators possess varying skill levels. So, too, in ancient times was a work necessarily at the mercy of some who may have rendered exceptional translations while others produced poor-quality works, missing sublime profundity and nuance, obscuring or, perhaps even worse, simply not understanding the meaning of passages, esoteric or otherwise. They may have introduced new errors or repeated errors in the copies from which they worked. They could have missed lines or repeated lines or words. These are just a few of the things scholars look for when they have a good control copy with which to compare a manuscript. But without the original composition or good copy of the original or other sources for comparison (the early church fathers sometimes copied an opponent's complete document to refute it) it would be difficult to know how well any ancient text has been translated, edited, or redacted.

Reasons for Alterations

It should seem obvious that if opposing groups desired to use the same sacred text but with different understandings of the work, they could modify the text to reflect their bias and further their agenda. For example, if a text contained a word or a line considered offensive or suggestive of something in conflict with a particular group's doctrine, the text could be rejected outright. In primitive Christianity, orthodox fathers could label it as heresy. Or the Gnostics could determine that the "real" interpretation was too esoteric for the orthodox and the masses and therefore keep it secret. An offending line could be changed or deleted. On a larger scale, a new beginning could be tacked on or a different ending given, pronouns could change, and other manipulations could be done. Of course, unintentional error was a possibility as well. Evidence of alterations of texts has been observed in the Gnostic texts as well as the New Testament writings.

Documents Surviving in Epitome

Epitome means a shortening of a text into a summary or miniaturized form. Some works of the ancient Greco-Roman world exist today only in the form of the epitome, or a kind of synopsis. Large works lost to antiquity would at a later time be re-created in the form of an epitome by writers attempting to stay close to the point of view and spirit of the original work. In this way, some semblance of the work continued. Here again, the writer could stay close to the original author's intent and composition, or introduce a bias not found in the original. Epitomes, in some cases, are all that the modern world has of certain lost works such as the precis (written by John Xiphilinus) for the *History of Rome* by Cassius Dio and the epitome of the Act of Peter.

The epitome of the Act of Peter is a Christian manuscript found in the Berlin Codex 8502. It details the story of Peter's beautiful virgin daughter who is paralyzed on one side. A rich man named Ptolemy observed Peter's ten-year-old daughter bathing with her mother and desired her for his wife. The manuscript then has missing text, but when it resumes, Peter must have agreed to allow Ptolemy to have his daughter because the servants are depositing the girl at Ptolemy's house. There she praises the Lord for allowing her to escape defilement. Ptolemy then has a vision in which God tells him he should not defile the girl and instead see her as his sister. God declares he is the one Spirit for both of them. Ptolemy bequeaths a piece of land to Peter's daughter. Because of her, he believed in God and was "saved." The story ends with Peter selling the land and giving the money to the poor.

Why Mary Magdalene Is Missing

Some feminist theologians have suggested that Mary Magdalene posed a problem for the emerging church. The fledgling Christian church survived through unification and organization based on a hierarchy of male clergy who wielded ecclesiastical power to varying degrees. Because of her role as eyewitness to the risen Jesus, so central to Christian doctrine, Mary Magdalene was too important and well known to be completely edited out of the canonical gospels. However, the writers and possibly later editors or scribes may have marginalized her story to serve the patriarchal orthodox bias, according to some religious scholars.

In the Gnostic Gospel of Mary, the Savior warns his disciples to be on their guard for error and to know that he is within them. It seems that they must first understand those important ideas before he will commission them to preach the good news.

It is unlikely that a faith with a woman at the center (as its founding mother) would have appealed to the patriarchal religious men of that time, and it might have posed a problem for recruiting new converts. Mary Magdalene's story was further shifted in an erroneous portrait painted by Pope Gregory the Great in the sixth century as a penitent prostitute. From that time on, she embodied the "fallen woman" with its resonance back to Eve and the Original Sin.

Mary Magdalene in the Canon

The canonical gospels mention Mary Magdalene a total of fourteen times, mostly as a name in a list. When she is included in lists of other women, her name often appears at the beginning of the list, or behind Mother Mary, an indication of her stature and importance. Those texts also say that Jesus healed her by casting out seven devils. She became his faithful follower and with other women provided for him and his entourage, out of her means. She stood at the base of his cross with his mother Mary. She and some of the other women followers went to the tomb to anoint Jesus' body with spices and found the stone rolled away and the tomb empty. Mary Magdalene witnessed the transcendent form of Jesus and bore testimony to it. She obeyed Jesus' commission to find the other disciples and tell them the good news. Following that, she disappears from the New Testament.

Mary Magdalene in the Gnostic Gospels

The Gnostic Gospels reveal that Mary Magdalene was recognized as the closest female disciple to Jesus, his companion and confidante. Jesus praised her brilliant understanding of his teachings and told her he would "complete her" in the mysteries of the Divine. He defended her when Peter asked that she be made to leave them because she was a woman. Jesus loved her more than all the other women (according to Peter in the Gospel of Mary), and kissed her often, much to the consternation of the other disciples (according to the Gospel of Philip). After the Resurrection, Mary shared a secret vision with the Peter and the others in which she saw Jesus, who praised her for not being afraid and explained how it was possible for her to see him. She did not back down as Peter challenged her secret teaching. She had proximity to the Savior, a reputation for understanding his teachings, and an ability to eloquently articulate his ideas, and she proclaimed the good news in integrity and boldness. Many would naturally flock to her after Jesus' death. Some may have considered her Jesus' heir apparent and mother of the church, an assertion that most assuredly would have been hotly disputed by the dominant orthodox branch of Christians.

FACT

The word presbytera has been found on some ancient tomb inscriptions. Since a presbyter in early Christianity was the term used for priest, some say this proves that the tombs belonged to female priests. However, others point out that the term was also used to designate an office bearer such as an administrator or teacher. In later centuries, it meant a priest's wife or an abbess.

Mary Magdalene's tradition survived centuries, emerging especially in places where Gnosticism flourished. Although she embodied the perfect apostle, the writers of the New Testament gospels did not call her one. Today, however, the Roman Catholic Church refers to Mary Magdalene as "Apostle to the Apostles" and the Greek Orthodox Church calls her "Equal Unto the Apostles." Modern Gnostics continue to revere her, and many modern women and men see in her the perfect spiritual exemplar. There is a speculation, although it is highly disputed, that she may have been the Beloved Disciple and perhaps wrote or served as the eyewitness source for the Gospel of John.

Redaction of the Gospel of John

The Gospel of John, also called the fourth gospel of the New Testament because of its order in sequence, differs greatly from the synoptic Gospels. However, that reason alone is not why religious scholars think that the gospel had a little redaction. The Gospel of John contains sayings of Jesus and some of the events in his ministry such as the feeding of the multitudes, the marriage at Cana, and the raising of Lazarus from the dead, among others. However, some biblical scholars have questioned the authorship of the

Gospel of John and have suggested that the present version shows work on the text that must have come at a time later than the original composition.

What is redaction?

Redaction means to edit, revise, or manipulate written material in order to position it in a suitable literary form. Ways in which something could be redacted include shifting the sequence of the order of things, inserting a new beginning, rearranging material, weaving new words into a document, affixing a different ending or conclusion, or framing a text in a certain way.

The suggestion of tampering with the Gospel of John prior to its inclusion into the canon comes from Greek language peculiarities found within the composition. There are breaks in odd places, repetitions in dialogue or sections of discourse, and passages of text that appear in the wrong place for the context. Biblical scholars assert that after the gospel was completed, chapter 21 was tacked on because the Greek style for that chapter differs from the rest of the gospel. John 14:31 and John 18:1 show two different endings to the Last Supper discourse of Jesus in the Upper Room. The magnificent prologue contains a hymn to open the work, but was most likely added later to open the piece and lengthen the work. The entire narrative of the gospel seems to have been arranged and adapted in a way to serve the author's theological agenda. For example, John seems to show through the writing of the gospel an opposition to the followers of John the Baptist in order to exalt Jesus, perhaps to emphasize a belief in Jesus' divinity, and to advocate the need for all Christians to be anchored in that belief. There is a touch of polemic in the narrative as well, showing the synagogue and the church at opposite poles and with references to Sadducees and Pharisees who harshly treated Jesus being referred to as "the Jews."

Marcion eviscerated the Gospel of Luke and edited out some of the letters of Paul (the pastoral Epistles) to create a canon for use in his churches. Marcion felt the God of Israel was an inferior god, subordinate to the higher God whom Jesus Christ revealed. His movement rivaled the traditional church in the early centuries. In 144 A.D., the Roman church excommunicated Marcion.

All these observations of redaction of the Gospel of John are not new. Scholars began doing the research on the inconsistencies in the 1800s. In fact, redaction criticism is now a scholarly discipline in which the expert scrutinizes the material to determine the theological agenda or bias of the author or editor. There are three things in particular that critics can search for to determine editing. They look for themes that seem to be hit upon repetitively. They compare two versions of the work to see if the latter piece has omissions or additions. Finally, the experts study the words to figure out the words that the author commonly used; if there are words the author would never use, it suggests the work of an editor on the piece. From studying a manuscript that way, experts can determine the theological leanings of the writer and editor.

QUESTION?

Why are Bibles revised?
The scriptures are timeless, but cultural changes and an explosion of biblical studies account for some of the reasons why Bibles are revised. New translations and explanations are necessary to adjust the materials to keep up with biblical scholarship and new understandings.

The Gospel of Mark stands apart from the other texts of the canon as having verifiable evidence indicating revisions of the text. Scholars know about at least four endings to that gospel and believe they were created in the earliest centuries of the church. Twelve new verses were added onto a Greek copy known as the Codex Washingtonianus. Those twelve verses cannot be found in the oldest version of that gospel. Even the early church fathers like Clement of Alexandria and Origen did not know about those verses. Scholars believe they were the work of a later editor or scribe.

Forgeries and Falsifications Exposed

Sacred theology, some say, begins and ends on the written word of God. But forgeries of texts thought to be sacred, authentic, and inspired have surfaced from time to time—not only in the modern world, where manuscripts dating to antiquity are priceless, but in ancient times as well. Before the New Testament writings, there existed the oral tradition. The ancient Hebrews lived in a heightened sensitivity of the divine presence in their lives and relied on both oral and written tradition. In the first and second centuries, there were many claiming to be messiahs and prophets with personal revelations and apocalyptic visions. The scriptures reveal that the Apostles of Jesus were empowered by the gifts of the Holy Spirit. Some of the Gnostic sects found visions and inspired revelation to be divine blessings upon the spiritually advanced or mature, and their sacred texts boldly declare their beliefs. Inherent, however, in any spoken teaching or text is the possibility of deception. The Apostle Paul wrote to the Corinthians to beware of ministers of Satan and false apostles.

For such are false apostles, deceitful workers, transforming themselves into the apostles of Christ. And no marvel; for Satan himself is transformed into an angel of light. Therefore it is no great thing if his ministers also be transformed as the ministers of righteousness; whose end shall be according to their works.—2 Corinthians 11:13–15

Many works of antiquity must be scrutinized by academics in a variety of fields to determine if the material is a forgery or has been falsified. One such work in dispute is the Mar Saba letter, alleged by some to be a modern forgery. The work was unknown to religious and historical scholars until it was discovered by Morton Smith, who published a book in 1973 about a letter supposedly written by Clement of Alexandria that Smith had discovered when he was cataloging documents at the Mar Saba monastery in 1958. He claimed that endpapers in a printed edition of *Ignatius of Antioch* (from the seventeenth century) contain the letter's text. Smith took some photographs of the letter after his discovery of it. In the letter, Clement writes to Theodore, the intended recipient of the letter, that Mark, author of the Gospel of Mark, wrote a second, more mystical and secret gospel that contained falsehoods, added by the Carpocratians. But Clement emphasized that Theodore was to deny ever knowing that such a gospel existed even if he were sworn to an oath. Clement references two sections of the secret gospel that have to do with Jesus spending the night with a rich young man (wearing only a linen cloth) as he teaches the youth about the kingdom of God, perhaps some kind of mystical or metaphysical initiation.

FACT

The Carpocratians were Gnostics who believed that Jesus was not divine but that his soul was pure and that he could remember the sphere of the unbegotten God from which he came. The Carpocratians were not bound by rules of morality or Mosaic Law because they believed both belonged to the powers of the material world.

Three years after Smith's book came out, four scholars visited the monastery to have a look at the letter and to take some photographs. Then one year after that, the volume with the letter was transferred to the Patriarchate library in Jerusalem. The librarian removed the manuscript pages, had them photographed, and, in 2000, the photographs were published. Since then, scholars have not been able to view the manuscript. No other copy of the secret gospel exists with which to compare the brief references in Clement's letter. The veracity of the letter as well as the secret gospel is being disputed.

The recent finding of a gospel bearing the name of the most reviled of Jesus' followers has also stirred controversy and raised questions of authenticity.

Some Christians have opined that the Gospel of Judas, which was only recently made available to the world to read, is a forgery. They note that it offends Christian sensibility because of its revelation that Jesus understood that Judas had to betray him, that Judas was loyal to Jesus and carried out the action as necessary, and that Jesus encouraged him to do it. Further, the Gospel of Judas, like so many of the Gnostic gospels written about in this book, points to salvation through knowledge rather than through the death and resurrection of Jesus. Those claiming the text is a fraud assert that Christians should heed the Apostle Paul's warning to the Galatians of certain persons preaching a different Christ. They noted that they did not recognize the Christ in the Gospel of Judas and emphasized that the gospel simply does not stand up to scholarly scrutiny or have any credibility as a historical document because its language places it in the wrong language at the wrong time.

The Apocryphon of James had expanded versions of sayings found in the New Testament gospels, and it made reference to other secret texts used by the spiritually advanced. Modern scholars are aware of more than fifty Christian gospels and secret writings that circulated among Christian sects in the first century.

But there are those on the other side of the argument who believe the text is genuine. For example, James Robinson, editor of *The Nag Hammadi Library* and professor emeritus of religion at Claremont Graduate University, was quoted in the *Boston Globe* as saying he was convinced that the document was not a forgery. No one likes to be duped, but everyone enjoys a good mystery.

Any text bearing the name of a famous person or sect of antiquity should be critically examined, scrutinized by scholars, and tested in every way possible to determine the truth. Otherwise, there is simply mystery, wild speculation, controversy, and dissenting opinion. The Dead Sea Scrolls, for example, illustrate the necessity for tests. Discovered in eleven caves near

Khirbet Qumran, the scrolls were believed to date from the third century B.C. to the first century A.D. Professor Solomon Zeitlin at Philadelphia's Dropsie University argued vigorously to reject the antiquity of the Dead Sea Scrolls, based on philological assessment (the classical scholarship of words and their meanings). However, carbon-14 dating proved that the linen wrappers of the scrolls dated to the late Second Temple Period. The tests confirmed that the scrolls were genuine.

Chapter 20

Gnostic Themes and Images in Pop Culture

Suddenly it seems that pop culture has fallen in love with all things Gnostic. Scholarly translations and commentaries of the Gnostic Gospels and other Gnostic texts are now published for a mainstream audience. Gnostic influences certainly have emerged in artistic creations belonging to other centuries; however, today Gnostic elements and themes are showing up in mass-market books, movies, television shows, comics, cartoons, and music. And while some observers of pop culture declare that it's only a fad, others say it's here to stay.

20

Gnosticism in Books

The Da Vinci Code is believed to be the eighth best-selling book ever, with more than 60.5 million copies in print and translations in forty-four languages. The book single-handedly sparked interest in the Catholic Church, Opus Dei, the Gnostics, Mary Magdalene, the Holy Grail, and the history of Christianity. That mystery novel builds upon the premise that a conspiracy spanning centuries has been perpetrated within the Catholic Church to cover up the truth about Jesus' story and, furthermore, that the Vatican knows the truth but hides it to stay in power. Author Dan Brown, according to the partial bibliography listed on his Web site, derived inspiration from many sources, including *The Templar Revelation*; *Holy Blood, Holy Grail*; and books about Mary Magdalene and Jesus by Margaret Starbird. Brown has his characters noticing, interpreting, and debating various topics such as the Gnostic Gospels, the holy rite hieros gamos (sacred marriage), the symbolic presence of Mary Magdalene in Leonardo da Vinci's painting of the Last Supper, a marriage of Jesus and Mary Magdalene, the Holy Grail as being not a cup or goblet but Mary Magdalene, and their child (the bloodline of Jesus) becoming ancestress to European royalty.

Among the esoteric references skillfully interwoven, the novel reveals that man requires woman to be complete or whole and also that it is possible to experience contact with the God through sacred sex in an instant during orgasm when the mind is quiet and thoughts are stilled. This "sacred sex" suggests the mysterious Gnostic ritual known as the Bridal Chamber or the sacred rite *hieros gamos* and is a topic mentioned in a number of books about the Gnostics and their religious beliefs that the novelist included in his bibliography.

Yale scholar and writer Harold Bloom is another author who has explored Gnostic elements and themes in his philosophical novel, *The Flight to Lucifer: A Gnostic Fantasy*. Bloom's work features an alien planet named Lucifer that was created by a Demiurge (whose mother is the "Dark Intention"). The story involves a veritable trove of Gnostic elements: pure being, a pleroma and transcendent fullness, archons, Aeons, a corrupt cosmos, an early Christian heresy, unpolluted Light, and a missing god. In *Geniuses*, a study of literary figures and their unique geniuses, Bloom claimed that

Gnosticism is the "religion of literature." He also wrote *The Book of J,* in which he suggested a woman was the author of the J-text (the oldest strand of narrative found in the Old Testament books of Genesis, Exodus, and Numbers). Bloom also wrote *Omens of Millennium: The Gnosis of Angels, Dreams, and Resurrection.*

Bloom's book *Omens of Millennium* was written, according to the author, from the ancient conviction that gnosis is what frees humans. The author claims that a belief in angels apart from God is pointless, regardless of whether the angels are administrators, messengers, or warriors in opposition to the Divine.

Author and philosopher Umberto Eco has a character in his novel *Baudolino* provide a detailed description of the Gnostic creation myth. Another Eco novel, *Foucault's Pendulum,* also deals with Gnostic aspects and esoteric elements, including the ten Sephirot (attributes of God) of the Kabbalah system of Jewish mysticism, alchemy, conspiracy theories, the Knights Templar, and an actual pendulum. But though those elements appear in the book, Eco's story actually appears to criticize metaphysical thinking as flawed, focusing on the search for power and the veneration of evil. Three main characters populate his story. One serves as the embodiment of the Gnostic Sophia, another is convinced that his people are the Jews, and the third holds a doctoral degree with a dissertation on the Knights Templar. Answering the archetype hero's call to action, the three become engaged in plot and counterplot in a battle of good against evil and the forces of light against darkness (a favorite theme of the Gnostics).

In his book *The Last Temptation of Christ,* Nikos Kazantzakis, Greek novelist, poet, and playwright, explored the possibility that Jesus, in his last moments, envisioned an ordinary life that included marriage and sex. The Jesus/Mary Magdalene coupling would find echoes in the Gnostic male/female or Christ/Sophia pairing. The movie of his book *Zorba the Greek* brought Kazantzakis the attention of the world, but *The Last Temptation of Christ* brought condemnation of him by those opposing the idea of Jesus as a married Jewish man with doubts. The Martin Scorsese movie *The Last Temptation of Christ* drew huge audiences and critical acclaim despite any opposition to the content.

QUESTION?

What is the Foucault pendulum theory?
Jean Bernard Léon Foucault, who studied sciences such as astronomy and physics, showed that a pendulum suspended by a wire or string swung in exactly the same arc and direction regardless of the position of its point of suspension. The idea, put to the test, provided visual proof of the earth's rotation.

Contemporary authors writing about the Gnostics and their beliefs and practices include writers working in both nonfiction and fiction, the latter in genres ranging from science fiction and fantasy to historical fiction. The nonfiction work of Timothy Freke and Peter Gandy titled *The Jesus Mysteries* deals with Gnosticism and explores the subject of Jesus as a mythical creation. The late novelist Philip K. Dick borrowed from the Gnostic tradition ideas for two novels, *The Divine Invasion* and *Valis*. Novelist Ki Longfellow presented a Gnostic Mary Magdalene in her historical novel titled *The Secret Magdalene*. Science fiction/fantasy writer John Crowley drew inspiration and elements from Gnosticism for his four-novel series *Aegypt*. Anatole France wrote a satirical work, *The Revolt of the Angels*, that features the Demiurge Yaldabaoth's doctrine and a guardian angel. And English-born writer Philip Pullman's fantasy novels *Northern Lights*, *The Subtle Knife*, *The Amber Spyglass*, and *His Dark Materials* all show Gnostic influence.

The preceding authors only partially represent the number of writers today whose works show some Gnostic influences. Gnostic belief systems provide a rich reservoir of themes, characters (especially in their cosmologies), and myths from which moderns can draw inspiration and detail for their narratives, even those of a futuristic nature requiring alternative worlds.

Gnostic Elements in Film and Television

With the worldwide success of *The Da Vinci Code* novel, a movie had to follow. But other Hollywood movies have shown Gnostic influence—for example, *The Matrix* trilogy with its religious/philosophical view of the world at some future time. The theme of *The Matrix* and *The Matrix: Reloaded* dealt with human perception of reality that is illusory because it is based on the habitual choices people continue to make due to their human nature. In many ways it was an allegory for some Gnosticism belief systems. The movies seem to say that humanity necessarily had to break free of the day-to-day world we live in to embrace the real world, to make new choices. The second film's references to the Dead Sea Scrolls and Origen of Alexandria, the early Christian orthodox father, may be missed by those unfamiliar with the scrolls or the historical figure. But the movie has resonance with modern viewers because it is about the ancient myth of the hero's journey. There is even an Oracle who beckons the hero to undertake his mission. Other elements include the Architect, the One, and Neo (as in new).

Stigmata, a film released years before the *Da Vinci Code*, dealt with a Roman Catholic Church cover-up over a lost gospel (as it turns out, the Gnostic Gospel of Thomas). The gospel's teachings, especially about God's eminence, were of concern to the church, supposedly posing a threat to the existing hierarchy.

In the movie *Pleasantville*, it is difficult to miss the pointed Gnostic-type references to an alternative world. The characters, a sister and a brother, become transported to the old TV world of Pleasantville, a joyless place where "black and white" people are ensnared in traditional morality. There is even a scene where a female plucks an apple from the tree to eat it, suggesting that when one eats of the Tree of Knowledge of Good and Evil, one becomes mature or evolves into enlightened being. In that movie, people began to be "colorized" only when they abandoned the rigid morality of the old world in order to live freer and more joyfully in awareness of their true natures.

Pleasantville and other movies like *The Truman Show*, *Vanilla Sky*, *Dark City*, *The Thirteenth Floor*, and *Twelve Monkeys* put forth in various ways the Gnostic idea that an illusory cosmology has been created to enslave or restrict humanity, and only through enlightenment or self-knowledge that illuminates the truth can humans break free of the illusion. *The Da Vinci Code* and *Stigmata* portray the Roman Catholic Church, or factions within it, as villains.

FACT

The Roman Catholic Church defines stigmata as marks of the torturing and suffering of the Christ. An invisible stigmata is where an individual experiences the suffering but not the visible signs of Christ's Passion. Saints and mystics, including Francis of Assisi, Catherine of Sienna, Catherine of Genoa, John of God, and others showed visible signs of the stigmata.

Tommy Gnosis is the name of a character in the movie *Hedwig and the Angry Inch*. The movie follows a transsexual punk rocker from East Berlin who desires to take on his mother's identity and undergoes a sex change operation. The procedure is botched and he remains with only "an angry inch." The protagonist flees to America, forms a rock band, and searches for a soul mate. The movie revolves around a pseudo-Gnostic myth and explores the Gnostic belief in the superiority of the androgynous state to symbolize spiritual maturity and higher realities.

There are a number of *anime* (Japanese-style animated TV series/cartoons) and *manga* (Japanese-style printed comics) that show Gnostic symbols, elements, influences, and themes. Seen on the Cartoon Network and elsewhere, some include *Revolutionary Girl Utena, Fullmetal Alchemist,* and *Big O.*

Revolutionary Girl Utena, a *manga* launched in 1996 and the *anime* in 1997, was inspired by a number of sources, among them Hermann Hesse's *Demian* for its Gnostic themes. The series features an androgynous teenage girl protagonist Utena who must confront conflict with different powers or rivals in each segment. There are many obscurities of motive and many mixed metaphors that are best understood on a metaphysical level. Viz Communications publishes the *manga* or comic book series for *Revolutionary Girl Utena.*

Hermann Hesse wrote many works, including *Siddhartha*, *Steppenwolf*, and *Narcissus and Goldmund*, among others. Hesse often drew upon aspects of his own personality for his characters. In *Narcissus and Goldmund*, the characters are a man of the cloth and a man of the world. Hesse explores the Gnostic idea of opposites as competing forces within each human being and both being equally necessary for wholeness.

Fullmetal Alchemist, another *manga* and *anime* with a movie spin-off as well as novelizations and video games, deals with an alternate Earth, a world called Amestris that relies on the science of alchemy to change matter into different material using transmutation circles. The protagonist is young Edward, who has lost his left leg and his right arm as a result of alchemical errors. He and his brother were trying to bring their mother back from the dead but the attempt failed. Edward lost his leg and Alphonse lost his body. To save his brother's soul, Edward gave up his arm to affix his brother's soul to a piece of armor. Edward continued his quest once his limbs were replaced with pieces of Automail. The boys become State Alchemists, learn of the Philosopher's Stone, and embark on a quest to find it. The series contains considerable Gnostic aspects throughout and are attributable to the Gnostic influences on certain real-world medieval alchemists.

Big O has been called a Gnostic drama of the modern world because it is loaded with elements entrenched in ancient Gnosticism. The plot of *Big O* revolves around its protagonist Roger Smith, a negotiator, and his attempts at conflict resolution between individuals within the doomed Paradigm City and others, including criminals. He also secretly pilots Megadeus, a giant robot (called "the Big O") left over from the world that existed prior to "The Event." It is the job of Smith to discover the truth about that event, the world (both past and present), and Paradigm City while also trying to ward off attacks on the city by various factions, internal and external.

The notion of ascension to higher states of existence and a race of ascended beings with the power and will to oppress humanity in order to steal its energy has prompted some to assert that *Stargate SGI*, the science fiction TV series, has Gnostic elements of false gods. Human energy serves as the fuel that the race of people known as the Ori used to reach higher levels of ascension.

QUESTION?

What is alchemy?
Alchemy is a pseudoscience in which base metals, or so it was thought, could be turned into gold; it also has associations with magic. The vocabulary of alchemy consists of metaphors that suggest spiritual initiation, a concept that psychologist Carl Jung explored in the world of analytical psychology. Others believe alchemy is a metaphor for sex magic.

In the world of comics, it is worth mentioning the *X-Men* series for its use of Gnosticism's philosophy of pessimism with the human world. The pessimism had resonance in Gnostic thinking and actually extended further back to Platonic ideas about social organization and the advantages of the stronger, in positions of power, to impose their will and decree what was thus right or wrong. In *X-Men*, the mutants, or homo superiors, represented evolutionary successors of humankind. Gnostic beliefs, too, included a superior spiritual elite. The Gnostic Valentinian sect embraced the tripartite division of humans as espoused by an earlier philosopher, Plato. The Manichaeans, or followers of Mani, called their spiritual elite "the Elect." The medieval Cathars referred to theirs as *Perfecti* or *Parfaits*.

Gnostic Influence on Music

Musician Tori Amos's book *Piece by Piece*, written with journalist Ann Powers, devoted two chapters to exploring the Gnostic belief that Mary Magdalene wrote the canonical Gospel of John. Amos's book emphasizes how all the experiences and influences of her life so far have contributed to her musical compositions. A hallmark of her music is haunting and beautiful lyrics that mix elements of the personal with religion and mythical archetypes, including the sacred feminine. In a series of conversations with

Powers detailed in the book, Amos ruminated on the challenges of reconciling the sexual and the sacred in women's lives and also discussed the roots of femininity and creativity. She revealed the inspirations for some of her songs. As she prepared for her ninth album, *The Beekeeper*, Amos noted that she began to research the roots of early Christianity and read *The Gnostic Gospels* by Elaine Pagels as well as the translated Gnostic Gospels themselves from the Nag Hammadi library. Amos's research into the life of Mary Magdalene and Gnostic beliefs influenced *The Beekeeper*. She sounds a call to get ready for an allegorical "coming storm" in that album.

For the lips of a strange woman drop as a honeycomb, and her mouth is smoother than oil: But her end is bitter as wormwood, sharp as a two-edged sword. Her feet go down to death; her steps take hold on hell. Lest thou shouldest ponder the path of life, her ways are moveable, that thou canst not know them.—Proverbs 5:3–6

Bill Nelson, from Yorkshire, England, is not only a guitarist but also a songwriter and painter who has found the Gnostic world fecund ground for inspiration. Nelson has been pursuing Gnostic interests for over twenty years. His album *Chance Encounters in the Garden of Lights* features Gnostic elements and titles that suggest Gnostic influences. In the album's dedication, he wrote that he offered the creation to his fellow initiates as testament to "the gnosis and a confirmation of the world within."

David Bowie, in his music, song lyrics, and stage personas, expresses an esoteric fragmentation of the world through his art. Some of his song lyrics sound an appeal for a salvation from the evil world while others explore dichotomies, polarities, and alienation (Gnostic ideas). Bowie entertains as much through his various "emanations" on stage as through his Herculean endeavors to reinvent and express himself through his music.

The title of "Spirits in a Material World" clearly reflects an ages-old Gnostic concept. The song by the pop rock group The Police was a hit in the 1980s.

Gnostic Imagery in Art

The nineteenth-century artist and poet William Blake expressed a distrust of the material world in his prolific writing and works of art. Blake, a mystic, created many images that resonate with those found in the ancient world of the Gnostics. Most scholars hesitate to call Blake a Gnostic, yet many of his mythological images suggest parallels in Gnostic cosmological angels, demons, and even the Gnostic Demiurge. Blake's series of line engravings for illustrations in the Book of Job combines images from his own personal mythology along with quotes from the Bible. Job's spiritual awakening, in Blake's view, had a parallel with the spiritual awareness and vision of the poet and artist. In his watercolor renderings for Dante's Divine Comedy, Blake painted Dante attired in a red color throughout the series to represent the carnal world of experience, and he depicted Virgil in blue to convey the world of spirit. These two worlds remain in conflict in Gnostic belief.

The painting of Sophia by artist Alex Grey is part of a series he calls "Sacred Mirrors." The visionary artist has rendered many ancient mythological and Gnostic ideas into images of the archetypal beings who must struggle toward cosmic understanding and unity. Grey's paintings are as anatomically detailed as could be found in an atlas of human anatomy. His artistic vision is for a humanity that is flawed but that can become perfected. Grey's own personal journey into the world of transcendence through his own spiritual search enabled him to create twenty-one paintings, the Sacred Mirrors, that allow viewers to embark upon a journey into their own divinity. Recognition of an individual's divine nature and journey toward self-knowledge echo ancient Gnostic concepts.

Gnostic Games

Gnostic elements in popular culture are also found in popular games (including video and computer games), especially those that are interactive and involve role-playing. Dungeons & Dragons has been around for many years, but continues to excite players. Complementing the game now are companion books replete with Gnostic ideas. One, for example—*The Book of Exalted Deeds*—reveals details about a figure that appears to be Pistis Sophia, the archon of the game's monks (who are experts in martial arts).

The Book of Exalted Deeds serves as a sourcebook for the interactive game of Dungeons & Dragons. It reveals a magical artifact considered extremely powerful for the game. The book helps players who wish to wage campaigns utilizing good forces and good alignment. Other supplement books include *Complete Arcane* and *Book of Vile Darkness*.

Final Fantasy VII and *X* feature Gnostic elements, themes, and references, as does *Kult* and *Aeon Flux* (the latter is an MTV animated science-fiction TV series). Elder God is a character of *Defiance*, the most recent of the games in the series called the *Legacy of Kain*. *Defiance* contains numerous Gnostic elements and references. Finally, one other game worth mentioning that is replete with Gnostic ideas and images is a game called *Tales of Symphonia*. It features two worlds, one declining and one emerging. Angels are not the divine beings traditionally portrayed. The quest, the central element of any game, is based on an untruth perpetrated by the church and necessitates the overcoming of the powers of Lord Yggdrasil, who is unquestionably a demiurgical character and the game's main villain.

Appendix A

Glossary

anoint
To rub with olive or scented oil as an act of consecration.

Aramaic
The first-century language spoken by Jesus and many of his disciples.

Apostle
One of the twelve disciples Jesus commissioned to teach the gospel.

Achamoth
The lower Sophia as opposed to the original (or higher) Sophia in Valentinian Gnosticism.

Aeon
Derived from the Latin aeon, meaning "forever," an Aeon was an emanation of the Supreme Being much as the Judeo-Christian angel is a being of light. However, in Gnostic doctrine, the first being is an Aeon with its own inner being, Ennoea (Thought).

Adamas
Divine Adam and father of Seth in the Pleroma, not to be confused with Adam, the father of humanity.

androgynous
Being both male and female. Adam, the first human, was created as an androgynous being. In Gnostic doctrine, many emanations (Aeons or attributes of God) are male-female.

apocalyptic
Pertaining to the biblical prophecy of the apocalypse or end-time. Revelatory prophecy of the destruction of the universe.

Apocrypha
Various religious literary works of questionable origin. Some people regard such works as inspired, but others reject them because of questionable authenticity or authorship.

Apologists
Early Christian writers who defended and explained Christianity.

archon
Ruler, notably an angel of the world of matter associated with the chief archon, the Demiurge.

Arimanios
The Pharisee's name in the Apocryphon of John.

Autogenes
One who is "self-begotten" or "self-generated." In a number of Gnostic texts, Autogenes is an epithet for the Divine.

Barbelo
The first emanation of the Unknowable Father of All. In Sethian Gnostic writings, Barbelo is the Divine Mother. She is also referred to as the forethought of the Invisible Spirit.

Basilides
A teacher of Christianity who lived in the early part of the second century and whose school of Gnosticism was eclipsed by Valentinus.

Bridal Chamber
A mysterious Gnostic sacrament that might have involved a sacred sexual act or the mystical merging of male/female energies using esoteric knowledge and techniques such as meditation.

Coptic
One of the ancient Egyptian languages. Many Gnostic texts that survive from antiquity are translations from the ancient Greek into Cop-

tic. The Egyptian Coptic Church still uses the language in its liturgy, although the language is considered extinct.

codex
The earliest form of a book, used by the Christians from the first century onward. A codex usually contained a stack of manuscript pages stitched together and placed inside of a leather cover and tied. The codex replaced scroll and wax tablets of earlier times.

creed
A formal declaration of the chief articles of Christian belief.

Demiurge
Creator god or supreme craftsman in the various creation stories, especially in Platonic philosophy and the Gnostic narrative of Genesis. The Demiurge and lesser gods fashioned the material world out of chaos.

Docetists
Early Christians who believed that Christ only appeared to die on the cross. Some ancient Gnostics favored the belief that Jesus did not have a body and therefore neither suffered nor died.

Error
Error (female in gender) is personified in Valentinian Gnosticism as the opposite of Wisdom.

Essenes
A sect of first-century Palestinian Jews who practiced asceticism. The Dead Sea Scrolls, believed by experts to have been manuscripts of the Essenes, were discovered at Qumran, a village in which the sect members lived.

Eucharist
The ritualistic eating of blessed bread and wine in Christian worship. The Eucharist is also one of the five sacraments of Gnostic tradition.

Eve
In the book of Genesis, Eve is the first mother of human beings. Her name in the Septuagint is Zoe, the Greek word for "life."

five seals
In Sethian Gnostic ritual, the five seals are associated with the sacrament of baptism. Possibly linked to the inner mystical ascent to the Divine or heavenly realms.

gnosis
Gnosis is the mystical revelation of all things sacred through experiential inner "knowing" as a path to enlightenment. Gnostics believed gnosis was necessary for their salvation.

heresiologists
Proto-orthodox Christian leaders who sought to stamp out heresy and unorthodox ideas as such ideas emerged and crept into Christian faith and teachings.

hylic
In Gnostic doctrine, hylic is the lowest level of human beings. The highest level was the pneumatic Gnostics, followed by the psychic Christians.

Irenaeus
Proto-orthodox Christian leader who lived from A.D. 130 to 202. He served as Bishop of Lyons. Vigorously defending the Christian church against Gnosticism, he wrote a book titled *Against All Heresies*.

James the Just
The brother of Jesus and head of the early Christian church in Jerusalem. Assumed to have written the Secret Book of James.

Josephus
Jewish historian (circa A.D. 37 to 107) whose writings about Jews of the first century helped scholars from that time forward to understand and write about that period in antiquity.

John the Baptist
Jewish teacher and a messianic figure. He is accorded second position in Christianity, after Jesus. He baptized Jesus in the Jordan River.

Logos
Word of God personified. Gnostics equated Logos or Word with the wisdom of God.

Mary of Magdala
Mary Magdalene, the pre-eminent female disciple of Jesus whom he "kissed often," according to the Gospel of Philip. The Gnostics held her in high esteem, and she may have been the leader of an early Gnostic sect. The Catholic Church calls her "Apostle to the Apostles" and she is similarly referred to in the Greek Orthodox tradition.

Montanists
Followers of Montanus, a prophetic leader of a second-century charismatic movement. Montanus, who believed the Holy Spirit spoke through him, espoused an apocalyptic view that the Second Coming of Christ was imminent.

mystic
A person who seeks a personal relationship with the Divine through regular sessions of contemplation, meditation, prayer, fasting, and other ascetic practices.

Naassenes
Serpentine Gnostics whose cult name derives from the Hebrew word nahash, meaning "serpent." To the Naassenes, the serpent symbolized wisdom.

Pistis
Faith; in the Gnostic tradition often used as Pistis Sophia or the embodiment of Faith Wisdom in Gnostic texts.

Pleroma
Fullness. Encompasses all the Aeons and Divine emanations and the realm of the transcendent god in which they are found.

pneumatic
In Gnostic belief, a pneumatic is a spiritual person. Pneumatic was also taken to mean "seed of Seth," or a Gnostic. In Valentinian Gnosticism, pneumatic was the highest level of human, followed by psychic, and then hylic, the lowest.

pronoia
Forethought. See Barbelo.

Protennoia
First Thought (as opposed to Forethought/Barbelo). In Sethian doctrine, Protennoia is the First Thought personified as female from the Divine.

right
Right referred to the psychical people, according to the Valentinian tradition. The Valentinians also equated those of the left as material people.

rest
Derived from the Greek word *anapausis*, the word describes divine rest and repose. In

Gnostic belief, people who attain gnosis rest in a blessed state of silence and peace.

Seth

Son of Adam and Eve. Seth, according to Genesis, was another seed of his mother Eve after her son Cain slew his brother. The Gnostics called themselves the spiritual seeds or offspring of Seth.

Simon Magus

A Samaritan religious teacher who lived during the Apostles' lifetimes. The heresiologists of the fledgling Christian church called him the founder of Gnosticism. Simon Magus is often associated with his "first thought," a woman named Helena. The Acts of Peter and the Acts of the Apostles referred to him as a magician.

Sophia

Divine Wisdom personified. In Gnostic texts, Sophia brings forth the Demiurge who, with Aeons, creates the material universe and rules over it. She falls from grace, is redeemed, and is restored in Gnostic myth.

synoptic Gospels

Term for the first three gospels of the New Testament—Matthew, Mark, and Luke. These are so similar in content when placed side by side that scholars have suggested that they possibly relied on the same source material.

Tertullian

A powerful orthodox apologist and religious writer in the second and third centuries of the Christian Church. Tertullian knew both Latin and Greek, and many of his writings reveal the religious beliefs and disciplines of his time. He later left the traditional Christian church to join the Monatists and then left that cult to start his own group.

Valentinus

Popular poet, thinker, teacher, and founder of the Gnostic movement named after him. His Gnostic ideas and practices, placed upon the framework of emerging orthodox Christianity, had wide appeal and he gained a large following—so much so that the church saw his movement as its biggest internal threat.

Yaldabaoth

The name in Sethian Gnostic texts of the Demiurge or the creator of the physical universe. Yaldabaoth comes from the Aramaic, meaning "child of chaos." Other names for the Demiurge are Sakla ("fool" in Aramaic) and Samael ("blind god" in Aramaic).

Appendix B

Web Site Resources

B

The Gospel of Mary

This site provides links to the online text of The Gospel of Mary, as well as further information and expert commentary on the gospel.

www.earlychristianwritings .com/gospelmary.html

The Gnosis Archive

This site is a storehouse of information on Gnosticism, including The Gnostic Society Library, which contains an exhaustive selection of Gnostic documents.

www.gnosis.org

The Secret Gospel of Mark

This site is a source of information and links to other sites about the Secret Gospel of Mark.

www.historian.net/secmark.htm

Plato's Timaeus

This site contains the translation of the entire text of *Timaeus*, wherein Plato mentions Demiurgos, which probably influenced the Gnostic concept of the Demiurge.

http://classics.mit.edu/Plato/timaeus.html

The Gnostic Society Library

This site displays a letter attributed to Clement of Alexandria that appears to include some material from the Secret Gospel of Mark.

www.webcom.com/gnosis/ library/secm.htm

New Advent Catholic Encyclopedia

This site provides a definition and description of the Gospels.

www.newadvent.org/cathen/06655b.htm

A Synoptic Gospels Primer

This site introduces the synoptic problem to beginning scholars.

http://virtualreligion.net/primer/

The Gospel of Q

This site compares the opinions of various contemporary scholars on the Q Source (the suspected additional source for the synoptic Gospels).

www.earlychristianwritings.com /q-contents.html

The Real Jesus of the Q Gospel

This is the Web site of religion professor and Q gospel scholar James M. Robinson.

www.religion-online.org/showarticle .asp?title=542

Mary Magdalene: Author of the Fourth Gospel?

The Web site of Ramon K. Jusino, M.A., this site offers new insight on the authorship of the Gospel of John.

✐*http://ramon_k_jusino.tripod.com/ magdalene.html*

The Internet Christian Library's Guide to Early Church Documents

This site contains information on early Christian writings as well as the New Testament canon.

✐*www.iclnet.org/pub/resources/christian-history.html*

Ancient Book Forms

To see examples of ancient books of the type used by Christians (such as the book roll and the codex), go to this site.

✐*www.lib.umich.edu/pap/k12/bookforms .html*

Reluctant Messenger

A list of the canons decreed at the Council of Laodicea can be found at this Web site.

✐*http://reluctant-messenger.com/ council-of-laodicea.htm*

The Gospel of Truth

To read the text from Irenaeus referencing the Gospel of Truth, see book 3, chapter 11, verse 9 at this site.

✐*www.ccel.org/fathers2*

Early Christian Writings

Read The (Coptic) Gospel of the Egyptians, also known as The Holy Book of the Great Invisible Spirit, at this Web site.

✐*www.earlychristianwritings.com/ text/gospelegyptians.html*

History of Gnosticism

To read about the history of Gnosticism, go to this Web site.

✐*http://en.wikipedia.org/wiki/ History_of_Gnosticism*

The Twelve Apostles

For a Greek Orthodox source on the Apostles, go to this site.

✐*www.goarch.org/en/ourfaith/articles/ article7065.asp*

Appendix C

Text Resources

Scriptural Texts

The Biblical and catechism texts quoted in this book are drawn from:

The Holy Bible: Old and New Testaments
Self-pronouncing edition, conforming to the 1611 edition, commonly known as the Authorized or King James Version.
Cleveland and New York: The World Publishing Company. (No copyright or publication date available.)

The New Testament of Our Lord and Saviour Jesus Christ
Translated from the original Greek, Dutch-English edition.
New York. American Bible Society, 1869.

Catechism of the Catholic Church
Revised in accordance with the official Latin text promulgated by Pope John Paul II.
New York: Random House, Doubleday, 1997.

Other Texts

Additional, supporting sources are as follows:

Armstrong, Karen. *A History of God, The 4,000-Year Quest of Judaism, Christianity, and Islam.* New York: Random House, Ballantine Books, 1993.

Barnstone, Willis and Marvin Meyer, eds., *The Gnostic Bible, Gnostic Texts or Mystical Wisdom from the Ancient and Medieval Worlds.* Cambridge: Harvard University Press, 2003.

Brock, Ann Graham. *Mary Magdalene, The First Apostle: The Struggle for Authority.* Cambridge: Harvard University Press, 2003.

Carmichael, Joel. *The Birth of Christianity, Reality and Myth.* New York: Dorset Press, 1992.

Ehrman, Bart D. *The Lost Christianities, The Battles for Scripture and Faiths We Never Knew.* New York: Oxford University Press, 2003.

Ehrman, Bart D. *Lost Scriptures, Books that Did Not Make It into the New Testament.* New York: Oxford University Press, 2003.

Ehrman, Bart D. *Misquoting Jesus: The Story Behind Who Changed the Bible and Why.* New York: HarperCollins Publishers, HarperSanFrancisco, 2005.

Freke, Timothy and Peter Gandy. *Jesus and the Lost Goddess: The Secret Teachings of the Original Christians.* New York: Three Rivers Press, 2001.

Freke, Timothy and Peter Gandy. *The Jesus Mysteries: Was the "Original Jesus" a Pagan God?* New York: Three Rivers Press, 2001.

Gaffney, Mark H. *Gnostic Secrets of the Naassenes: The Initiatory Teachings of the Last Supper.* Rochester, Vermont: Inner Traditions, 2004.

Haskins, Susan. *Mary Magdalen, Myth and Metaphor.* New York: Berkeley Publishing Group, Riverhead Books, 1993.

Kasser, Rodolphe, Marvin Meyer, and Gregor Wurst, eds., with commentary by Bart D. Ehrman. *The Gospel of Judas.* Washington, D.C.: National Geographic Society, 2006.

King, Karen. *The Gospel of Mary of Magdala: Jesus and the First Woman Apostle.* Santa Rosa, California: Polebridge Press, 2003.

Klein, Peter. *Catholic Source Book, a Comprehensive Collection of Information about the Catholic Church.* Dubuque: Harcourt Religion Publishers, 2000.

Krosney, Herb. *The Lost Gospel: The Quest for the Gospel of Judas Iscariot.* Washington, D.C.: National Geographic Society, 2006.

Layton, Bentley, translator. *The Gnostic Scriptures.* New York: Random House, Doubleday, 2003.

LeLoup, Jean-Yves. *The Gospel of Mary Magdalene.* Rochester, Vermont: Inner Traditions International, 2002.

Lester, Meera. *The Everything Mary Magdalene Book.* Avon, Massachusetts: Adams Media, 2006.

Lockyer, Herbert. *All the Women of the Bible.* Grand Rapids, Michigan: Zondervan, 1967.

Meeks, Wayne A. *The First Urban Christians: The Social World of the Apostle Paul.* Second Edition. New Haven and London: Yale University Press, 2003.

Meyer, Marvin. *The Gnostic Discoveries: The Impact of the Nag Hammadi Library.* New York: HarperCollins Publishers, HarperSanFrancisco, 2005.

Meyer, Marvin with Esther A. De Boer. *The Gospels of Mary: The Secret Tradition of Mary Magdalene, the Companion of Jesus.* New York: HarperCollins Publishers, 1994.

Meyer, Marvin with commentary by Harold Bloom. *The Gospel of Thomas, The Hidden Sayings of Jesus.* New York: HarperCollins Publishers, 1992.

Miller, Robert J., ed., with an introduction by Karen King. *The Complete Gospels: Annotated Scholars Version.* Sonoma, California: Polebridge Press, 1992.

Pagels, Elaine. *Beyond Belief: The Secret Gospel of Thomas*. New York: Random House, 2003.

Pagels, Elaine. *The Gnostic Gospels*. New York: Random House, Vintage Books Edition, 1989.

Picknett, Lynn. *Mary Magdalene*. New York: Avalon Publishing Group, Carroll & Graff Publishers, 2003.

Robinson, James M., ed. *The Nag Hammadi Library in English: The Definitive Translation of the Gnostic Scriptures Complete in One Volume*. New York: HarperCollins Publishers, 1990.

Wylen, Stephen M. *The Jews in the Time of Jesus, An Introduction*. Mahwah, New Jersey: The Paulist Press, 1996.

Index

A

Act of Peter, epitome of, 144, 242, 245

Acts of Peter and Twelve Apostles, 218–20

Adoptionism, 122

Aeon(s)
  creation and, 183–84, 186
  defined, 21, 80, 81
  as Divine emanations, 21, 22, 84, 185, 222, 228, 236, 238
  original, 27
  restoring order in Pleroma, 180

Anointing at Death, 30, 98

Antinomian discipline, 114–17

Apocalypse
  defined, 3–4
  expectations of, in Jesus' time, 4, 234

Apocalypse of Peter, 228–30

Apocalyptic ideology, 4

Apocrypha, defined, 10

Apocryphon of John. *See* Secret Gospel (Apocryphon) of John

Apollinarianism, 68, 70, 122

Apologetics, 38–39

Apostolic Christians, 16

Archon, defined, 21

Arianism, 68, 69

Art, Gnostic imagery in, 264

B

Baptism
  Cathari view, 127

Council at Nicaea and, 50

dissolving gender, 101

early Christian views, 14

Essene view, 137

gnosis through, 188, 189, 225–26

Gnostic views, 31, 82, 83, 110, 179–80, 188–89, 225–26, 236

by Holy Spirit, 80

hymn for, 190

of Jesus, 49, 56, 63, 80, 122

Menandrian view, 116

women and, 13, 97

Bardesanes, 163

Basilidians, 37, 111

Book of Thomas the Contender, 158

Books. *See also* Canonical Christian texts; Gnostic texts; Gospels; *specific gospels*
  Gnostic themes in, 256–58
  text resources, 278–80

Bridal Chamber, 30, 31–32, 108, 112, 170, 172–73, 180, 256

Burial, of sacred texts, 135–36

C

Cainites, 110

Canon, term origin, 72

Canonical Christian texts, 35–51, 71–73. *See also* Gospels; Orthodox vs. Gnostic views; *specific gospels*

accuracy/completeness of, 75–77

call for unity, 43–45

Council at Nicaea and, 48–50

establishment of, 40–41

fight over, 47–48

Gnostic texts compared to, 58–60, 62–64, 140–41

Gospel of Thomas
  excluded from, 164–65
  language of, 76
  letters opposing Gnosticism and, 36–37

Mary Magdalene in, 246

other significant writings, 39–41

Sayings Gospel Q and, 46–47, 73, 94, 160, 161, 166, 171, 204

standard texts, 71–73

surviving fragments of, 75

timeline of, 73

Trinity controversy, 48–49

views of salvation and, 42–43

writing favoring Gnosticism and, 37–39

Carpocratians, 41, 114–15, 251

Cathars, 126–28, 129, 238, 262

Chaos, ruler, 186

Chrism, 30, 172, 180

Circumcision, 5–6, 14

Clement of Alexandria, 40–41, 56, 115, 176, 229, 251

Copper Scroll, 139

Council at Nicaea, 48–50. *See also*
   Nicene creed
Creation
   dual-realm view, 22
   Genesis on, 24–26
   key terms for describing,
      21–22
   myths, 21, 57–58, 82, 84–85,
      110, 182, 185–88, 211, 220
   opposition to Gnostic view,
      37
Creed, defined, 237
Crusades, 129

D
Dead Sea Scrolls
   burial of, 242
   Copper Scroll, 139
   discovery of, 10, 11, 132,
      136, 138, 139, 142
   examination of, 252–53
   Nag Hammadi treasures
      and, 137
Demiurge
   alternative names for, 21
   creation story and, 22, 28,
      127, 185–86
   defined, 21
   Marcionite view of, 113
   Plato influence, 22–23
   Sophia's fall and, 81–82, 84,
      174, 183
   Trinity and, 27
Destruction of writings, 123–24,
   176, 237
Dialogue of the Savior, 224–27
Didymos Judas Thomas. *See*
   Gospel of Thomas; Thomas

Divine beings, 184–85. *See also*
   Aeon(s); Unknowable One
   (Unknowable Divine Being)
Divine feminine, 79–90. *See also*
   Mary Magdalene; Sophia
   Peter challenging Mary
      Magdalene, 87
   wisdom as female, 80–81
Docetism, 21, 36, 38, 123
Donatism, 123
Doubting Thomas, 162–63
Dualism, 21, 24, 37, 148
Dualistic discipline, 112–13

E
Early Christianity. *See also* Heresy;
   Orthodox vs. Gnostic views
   call for unity, 43–45
   cultural influences on, 7–8
   dissension/multiple views
      in, 6, 7, 10–12, 16–17, 44,
      233–34
   evolution of, 232
   first followers of, 2–4
   Palestinian Jews, 9–10
   practices of, 12–16
   radical originators of, 5–7
   roles of men and women,
      12–13
   spreading Good News,
      234–35
   use of word "Christian," 2
Early Christianity and Gnostic
   texts, 231–40. *See also*
   Canonical Christian texts;
   Gospels; Orthodox vs. Gnostic
   views; *specific gospels*
   destruction of texts, 32,
      123–24, 176, 237

   fear of Gnostic views,
      238–40
   Gnostic variants, 235–36
   secret teachings and. *See*
      Secret teachings of Jesus
   spreading Good News,
      234–35
Earthenware jars, scriptures in,
   132, 133, 136, 242. *See also* Nag
   Hammadi treasures
Egyptians. *See* Gospel of the
   Egyptians
Epitomes, 244–45
Essenes, 9, 10, 11, 136–37, 139,
   242–43
Excommunication, 125–26, 237
Exegesis on the Soul, 54, 83, 172
Extreme Unction, 30

F
Film and TV, Gnostic elements in,
   259–62
Five seals, 183, 187, 188

G
Games, Gnostic, 264–65
Gender equality, 54–55, 94–95,
   101–2, 128, 168. *See also*
   Women
Genesis, 24–26
   Apocryphon of John and,
      85
   esoteric interpretation, 212
   prologue to, 185–86, 187
   Sethian mythology and,
      26–28
Glossary, 268–71
Gnosis. *See also* Transcendence

as cornerstone of Gnostic
view, 6, 200–201
defined, 2, 21–22
salvation through, 82–83,
123, 166
through baptism, 188, 189,
225–26
Gnosticism
as heresy. *See* Heresy
main branches today, 238
roots of, 20–22
Gnostics
in England, 238
in France, 70, 112, 126–28,
129, 176, 238
key terms used by, 21–22
origins of, 20–22
orthodox views vs., 6
Plato influence on, 22–24
reinterpreting orthodox
views, 239
who they were, 2
Gnostic texts. *See also* Early
Christianity and Gnostic texts;
specific texts and gospels
canon and. *See* Canonical
Christian texts; Gospels;
Orthodox vs. Gnostic
views
destruction of, 32
discovery of. *See* Nag
Hammadi treasures
Gospels, 56–58, 62–64
manipulation of copies/
translations, 243–45
revealing Gnostic
perspective, 237–38
summary-version texts,
244–45
Gnostikoi, defined, 2
Gospel According to Hebrews, 233

Gospel of the Egyptians, 181–91
arrogance of Sakla, 186–88
author of, 57
divine beings described,
184–85
emergence of Christ, 183
emergence of man
(Adamas), 183–84
gnosis through baptism,
188, 189
Hades/Chaos rulers, 186
Unknowable Divine Being
and, 182–84
Gospel of John (canonical),
59–60. *See also* Secret Gospel
(Apocryphon) of John
approximate composition
date, 73
author of, 59, 60, 61, 152–53,
247, 262
Gnostic texts compared to,
140–41
Gospel of Philip and, 177
Gospel of Truth and, 213–14
on Judas, 202, 205
mystery in, 59–60
redaction of, 247–50
on salvation, 42
synoptic gospels vs., 56, 59
on Thomas, 162–63, 205
Gospel of Judas, 193–206. *See also*
Judas
brief history of, 201–2
disciples' vision in, 197–98
divergent view of Judas,
194–95, 199–200, 202–6
gnosis as focus of, 200–201
Jesus' vision in stars, 199–
200
Sethian Gnostic teaching,
198–99

Gospel of Luke
approximate composition
date, 73
Gospel of Thomas and, 159,
161, 162, 165, 166
on inner Kingdom of God,
64
on Judas, 204, 205
Marcion editing, 48, 56, 71,
124, 141, 249
relying on Mark, 46
Sayings Gospel Q and, 161
synoptic Gospel, 13, 42,
45–46
Gospel of Mark. *See also* Secret
Gospel of Mark
approximate composition
date, 73
author of, 55
Gospel of Thomas and, 165,
166
on Judas, 196, 203–4
multiple versions of, 40–41,
249–50, 251
Sayings Gospel Q and,
46–47, 55
synoptic Gospel, 1, 13, 44,
45–46
Gospel of Mary (Magdalene), 143–
55. *See also* Mary Magdalene;
Mary Magdalene vision
articulating Jesus'
teachings, 151
author of, 56–57
Coptic vs. Greek versions,
145
Jesus' discourse and
departure, 146–47
original text fragments,
144–45

special revelation of, 145–48

Gospel of Matthew
approximate composition date, 73
author of, 55
Gospel of Philip and, 177
Gospel of Thomas and, 161, 162, 166
on Judas, 196, 198, 203, 204–5
relying on Mark, 46
salvation perspective, 42
Sayings Gospel Q and, 46–47, 73
synoptic Gospel, 13, 42, 45–46

Gospel of Peter, 75, 76

Gospel of Philip, 169–80
author of, 58
Bridal Chamber sacrament and, 172–73
consecrated sex and, 172–73
content summary, 170–74
Gnostic sacramental rites in, 179–80
on Jesus/Mary Magdalene relationship, 87, 178–79
New Testament Gospels and, 177–78
revealing statements of, 177–78
Valentinian ideas and, 175–76

Gospel of Thomas, 134, 157–68
approximate composition date, 158
author of, 56
Didymos Judas Thomas as Jesus' twin, 161–62, 163

discovery of, 132
dispute as Gnostic text, 158
doubting Thomas and, 162–63
excluded from canon, 164–65
Jesus responds to Peter, 167
myriad literary forms of, 160–61
New Testament Gospels and, 59
original text fragments, 158
parallels in New Testament, 165–67
source of, 161
wisdom sayings/interpretations in, 159–60

Gospel of Truth, 208–16
audience for, 210
author of, 57, 208–9
central ideas/concepts, 211–12
death of Jesus in, 212–13
hidden/revealed meanings, 213
parable for truth, 213–14
Ptolemy letter to Flora, 214–16

Gospels. *See also* Canonical Christian texts; Synoptic Gospels; *specific Gospels*
authors of, 55–58
canonical, approximate composition dates, 73
comparison of Gnostic/canonical, 58–60, 62–64, 140–41
content of, overview, 45
defined, 45
Gnostic, 56–58, 62–64
Jesus in, 63–64

New Testament, 55–56
scribes of, 60–61
source material for, 45–47
total number of, 57
Greek discipline, 110–12

H

Hades, ruler, 186
Healings, in name of Christ, 190, 219
Healings, of Jesus
of Mary Magdalene, 89, 246
on Sabbath, 4–5
of women, 89, 92, 167, 246
Heresy, 2. *See also* Polemics
consequences of. *See* Heresy consequences
defining, within Christianity, 67–70
emergence of, 120–21
Gnostic writings and, 33
Ignatius on, 36–37
Irenaeus and, 32, 37, 48, 58–59, 85, 121, 124, 208
issues/instances of, 121–23
modern requisite for, 120
Nicene creed and, 67–68, 70
origins of, for Gnostics, 32–33
refutation of all, 74
syncretism and, 32–33
term origin, 121
Theodosius eradicating, 68–69
top ten heresies, 122–23
Heresy consequences, 119–29
for Cathars, 126–28, 129, 238
Crusades, 129

destruction of writings, 32, 123–24, 176, 237
emergence of heresy and, 120–21
excommunication, 125–26, 237
Inquisition, 129, 238
Holy Eucharist, 14, 30, 50, 127

I

Infancy Gospels, 48, 164
Inquisition, 129, 238

J

Jesus. *See also* Secret teachings of Jesus
baptism of, 49, 56, 63, 80, 122
in canon and Gnostic belief, 63–64
canonical view, 63–64
differing interpretations of, 16–17
discourse and departure of, 146–47
first followers of, 2–4
on gender equality, 94–95
Gnostic views, 64
marriage of, 154, 179, 256, 257–58
Mary Magdalene and. *See* Mary Magdalene
radical followers of, 5–7
radical practices of, 4–5
secret teaching to from, 40–41
view of, in his time, 7
vision of Judas' act, 199–200

world at time of, 3
John. *See* Gospel of John (canonical); Secret Gospel (Apocryphon) of John
Judas. *See also* Gospel of Judas
betrayal by, canonical version, 195–96
divergent view of, 194–95, 199–200, 202–6
portrayal of, in church writings, 196, 204–5
vision of, interpreted, 198
wisdom revealed to, 197

L

Luke. *See* Gospel of Luke

M

Magic, Gnosticism and, 116, 190–91
Mandaeans, 109, 110, 189, 236
Manichaeanism, 56, 123, 262
Marcion
about, 37–38
belief in two gods, 74, 112
editing Gospel of Luke, 48, 56, 71, 124, 141, 249
as heretic, 48
New Testament version, 107
view of reality, 107, 112–13
Mark, teachings of, 131, 164. *See also* Gospel of Mark; Secret Gospel of Mark
Marriage
early Christian views, 14–16
Gnostic views, 38, 87, 99, 103, 107
Jesus and Mary Magdalene, 154, 179, 256, 257–58

making Mary male and, 167–68
Mary Magdalene. *See also* Gospel of Mary (Magdalene); Mary Magdalene vision
alternative names of, 80
as Beloved Disciple, 152, 153, 247
in canon, 246
as Christian leader, 89, 146, 152
as counterpart of Jesus, 98–99
divine Wisdom of, 88, 96–97
elevated status of, 152–55
fear of Peter, 88
Gnostic perspective, 43–44, 62, 98–99, 246–47
as Gospel of John author, 152–53
as Jesus' elect, 89–90
Jesus' response to Peter about, 167
legacy of, 103–4
making her male, 167–68
Peter challenging, 87–88, 233
Pistis Sophia focusing on, 154–55
as problem for emerging church, 245–46
relationship with Jesus, 87, 147, 154, 178–79, 256, 257–58
Resurrection and, 13, 80, 89, 90, 93, 153
as Sophia, 88, 95–98
telling disciples of Resurrection, 103, 146

Mary Magdalene vision, 62, 147–50, 246
  explanation of, 148
  importance of, 148–49
  Peter disbelieving/bullying, 149–50
  recounted to Peter, 147
Matthew
  Gospel of. *See* Gospel of Matthew
  seeing light, 225–26
Mithraism, 8, 47, 123
Monophysitism, 70, 123
Muhammad Ali, 133–34
Muratorian Canon, 71–72
Music, Gnostic influence on, 262–63

N

Naassenes, 19, 96, 107–8, 168
Nag Hammadi treasures, 131–42. *See also* Dead Sea Scrolls
  burial of, 135–36, 242–43
  discovery of, xi, 2, 20–21, 33, 45, 132–34
  in earthenware jars, 132, 133, 136, 242
  Essenes and, 9, 10, 11, 136–37, 139, 242
  examination of, 140–42
  Gospel of Thomas and, 132, 158
  manipulation of copies/translations, 243–45
  Masada and, 136, 138
  Muhammad Ali and, 133–34
  for scholarly analysis, 142
  searching for more, 140

summary-version texts, 244–45
today, 242
translation to Coptic, 134–35, 242–43
writing surfaces of, 138
Neoplatonism, 70
Nestorianism, 70
New Testament. *See* Canonical Christian texts; Synoptic Gospels
Nicene creed, 25, 50–51, 67–68, 69, 70, 132, 237

O

Ophites, 108–9
Oral traditions, 67
Orthodox vs. Gnostic views, 6, 65–77. *See also* Canonical Christian texts; Gospels; *specific gospels*
  diversity and intolerance, 66
  fear of Gnostic views, 238–40
  Gnostics reinterpreting orthodox views, 239
  oral traditions on, 67
  outside sects, 69–70
  scriptural accuracy/completeness and, 75–77

P

Patriarchal view. *See also* Women
  challenge to, 92–94
  early Christian views, 12–13, 43–45, 94–95, 151, 167
  evolution from, 232
  Gospel of Mary and, 145, 146

Jesus view vs., 4
  making Mary male and, 167–68
  marginalization of Mary Magdalene and, 245–46
  marriage and, 14–16
Paul. *See also* Gospel of Luke
  on behavior of women, 40
  conflicts with Peter, 233–34
  dates of New Testament texts, 73
  evangelism of, 5
  purity law conflict, 5–6
  revelations about women, 101–2
  writings of, 39–40, 73
Pelagianism, 123
Peratai, 109
Peter
  Apocalypse of, 228–30
  challenging Mary Magdalene, 87–88, 233
  conflicts with Paul, 233–34
  Gospel of, 75, 76
  Jesus' response regarding Mary, 167
  Mary Magdalene fearing, 88
Pharisees, 4–5, 9, 10, 248
Philip. *See also* Gospel of Philip
  exploits/demise of, 171–72
  family of, 171
  as third disciple, 170–71
Pistis Sophia, 43, 86–90, 96, 145, 154–55
Plato, influence of, 22–24, 107, 111, 114, 208, 235, 262
Pleroma
  carbon copy of, 28
  characteristics of, 22, 23
  crisis in, 28, 81
  defined, 22

Godhead/gods in, 81, 185
Jesus descending from, 82
restoration of, 82, 180
Sophia falling from, 81–82, 174
Sophia inspiring return to, 22, 85–86
Polemics
against Arius, 39
defined, 38
driving Gnostics underground, 30–31
against Gnostics, 30–31, 55, 66, 73–74, 101–2, 109, 111, 112, 115, 126
of Irenaeus, 190, 196
against orthodoxy, 201
of Tertullian, 38–39, 174
Polytheism, 3, 8, 232
Pop culture, Gnostic themes in, 255–65
art, 264
books, 256–58
film and television, 259–62
games, 264–65
music, 262–63
Ptolemy, 112, 176, 208, 214–16
Purity rules, 4–6, 12, 42, 91

R
Redactions
defined, 248
of Dialogue of the Savior, 225
of Gospel of John, 247–49
of Gospels, by Marcion, 113
of other gospels, 141
of women in scriptures, 61
Redemption, 30, 43, 66, 87, 112, 172, 180, 185–86, 210, 221, 224

Reincarnation, 29, 114, 127, 221
Resources
books, 278–80
Web sites, 274–75
Revelations
Apocryphon of John and, 85
approximate composition date, 73
author/writing of, 60, 62
Gospel of John and, 62
Rites, of Gnosticism, 29–32, 179–80, 188, 190–91. *See also specific rites*

S
Sabellianism, 123
Sacraments. *See* Rites, of Gnosticism
Sadducees, 9, 10, 248
Sakla, 21, 186–88
Salvation
antinomian view, 114
Apocryphon of John on, 220
Arianism and, 122
canonical view, 64
Carpocratian view, 115
gnosis for, 82–83, 123, 166
Gnostic view, 2, 6, 7, 42, 82–83, 87, 106, 123, 180, 252
Gospel of Truth and, 210, 212–14
Holy Communion and, 14
Jewish Christian view, 7, 42
John on, 85
Menandrian view, 116
orthodox vs. Gnostic views, 66, 75, 106, 252

Pauline Christian view, 42–43
Paul on, 39
sharing knowledge of, 212–14
Thomas on, 59, 166
views of, 10, 42–43
for women, 167
Saturnilians, 109–10
Sayings Gospel Q, 46–47, 73, 94, 160, 161, 166, 171, 204
Scriptures. *See also* Canonical Christian texts; Early Christianity and Gnostic texts; Gnostic texts; Gospels; *specific scriptures*
favoring Gnosticism, 37–39
Gnostic beliefs in, 36–41
letters opposing Gnosticism, 36–37
myriad literary forms of, 160–61
other Gnostic literature, 217–30
Secessionist Christians, 16
Secret Book (Apocryphon) of James, 80, 239, 252
Secret Gospel (Apocryphon) of John, 54, 57–58, 60–61, 84–85, 184, 220–23
Secret Gospel of Mark, 75, 115, 251
Secret Gospel of Thomas. *See* Gospel of Thomas
Secret teachings of Jesus, 20
Clement on, 40–41, 251
for gnosis (self-knowing), 21–22, 64, 83, 236
Gnostics imparting, 239–40
Gnostic view of, 42, 64, 66, 82–83, 236, 239
heresiologists on, 132, 237

to John, 57
to Judas, 198–99, 251–52
at Last Supper, 107–8
Marcion belief of, 113
Thomas emphasizing, 166
to/from Mary Magdalene,
    43–44, 96, 108, 148–49,
    246–47
Valentinus and, 174–75
Sects, of Gnosticism, 105–17. *See
    also specific sects*
    antinomian discipline,
        114–17
    dualistic discipline, 112–13
    emergence of, 106–7
    Greek discipline, 110–12
    Syrian discipline, 107–10
    teachers disagreeing, 176
Self-knowledge. *See* Gnosis
Septuagint, 10, 17
Seth
    baptism rite and, 188, 189
    creation and, 187–88, 201
    as Father of Gnostic Race,
        57
    Gospel of Egyptians author,
        57
    Jesus as incarnation of, 122
    Second Treatise of, 58, 65,
        66
Sethian Gnostic teaching, 198–99
Sethians, 26–28, 109
Sicarii, 6–7, 195
Simonians, 115–17, 190
Simon the Cananaean (the
    Zealot), 7
Sophia
    defined, 22
    fall of, 81–82, 85
    Gnostic women and, 97–98

Mary Magdalene as, 88,
    95–98
as message of hope, 85–86
Pistis (Faith of Sophia),
    86–90
in Secret Book of John,
    84–85
as spirit of wisdom, 80–81
Sophia of Jesus Christ, 54, 144,
    227–28, 242
Stars, Jesus interpreting, 199–200
St. Pachomius, 135
St. Pachomius, monks of, xi, 2,
    136, 140, 242–43
Syncretism, 32–33
Synoptic Gospels. *See also specific
    Gospels*
    defined, 13
    Gospel of John vs., 56,
        247–48
    Gospel of Thomas and, 161,
        166
    problem of, 45–46
    Sayings Gospel Q and, 46–
        47, 161
    view of salvation in, 42
Syrian discipline, 107–10

T

Television and film, Gnostic
    elements in, 259–62
Theodosius eradicating, 68–69
Theodotus, 175, 176, 208
Thomas. *See also* Gospel of
    Thomas
    Didymos Judas Thomas,
        161–65
    taking Gospel to East,
        163–64
Thought of Norea, 54

Timothy (letters to), 26, 38, 40, 77,
    95
Timothy (man), 5–6
Tractates, defined, 229
Transcendence. *See also* Gnosis
    baptism and, 188, 189
    as central belief, 83, 140
    experiencing, 190
    liberation through, 20, 148
Transcendent God, 20, 22, 23, 29,
    96
Trinity
    beliefs before
        establishment of, 25–26
    Cathari view, 127
    defined, 27, 121
    dispute over, 48–49
    gender and, 54, 60–61
    Gnostic views, 27, 54, 82–
        83, 109, 182
    heretical assaults
        regarding, 121–22
    term origin, 38

U

Unknowable One (Unknowable
    Divine Being), 81, 84, 111, 182–
    85, 190, 228

V

Valentinians, 111–12. *See also*
    Gospel of Philip; Gospel of
    Truth
    apology for, 235
    freedom from relativity
        and, 31
    view of Jesus, 37, 122, 210
Valentinus, 57, 174–75, 208–9, 210

W

Web sites, 274–75

Women, 91–104. *See also* Gospel of Mary (Magdalene); Mary Magdalene; Patriarchal view

baptism and, 13, 97

as Christian leaders, 102

equality of, 12–13, 33, 54–55, 94–95, 101–2, 128, 168

Gnostic views, 12–13, 33, 54–55, 61

Jesus' egalitarian view of, 4

officeholders and bishops, 100

orthodox vs. Gnostic views, 12–13

Paul's revelations about, 40, 101–2

roles of, in early Christianity, 12–13

salvation for, 167

Sophia and, 97–98

strong/powerful, in scriptures, 61, 87

Z

Zealots, 5, 6–7, 9, 10, 204

Zoroastrian thinking, 2, 8, 47

THE EVERYTHING SERIES!

BUSINESS & PERSONAL FINANCE

Everything® **Accounting Book**
Everything® Budgeting Book
Everything® Business Planning Book
Everything® Coaching and Mentoring Book
Everything® Fundraising Book
Everything® Get Out of Debt Book
Everything® Grant Writing Book
Everything® Home-Based Business Book, 2nd Ed.
Everything® Homebuying Book, 2nd Ed.
Everything® Homeselling Book, 2nd Ed.
Everything® Investing Book, 2nd Ed.
Everything® Landlording Book
Everything® Leadership Book
Everything® **Managing People Book, 2nd Ed.**
Everything® Negotiating Book
Everything® Online Auctions Book
Everything® Online Business Book
Everything® Personal Finance Book
Everything® Personal Finance in Your 20s and 30s Book
Everything® Project Management Book
Everything® Real Estate Investing Book
Everything® Robert's Rules Book, $7.95
Everything® Selling Book
Everything® **Start Your Own Business Book, 2nd Ed.**
Everything® Wills & Estate Planning Book

COOKING

Everything® Barbecue Cookbook
Everything® Bartender's Book, $9.95
Everything® Chinese Cookbook
Everything® **Classic Recipes Book**
Everything® Cocktail Parties and Drinks Book
Everything® College Cookbook
Everything® **Cooking for Baby and Toddler Book**
Everything® Cooking for Two Cookbook
Everything® Diabetes Cookbook
Everything® Easy Gourmet Cookbook
Everything® Fondue Cookbook
Everything® **Fondue Party Book**
Everything® Gluten-Free Cookbook
Everything® Glycemic Index Cookbook
Everything® Grilling Cookbook

Everything® Healthy Meals in Minutes Cookbook
Everything® Holiday Cookbook
Everything® Indian Cookbook
Everything® Italian Cookbook
Everything® Low-Carb Cookbook
Everything® Low-Fat High-Flavor Cookbook
Everything® Low-Salt Cookbook
Everything® Meals for a Month Cookbook
Everything® Mediterranean Cookbook
Everything® Mexican Cookbook
Everything® One-Pot Cookbook
Everything® **Quick and Easy 30-Minute, 5-Ingredient Cookbook**
Everything® Quick Meals Cookbook
Everything® Slow Cooker Cookbook
Everything® Slow Cooking for a Crowd Cookbook
Everything® Soup Cookbook
Everything® Tex-Mex Cookbook
Everything® Thai Cookbook
Everything® Vegetarian Cookbook
Everything® Wild Game Cookbook
Everything® Wine Book, 2nd Ed.

GAMES

Everything® 15-Minute Sudoku Book, $9.95
Everything® 30-Minute Sudoku Book, $9.95
Everything® Blackjack Strategy Book
Everything® Brain Strain Book, $9.95
Everything® Bridge Book
Everything® Card Games Book
Everything® Card Tricks Book, $9.95
Everything® Casino Gambling Book, 2nd Ed.
Everything® Chess Basics Book
Everything® Craps Strategy Book
Everything® Crossword and Puzzle Book
Everything® Crossword Challenge Book
Everything® Cryptograms Book, $9.95
Everything® Easy Crosswords Book
Everything® Easy Kakuro Book, $9.95
Everything® Games Book, 2nd Ed.
Everything® Giant Sudoku Book, $9.95
Everything® Kakuro Challenge Book, $9.95
Everything® **Large-Print Crossword Challenge Book**
Everything® Large-Print Crosswords Book
Everything® Lateral Thinking Puzzles Book, $9.95
Everything® **Mazes Book**

Everything® Pencil Puzzles Book, $9.95
Everything® Poker Strategy Book
Everything® Pool & Billiards Book
Everything® Test Your IQ Book, $9.95
Everything® Texas Hold 'Em Book, $9.95
Everything® Travel Crosswords Book, $9.95
Everything® Word Games Challenge Book
Everything® Word Search Book

HEALTH

Everything® Alzheimer's Book
Everything® Diabetes Book
Everything® Health Guide to Adult Bipolar Disorder
Everything® Health Guide to Controlling Anxiety
Everything® Health Guide to Fibromyalgia
Everything® **Health Guide to Thyroid Disease**
Everything® Hypnosis Book
Everything® Low Cholesterol Book
Everything® Massage Book
Everything® Menopause Book
Everything® Nutrition Book
Everything® Reflexology Book
Everything® Stress Management Book

HISTORY

Everything® American Government Book
Everything® American History Book
Everything® Civil War Book
Everything® Freemasons Book
Everything® Irish History & Heritage Book
Everything® Middle East Book

HOBBIES

Everything® Candlemaking Book
Everything® Cartooning Book
Everything® **Coin Collecting Book**
Everything® Drawing Book
Everything® Family Tree Book, 2nd Ed.
Everything® Knitting Book
Everything® Knots Book
Everything® Photography Book
Everything® Quilting Book
Everything® Scrapbooking Book
Everything® Sewing Book
Everything® Woodworking Book

Bolded titles are new additions to the series.
All Everything® books are priced at $12.95 or $14.95, unless otherwise stated. Prices subject to change without notice.

HOME IMPROVEMENT

Everything® Feng Shui Book
Everything® Feng Shui Decluttering Book, $9.95
Everything® Fix-It Book
Everything® Home Decorating Book
Everything® Home Storage Solutions Book
Everything® Homebuilding Book
Everything® Lawn Care Book
Everything® Organize Your Home Book

KIDS' BOOKS

All titles are $7.95
Everything® Kids' Animal Puzzle & Activity Book
Everything® Kids' Baseball Book, 4th Ed.
Everything® Kids' Bible Trivia Book
Everything® Kids' Bugs Book
Everything® Kids' Cars and Trucks Puzzle & Activity Book
Everything® Kids' Christmas Puzzle & Activity Book
Everything® Kids' Cookbook
Everything® Kids' Crazy Puzzles Book
Everything® Kids' Dinosaurs Book
Everything® Kids' First Spanish Puzzle and Activity Book
Everything® Kids' Gross Hidden Pictures Book
Everything® Kids' Gross Jokes Book
Everything® Kids' Gross Mazes Book
Everything® Kids' Gross Puzzle and Activity Book
Everything® Kids' Halloween Puzzle & Activity Book
Everything® Kids' Hidden Pictures Book
Everything® Kids' Horses Book
Everything® Kids' Joke Book
Everything® Kids' Knock Knock Book
Everything® Kids' Learning Spanish Book
Everything® Kids' Math Puzzles Book
Everything® Kids' Mazes Book
Everything® Kids' Money Book
Everything® Kids' Nature Book
Everything® Kids' Pirates Puzzle and Activity Book
Everything® Kids' Princess Puzzle and Activity Book
Everything® Kids' Puzzle Book
Everything® Kids' Riddles & Brain Teasers Book
Everything® Kids' Science Experiments Book
Everything® Kids' Sharks Book
Everything® Kids' Soccer Book
Everything® Kids' Travel Activity Book

KIDS' STORY BOOKS

Everything® Fairy Tales Book

LANGUAGE

Everything® Conversational Chinese Book with CD, $19.95
Everything® Conversational Japanese Book with CD, $19.95
Everything® French Grammar Book
Everything® French Phrase Book, $9.95
Everything® French Verb Book, $9.95
Everything® German Practice Book with CD, $19.95
Everything® Inglés Book
Everything® Learning French Book
Everything® Learning German Book
Everything® Learning Italian Book
Everything® Learning Latin Book
Everything® Learning Spanish Book
Everything® Russian Practice Book with CD, $19.95
Everything® Sign Language Book
Everything® Spanish Grammar Book
Everything® Spanish Phrase Book, $9.95
Everything® Spanish Practice Book with CD, $19.95
Everything® Spanish Verb Book, $9.95

MUSIC

Everything® Drums Book with CD, $19.95
Everything® Guitar Book
Everything® Guitar Chords Book with CD, $19.95
Everything® Home Recording Book
Everything® Music Theory Book with CD, $19.95
Everything® Reading Music Book with CD, $19.95
Everything® Rock & Blues Guitar Book (with CD), $19.95
Everything® Songwriting Book

NEW AGE

Everything® Astrology Book, 2nd Ed.
Everything® Birthday Personology Book
Everything® Dreams Book, 2nd Ed.
Everything® Love Signs Book, $9.95
Everything® Numerology Book
Everything® Paganism Book
Everything® Palmistry Book
Everything® Psychic Book
Everything® Reiki Book
Everything® Sex Signs Book, $9.95
Everything® Tarot Book, 2nd Ed.
Everything® Wicca and Witchcraft Book

PARENTING

Everything® Baby Names Book, 2nd Ed.
Everything® Baby Shower Book
Everything® Baby's First Food Book
Everything® Baby's First Year Book
Everything® Birthing Book
Everything® Breastfeeding Book
Everything® Father-to-Be Book
Everything® Father's First Year Book
Everything® Get Ready for Baby Book
Everything® Get Your Baby to Sleep Book, $9.95
Everything® Getting Pregnant Book
Everything® Guide to Raising a One-Year-Old
Everything® Guide to Raising a Two-Year-Old
Everything® Homeschooling Book
Everything® Mother's First Year Book
Everything® Parent's Guide to Children and Divorce
Everything® Parent's Guide to Children with ADD/ADHD
Everything® Parent's Guide to Children with Asperger's Syndrome
Everything® Parent's Guide to Children with Autism
Everything® Parent's Guide to Children with Bipolar Disorder
Everything® Parent's Guide to Children with Dyslexia
Everything® Parent's Guide to Positive Discipline
Everything® Parent's Guide to Raising a Successful Child
Everything® Parent's Guide to Raising Boys
Everything® Parent's Guide to Raising Siblings
Everything® Parent's Guide to Sensory Integration Disorder
Everything® Parent's Guide to Tantrums
Everything® Parent's Guide to the Overweight Child
Everything® Parent's Guide to the Strong-Willed Child
Everything® Parenting a Teenager Book
Everything® Potty Training Book, $9.95
Everything® Pregnancy Book, 2nd Ed.
Everything® Pregnancy Fitness Book
Everything® Pregnancy Nutrition Book
Everything® Pregnancy Organizer, 2nd Ed., $16.95
Everything® Toddler Activities Book
Everything® Toddler Book
Everything® Tween Book
Everything® Twins, Triplets, and More Book

PETS

Everything® Aquarium Book
Everything® Boxer Book
Everything® Cat Book, 2nd Ed.
Everything® Chihuahua Book
Everything® Dachshund Book
Everything® Dog Book
Everything® Dog Health Book
Everything® Dog Owner's Organizer, $16.95
Everything® Dog Training and Tricks Book
Everything® German Shepherd Book
Everything® Golden Retriever Book
Everything® Horse Book
Everything® Horse Care Book
Everything® Horseback Riding Book
Everything® Labrador Retriever Book
Everything® Poodle Book
Everything® Pug Book
Everything® Puppy Book
Everything® Rottweiler Book
Everything® Small Dogs Book
Everything® Tropical Fish Book
Everything® Yorkshire Terrier Book

REFERENCE

Everything® Blogging Book
Everything® Build Your Vocabulary Book
Everything® Car Care Book
Everything® Classical Mythology Book
Everything® Da Vinci Book
Everything® Divorce Book
Everything® Einstein Book
Everything® Etiquette Book, 2nd Ed.
Everything® Inventions and Patents Book
Everything® Mafia Book
Everything® Philosophy Book
Everything® Psychology Book
Everything® Shakespeare Book

RELIGION

Everything® Angels Book
Everything® Bible Book
Everything® Buddhism Book
Everything® Catholicism Book
Everything® Christianity Book
Everything® History of the Bible Book
Everything® Jesus Book
Everything® Jewish History & Heritage Book
Everything® Judaism Book
Everything® Kabbalah Book
Everything® Koran Book
Everything® Mary Book

Everything® Mary Magdalene Book
Everything® Prayer Book
Everything® Saints Book
Everything® Torah Book
Everything® Understanding Islam Book
Everything® World's Religions Book
Everything® Zen Book

SCHOOL & CAREERS

Everything® Alternative Careers Book
Everything® Career Tests Book
Everything® College Major Test Book
Everything® College Survival Book, 2nd Ed.
Everything® Cover Letter Book, 2nd Ed.
Everything® Filmmaking Book
Everything® Get-a-Job Book
Everything® Guide to Being a Paralegal
Everything® Guide to Being a Real Estate Agent
Everything® Guide to Being a Sales Rep
Everything® Guide to Careers in Health Care
Everything® Guide to Careers in Law Enforcement
Everything® Guide to Government Jobs
Everything® Guide to Starting and Running a Restaurant
Everything® Job Interview Book
Everything® New Nurse Book
Everything® New Teacher Book
Everything® Paying for College Book
Everything® Practice Interview Book
Everything® Resume Book, 2nd Ed.
Everything® Study Book

SELF-HELP

Everything® Dating Book, 2nd Ed.
Everything® Great Sex Book
Everything® Kama Sutra Book
Everything® Self-Esteem Book

SPORTS & FITNESS

Everything® Easy Fitness Book
Everything® Fishing Book
Everything® Golf Instruction Book
Everything® Pilates Book
Everything® Running Book
Everything® Weight Training Book
Everything® Yoga Book

TRAVEL

Everything® Family Guide to Cruise Vacations
Everything® Family Guide to Hawaii

Everything® Family Guide to Las Vegas, 2nd Ed.
Everything® Family Guide to Mexico
Everything® Family Guide to New York City, 2nd Ed.
Everything® Family Guide to RV Travel & Campgrounds
Everything® Family Guide to the Caribbean
Everything® Family Guide to the Walt Disney World Resort®, Universal Studios®, and Greater Orlando, 4th Ed.
Everything® Family Guide to Timeshares
Everything® Family Guide to Washington D.C., 2nd Ed.
Everything® Guide to New England

WEDDINGS

Everything® Bachelorette Party Book, $9.95
Everything® Bridesmaid Book, $9.95
Everything® Destination Wedding Book
Everything® Elopement Book, $9.95
Everything® Father of the Bride Book, $9.95
Everything® Groom Book, $9.95
Everything® Mother of the Bride Book, $9.95
Everything® Outdoor Wedding Book
Everything® Wedding Book, 3rd Ed.
Everything® Wedding Checklist, $9.95
Everything® Wedding Etiquette Book, $9.95
Everything® Wedding Organizer, 2nd Ed., $16.95
Everything® Wedding Shower Book, $9.95
Everything® Wedding Vows Book, $9.95
Everything® Wedding Workout Book
Everything® Weddings on a Budget Book, $9.95

WRITING

Everything® Creative Writing Book
Everything® Get Published Book, 2nd Ed.
Everything® Grammar and Style Book
Everything® Guide to Writing a Book Proposal
Everything® Guide to Writing a Novel
Everything® Guide to Writing Children's Books
Everything® Guide to Writing Research Papers
Everything® Screenwriting Book
Everything® Writing Poetry Book
Everything® Writing Well Book